Strategic Job Modeling

Working at the Core of Integrated Human Resources

Strategic Job Modeling

Working at the Core of Integrated Human Resources

Jeffery S. Schippmann
Personnel Decisions International, Minneapolis

LEA LAWRENCE ERLBAUM ASSOCIATES, PUBLISHERS
1999 Mahwah, New Jersey   London

Lawrence Erlbaum Associates, Inc., Publishers
10 Industrial Avenue
Mahwah, NJ 07430

Cover design by Kathryn Houghtaling Lacey

Library of Congress Cataloging-in-Publication Data

Schippmann, Jeffery S.
      Strategic job modeling : working at the core of integrated human re-
   sources / Jeffery S. Schippmann
         p. cm.
      Includes bibliographical references and indexes.
      ISBN 0-8058-3052-9 (cloth : alk. paper). — ISBN 0-8058-3053-7
   (pbk. : alk. paper)
      1. Job analysis—Mathematical models.   I. Title.
HF5549.5.J6S35 1999
658.3'06—dc21   99-17929
                                                                    CIP

Books published by Lawrence Erlbaum Associates are printed on acid-free
paper, and their bindings are chosen for strength and durability.

Printed in the United States of America
10 9 8 7 6 5 4 3 2 1

*To two wonderful people,
who also happen to be my mom and dad,
Bobbi and Ed Schippmann*

Contents

III: THE FUTURE OF STRATEGIC JOB
MODELING

Preface

> *The real voyage of discovery consists not in seeking new lands, but seeing with new eyes.*
>
> —Marcel Proust

The concept of *job analysis* has a deep reach into the past of human history. Systematic procedures for identifying and describing the important work-related aspects of a job and the associated worker requirements can be traced back to the early Greeks. In discussing the needs of the ideal state, Socrates noted that different kinds of people, with different mixes of special skills, are required to satisfy different needs.[1]

The role of systematic analysis procedures gained prominence in the early 1900s when their information-generating properties were recognized by industrial engineers, management theorists, personnel specialists, and psychologists. The term *job analysis* evolved about this time, and enthusiasm for the subject grew as the basic ideas formed the foundation of Taylor's *scientific management.*[2]

Although the popularity of the practice has waxed and waned since the 1920s, the same fundamental ideas have been used to support a steadily increasing range of organizational applications. In the 1940s, Zerga identified more than 20 uses of job analysis information.[3] In the late 1990s, the results of job analysis practice are woven into the fabric of virtually every application involving an organization's people resources.

However, as the 21st century looms just ahead, job analysis is at a crossroad. Job analysis practices in the late 1990s are a product of the mass-production approach to thinking about work, where division of labor and job simplification are a prerequisite for high-volume production and interchangeable parts.[4,5,6] Just as it is questionable whether this philosophy of work will equip organizations for success in a business environment characterized by unprecedented competition and change, one can question whether current approaches to job analysis are capable of providing maximally useful information in this new environment.

I am not suggesting that human resource (HR) professionals and consultants toss this long-favored tool on the scrap heap. To the contrary, it is a scary, competitive, and changing business environment out there. Now more than ever, organizational decision makers need quality information to guide their thinking. However, using conventional job analysis approaches to develop HR applications is like using hand-operated drills, saws, and the like to build a house in an age of power tools. We need to leverage what is valuable in the approach while upgrading it from hand to power tool.

Strategic job modeling (SJM) is the term I use to describe the specific upgraded approach to job analysis presented in this book. At the risk of muddying the water by introducing new words, there are several reasons why I believe it is important to make the distinction. First, in many cases, conventional job analysis procedures are too short-sighted to meet the strategic and future-oriented needs of today's organizations. Out of necessity, organizations are busy planning for the future and pursuing strategies that will differentiate them from others in the market by creating competitive advantage. Although it is the responsibility of management to marshal the resources to achieve the organization's vision and strategy, those working in the HR arena are responsible for guiding and supporting the acquisition, development, deployment, and maintenance of the human capital portfolio. Therefore, it follows that decisions about the strategy and direction of the organization will have downstream impacts on work content and worker requirements. The next-generation job analysis approach presented here provides a process for understanding the ultimate objectives of an organization and translating this information into work requirements. In other words, conventional job analysis procedures frequently provide a past-tense description of something static, whereas strategic job modeling creates a future-tense description of something changing.

Second, many organizations are flattening, creating work environments that are highly matrixed, relying with greater frequency on self-managed teams, aligning their resources along value chains, or otherwise rethinking how best to structure work.[7] In fact, some professionals are writing about *the end of the job* or how the idea of an individual holding *a job* in an organization may be an outdated concept.[8,9,10] Although I do not buy into the idea that the era of the job is over, jobs are, like everything else, certainly changing; the way we define and measure the characteristics of jobs needs to change as well. Furthermore, although the focus of conventional job analysis has traditionally been a job, the target in today's workplace might be the job or it could be a job family, a mix of jobs in a value chain, a business unit, or an entire organization. Hence, although the use of the word *job* in SJM is something of a misnomer, the hope is that the use of a fresh phrase will underscore the shift in orientation represented in this book.

Third, the term *job analysis*, and much of the research and reporting of conventional job-analytic approaches, sends the message that we are analyzing jobs and worker functions into smaller and smaller parts, taking a reductionistic view of the research activities involved. While this activity often occurs, it is not the goal. The intent of using *modeling* rather than *analysis* is to underscore the importance of taking the pieces that have been examined and building a platform of information that can be used to support a particular application, cluster of applications, or all of the applications in an HR system. The creative and model-building component involved in this constellation of HR research activities often seems to get overlooked in discussions of conventional job analysis. In one small way, I hope the use of the word *modeling* better captures the developmental spirit involved in the approach presented here.

Finally, conventional thinking about job analysis is that it is a mundane, technical activity conducted on an as-needed basis to develop specific HR applications one at a time. However, we are operating at the intersection of the Information Age and the Learning Age; there is an intense demand to extract every ounce of meaning from information and put it to use quickly and broadly. In this context, efforts to systematically examine work and worker requirements have significant implications for broader organizational goals and management processes, and the findings can be compiled and used to advance the cause of the organization in a multitude of ways. Thus, the next-generation approach to job analysis presented here might be more appropriately thought of as an ongoing organizational intervention versus a loosely connected series of tactical projects.

In summary, few of today's organizations can be successful without talented people working together to implement the strategies of their respective organizations. Furthermore, there is no question that the level of success attained by individuals and work teams in an organization is directly influenced by the quality and success of the various HR applications that are designed to support the organization's people. The challenge of how to do this, and how to integrate these applications so they work together in a complementary fashion, is emerging as an exciting frontier, offering competitive advantage to organizations that rise to the challenge. This new frontier is SJM.

It makes sense, at this point, to explain how the terms *job modeling* and *job analysis* are used in this book. Any time I refer to conventional job analysis practice or specific approaches linked to early thought leaders in the field, the phrase that was prevalent at the time is used: *job analysis*. However, when referring to the future practice of job analysis in a general way, the term *job modeling* is used. When specifically referring to the approach presented in this book, the phrase *strategic job modeling* (SJM) is used.

The following pages contain ideas and techniques for planning and managing SJM projects. The results of these job modeling initiatives put one in a position to capitalize fully on the potential return from a wide range of HR applications. Because SJM is evolutionary versus revolutionary in nature, many of the ideas and techniques build on conventional job analysis methods and will be familiar to readers who know this literature. Other concepts and suggestions are likely to be quite new. However, everything is packaged in a practical framework for actually using what should be one of the most important and frequently used tools in the HR professional's toolkit.

Given the prominent role that job modeling plays in the development of virtually all applications affecting an organization's human capital, it is not surprising that individuals who specialize in this area of research are enthused by their work. Unfortunately, job modeling experts are rarely counted among the world's fun people. Notoriously insensitive to subtle shifts in mood, these individuals persist in discussing the virtues of good item-writing procedures and representative sampling plans long after the interest in polite company has waned.

Thus, although some important ideas and techniques need to be described to understand a process that is a critical part of most HR systems, the reader probably expects that covering this material will not be a great deal of fun. Henry David Thoreau had a point when he claimed that people learn more efficiently when they enjoy themselves. I have taken his dictum to heart and have interjected some humor here and there to help keep readers' attention as I present what I believe to be some of the leading thoughts and best practices in the field of job modeling.

Who are the readers this book is targeting? It was written with several potential audiences in mind. It should be useful to HR professionals and managers who want to learn more about how to conduct job modeling work to maximize the impact of the people-related applications and systems they are developing in their organizations. Consultants who work with organizations to create these kinds of applications are targeted as well. In addition, it should prove beneficial in teaching. Both students and scholars should profit from the practice-oriented design of the book, which may be used as a supplemental text in a variety of business and applied psychology courses dealing with personnel management and the development of specific HR applications (e.g., testing, training, compensation, performance management).

OVERVIEW AND CONTENTS

The book is divided into three sections. Chapters 1 and 2 comprise the first part. They provide some history for the practice, define the basic terms and concepts, and lead to a framework for thinking about SJM that summarizes crucial concepts by posing important questions and decision points in the process.

Part II uses the major steps of the job modeling process presented in chapter 2 as the organizing structure for the next five chapters; in short, it describes the mechanics of conducting SJM research. These steps in the job modeling process represent a series of decision points that guide the job modeler's thinking about subsequent decisions. Chapter 3 provides a structure for understanding an organization's vision, competitive strategy, and strategic initiatives. This information is key because it guides thinking about desired outcomes for the organization and relevant HR applications (e.g., revenue-based outcomes such as increasing the percentage of new product sales, to cost-based outcomes such as reducing project budget variances). It also helps frame the types of individual competencies that should be considered core or organization-wide competencies.

Chapter 4 begins by focusing on the application, or mix of applications, of interest. Different HR applications (e.g., recruiting programs, selection systems, performance management systems) need to be supported by the resulting information models in different ways, and different modeling approaches are more or less appropriate. Furthermore, the HR applications to be developed and supported also drive decisions about the type of information (e.g., work activities, competencies) that needs to be collected and the degree of detail or precision required of the descriptor content.

Chapter 5 involves decisions about the most relevant target population (e.g., management, clerical, hourly retail) for an intervention given the organization's strategies and target outcomes. These decisions then guide thinking about existing sources of information that can be leveraged in building the model. This chapter also covers interview and focus group procedures, sampling requirements, guidelines for writing descriptor content, and procedures used to create a rationally derived job model.

Chapter 6 focuses on issues that flow down from previous decisions and involves taking the rationally derived job model to the next phase and building it into a questionnaire. Again, the cumulative weight of previous decisions helps guide thinking about specific questions to ask about the descriptor content in the questionnaire (e.g., do we need data about the *Current Importance* of work activities, the *Difficulty* with which certain competencies are acquired, or some other mix of information?). This chapter also provides guidance in choosing appropriate subject matter expert respondent groups and developing sampling plans.

Chapter 7 addresses how the information collected in the previous step is analyzed and displayed. Ideas for evaluating the quality of the data and options for making various within- and across-job comparisons are presented. Choices at this point in the process guide the creation of decision rules that determine what descriptor content is used to form the empirically based job model.

Part III includes capstone chapter 8. This chapter covers the prospects and hopes for the future of job modeling. It also presents the changing role of HR in the "brave new world" of business, the impact of the second generation of computer technologies rumbling across the business terrain, and the associated influences on job modeling practice.

Part III also includes two appendixes. Appendix A provides a set of work activity and competency descriptors for management jobs. These categories of content illustrate some of the products of a typical modeling project. Furthermore, these taxonomies provide fairly comprehensive examples of two types of descriptor content and may be used for jump-starting job modeling work in this broad occupational group. Appendix B offers a detailed discussion on how to accomplish some of the more technical activities involved in modeling. Specifically, data-based techniques for consolidating jobs and creating job families are presented.

As we embark on this journey, please bear in mind that the general principles and guidelines presented in the following pages are just that. Each organization and job modeling situation offers unique opportunities and obstacles. As the point person conducting the job modeling work in a particular context, you will understand better than anyone else what the options and limits are. Thus, my hope is that you will *adapt* versus simply *adopt* the ideas presented here. If something in this book does not apply to a given situation, do not try to pound a square peg into a round hole. Experiment and innovate! In the final analysis, the job model you build must be your own, based on your own best judgment, understanding, and creativity.

ACKNOWLEDGMENTS

This is the really fun part of writing a book. How often does a person have the chance to offer a public "thank you" to the people who have been instrumental in providing help, guidance, motivation, and instruction on an undertaking? Not often enough! I plan to take full advantage of my opportunity now.

First and foremost, I would like to acknowledge my mentor, Erich Prien. Erich has been one of my teachers over the years and for this I am grateful. From him I have developed a strong appreciation of organizational functioning, of the men and women who staff organizations, and of the work they perform. Although he is referenced throughout this book, I suspect it is not enough to truly reflect the impact he has had on my thinking and the ideas represented here.

In addition to Erich, five other individuals graciously agreed to review the entire pre-publication version of the book: Bob Guion, Leaetta Hough, Kevin Murphy, Juan Sanchez, and Andy Vinchur all took time from very busy work and personal schedules to provide valuable feedback. I am fortunate to be the beneficiary of their ideas and support.

I am also indebted to a number of friends and colleagues who provided a more limited review of specific chapters or concepts at various stages of the book's creation. It is a pleasure to thank them. In alphabetical order, they include Dwain Boelter, Steve Cronshaw, Tom Dohm, Marv Dunnette, Maynard Goff, Dave Heine, Tom Janz, Steve Lammlein, Kal Lifson, Donna Neumann, Elaine Pulakos, Pete Ramstad, Mark Schmit, and Elaine Sloan.

Each these individuals made a number of suggestions, not all of which were included in the final draft. Although their input resulted in an improved product, it should not imply agreement with all the content of the book. Of course, I take responsibility for what is said and any errors, somewhat in the spirit of Sir

Thomas Moore, who said to his executioner on his way up the gallows, "Help me up. On the way down I can manage for myself."

Furthermore, a number of the ideas and tools presented in the book are extensions of the work of many writers and researchers. I have benefited from their efforts and have diligently tried to acknowledge the history of these ideas. However, over the 8 years I have been collecting materials and preparing the manuscript, it is possible I have made some oversights. To the extent there are errors of omission, I apologize and look forward to learning about them so that I may make corrections in the second edition of the book.

Next, I owe a debt of gratitude to Personnel Decisions International (PDI), my employer for the past 6 years. My colleagues at PDI possess an incredible blend of business savvy and technical expertise. As I pushed this project toward completion, this wonderful group of professionals proved to be a constant source of constructive criticism and cortical stimulation.

Thanks also to Ana Morel and Karen O'Grady, who typed the manuscript and did wonderful work translating my chickenscratching and convoluted illustrations, recorded on everything from notepaper to napkins, into readable text and exhibits. And thanks to Laurie Lippe and Johannah Bomster, who proofed the manuscript and taught me a thing or two about good grammar along the way.

In addition, the folks at Lawrence Erlbaum Associates proved to be terrific publishing partners. In particular it was a pleasure working with Anne Duffy, Robin Marks Weisberg, Joe Petrowski, and Kathryn Houghtaling Lacey.

Finally, my lovely wife Deborah deserves a tremendous "thank you." She not only proofed the final draft of the manuscript but demonstrated incredible patience while I brought this project to a close; Deb, I can help remodel the kitchen now!

AUTHOR'S NOTE

I ran into an unexpected problem while writing this book. Namely, how to handle the male-oriented emphasis of the English language. My initial strategy was to simply run away from the problem. However, this led to some pretty complex and contorted sentence structures. So, in the interest of smoother and more concise writing, I eventually settled on using the generic masculine pronoun when general concepts are discussed and, in specific examples, drawing on both male and female examples. Although I am not satisfied with this solution, it was the best way I could think of to handle this dilemma.

REFERENCES

[1]Plato. (1986). *The republic and other works* (B. Jowitt, Trans.). Buffalo: Prometheus.
[2]Uhrbrock, R. S. (1922). The history of job analysis. *Administration, 3,* 164–168.
[3]Zerga, J. E. (1943). Job analysis, a resume and bibliography. *Journal of Applied Psychology, 27,* 249–267.

[4]Sanchez, J. I. (1994). From documentation to innovation: Reshaping job analysis to meet emerging business needs. *Human Resource Management Review, 4*(1), 51–74.

[5]Cronshaw, S. F. (1997). Job analysis: Changing nature of work. *Canadian Psychology, 39,* 5–13.

[6]McLagan, P. A. (1990). Flexible job models: A productivity strategy for the Information Age. In J. P. Campbell & R. J. Campbell & Associates (Eds.), *Productivity in organizations* (pp. 369–387). San Francisco: Jossey-Bass.

[7]Howard, A. (Ed.). (1995). *The changing nature of work.* San Francisco: Jossey-Bass.

[8]Bridges, W. (1994). *Jobshift.* Reading, MA: Addison-Wesley.

[9]Arnowitz, S., & DiFazio, W. (1994). *The jobless future.* Minneapolis: University of Minnesota Press.

[10]Rifkin, J. (1995). *The end of work: The decline of the global labor force and the dawn of the post-market era.* New York: Putnam.

I

THE BASICS
OF STRATEGIC JOB MODELING

Chapter 1
Introduction to Strategic Job Modeling

> *... it is not what the [informed man] believes that distinguishes him, but how and why he believes it. ...*
>
> —Bertrand Russell

It is still possible to find people who believe Earth is flat. To the *flat earther*, the Earth is formed in the shape of a disk, with the North Pole at the center and the South Pole ringing the outer edge. These are not foolish people who are intent on believing silly things. They feel the Earth is flat on the basis of sound evidence.[1] For example, flat earthers point out that the opposite side of large lakes can be seen through binoculars; therefore, Earth's surface must be flat. Also, they say Earth cannot be a rotating globe because when people jump up in the air for 1 second they will not come down miles away.

Most of us would agree that the flat earthers have made the wrong observations and drawn the wrong conclusions if they are interested in the truth. Individuals who work in or with organizations must avoid similar traps of faulty observation. If faulty or uncritically examined information forms the basis of a belief, all subsequent decisions based on that information will be flawed. A tool available to those working with the human side of organizations is strategic job modeling (SJM), which can be used to collect information about people and jobs and guide efforts to select, build, or modify the components of a human resource (HR) system designed to achieve an organizationally relevant outcome. The result of using this tool is a richer and more accurate set of information for guiding decisions that ultimately have real organizational consequences. To drive this point home, it is becoming increasingly clear that companies that use sound HR data to guide decisions are more likely to show higher returns on equity, assets, and investments, in addition to increased stock appreciation and dividends per share.[2,3,4]

The prior claim deserves some clarification. Although there is a growing body of evidence to suggest a link between organization performance and individual HR applications such as compensation,[5] training,[6,7] selection,[8] and so on, this is only part of the picture. Evidence is also accumulating that suggests the financial impact of HR is not just additive, but that the whole system is greater than the sum of its parts (i.e., organization impact > compensation payoff + training payoff + selection payoff). In other words, HR systems achieve status as a truly unique source of competitive advantage when the specific applications have a high degree of horizontal and vertical fit.[9,10,11,12] *Horizontal fit* means that the various applications of the HR system are integrated and complementary. *Vertical fit* means the specific applications in the HR system and the overarching HR plan are congruent with the organization's vision and business strategy. When these horizontal and vertical alignments occur, positive relations are found with organization success factors such as financial strength, technological progress, market breadth, quality, resource levels, or product innovation.[13,14,15,16] Although the true range of these economic impacts are still being investigated, early work suggests that an integrated HR system can raise the organization's market value by $15,000 to $45,000 per employee[17,18,19] and can impact the probability of survival for a new firm by 22%.[20]

Where does job modeling fit into the picture of an impactful and integrated HR system? A quality HR system is not something that can be bought like a refrigerator. It has to be made. Down beneath the surface, working to piece together the various applications of the HR system to achieve horizontal fit and establish linkages with the organization's strategic objectives and initiatives to achieve vertical fit, is the job modeling engine. This engine is working at the core of an integrated HR system to build the information platform that supports the applications and guides HR decisions for creating and sustaining organizational performance and competitive advantage.

A definition of SJM, might be useful at this point. *Strategic job modeling* is: The source of certainty, the fount of clarity, and the origin of all that is good.

Just kidding! While I do not necessarily think the above is untrue, a more widely accepted definition follows.

> Strategic Job Modeling: An ongoing set of organizational activities that involve using methodologically sound research procedures to systematically investigate, study, verify, display, and apply all the relevant information about a job, job track, set of jobs in a value chain, and so forth, and the relevant person requirements for either a specific application or an entire array of applications comprising an HR system.

The definition just given is somewhat lacking, however, because it does not convey the fun and challenge inherent in the work. A good job modeler should be part detective and puzzle-solver, part writer, and part coach. Think about it. As a detective, the modeler is in search of a missing suspect. The target of the investigation is a strategic description of the requisite components of success for a job, job group, or whatever. We know our suspect exists, but we do not yet know his appearance. Our mission is to discover the facts. Next, we must piece the facts together so they make sense and then put them down on paper in a way that communicates the richness of the information contained in the results. Finally, we often need to coach others in the organization on how best to leverage the information broadly across the system to manage human capital and develop strategically aligned HR applications. To my thinking at least, this more elaborate description fits pretty well.

You have probably deduced at this point that the results of a modeling effort are seldom viewed as an end product. Instead, they provide an intermediate product used to select (or develop or modify) a selection system, a multirater feedback instrument, an assessment center, and so on. Hence, although SJM may not, by itself, result in a usable system, the fit between the applications that are developed and an organization's needs will be no better than the quality of information produced by this essential first step.

As an illustration, when building a house, one obviously wants to start with a solid foundation. Similarly, when building a training program, performance appraisal system, or assessment center, one would be well advised to reject loose earth and sand in favor of rock and mortar. That is, it is important to have a solid information base of descriptive data for the jobs targeted by the intervention. An important concept embedded in the previous sentence is the reference to a direct link among an organization's needs, the recommended application or applications, and the type of information collected in job modeling. In fact, different applications require different procedures for managing, analyzing, and displaying the job modeling information. In other words, the type of information collected and the way it is analyzed can be different in different situations (i.e., when supporting different applications).

Having said this, it should be noted that, over the past few years, there has been a marked increase in the development and promotion of off-the-shelf products for analyzing jobs. A primary selling point of these products is that "one size fits all."[21] However, these instruments have met with mixed success at best. Mumford and Peterson, in their work to create a replacement for the Department of Labor's *Dictionary of Occupational Titles (DOT)*, made no bones about the fact that there is no one set of descriptors that provides a fully comprehensive description of people's activities in an occupation.[22] Similar views have been expressed by a number of other researchers.[23,24] These views bring to the forefront an inherently troubling question: Do ready-made and fixed modeling products yield information that is useful to guide the development of subsequent applications?

While thinking about this question, also consider whether:

- one preemployment test (e.g., a test of mechanical aptitude) predicts job performance equally well in all jobs regardless of content (e.g., aircraft mechanic, vice president of marketing, or bakery route salesperson);

- one off-the-shelf training program is equally useful to all employees in all jobs across all organizations (i.e., regardless of work functions or whether the individuals targeted for training are good performers or poor performers); and
- one pay scale is equally suited to all classes of jobs across all organizations and across different parts of the country (e.g., from New York City to Bald Knob, Arkansas).

The obvious answer to these questions is *no*. By now it should be clear that I take issue (it has been said that nothing gets the adrenaline squirting like taking a little issue) with the one-size-fits-all concept. In fact, this book is predicated on the idea that no single prepackaged job analysis system with a fixed set of content provides all of the information needed for all jobs in all organizations or all possible HR applications.

LEGAL ENVIRONMENT

There is yet another reason for paying close attention to the quality of job information that is used to develop various HR applications. The legal environment in which businesses operate (collectively viewed as the exorcist of the HR world because it scares the devil out of everybody) has become a critical issue to be considered. A variety of laws passed since the 1960s, including Title VII of the Civil Rights Act of 1964,[25] The Equal Pay Act of 1963,[26] and the Age Discrimination Act of 1967,[27] have increased the importance of clear, logically derived job information as a vital part of establishing the job relatedness of various HR practices. Of course, the Civil Rights Act of 1991[28] and the Americans With Disability Act[29] created a new series of twists and turns along what was already a difficult-to-follow path.

Although none of these statutes specifically legislates job analysis, agency guidelines based on some of these statutes do require a systematic analysis of jobs and work to establish the job relatedness of resulting procedures.[30] The most definitive statement of these guidelines is embodied in the *Uniform Guidelines on Employee Selection Procedures*[31] (hereinafter the *Uniform Guidelines*). These administrative guidelines clearly establish job analysis as a prerequisite for demonstrating that employment practices are job related. In part, these guidelines state:

> There should be a review of information to determine measures of work behavior(s) or performance that are relevant to the job or group of jobs in question. These measures or criteria are relevant to the extent that they represent critical or important job duties, work behaviors or work outcomes as developed from the review of job information.[32]

Furthermore, the *Uniform Guidelines* state:

There should be a job analysis which includes an analysis of the important work behavior(s) required for successful performance and their relative importance and, if the behavior results in work product(s), an analysis of the work product(s). Any job analysis should focus on the work behaviors and tasks associated with them. If work behavior(s) are not observable, the job analysis should identify and analyze those aspects of the behavior(s) that can be observed and the observed work products. The work behavior(s) selected for measurement should be critical work behavior(s) and/or important behaviors constituting most of the job.[33]

The belief that accurately captured job information should precede most human resource management (HRM) practice is also firmly expressed in the *Standards for Educational and Psychological Testing*[34] and the *Principles for the Validation and Use of Selection Procedures*.[35] Hence, as various federal and professional guidelines indicate, the importance of job modeling information for supporting various HRM practices is well established. In fact, in light of recent legislation, quality job information appears to be becoming more important.[36,37,38,39]

ANTECEDENTS OF SJM

As noted in the preface, systematic procedures for identifying and describing work functions and worker requirements have been considered important work activities since the time of the early Greeks[40] and certainly through the Middle Ages.[41] Formal descriptions of practice started appearing around the turn of the 20th century, and the prominence of the work grew with the success of time-and-motion experts and efficiency engineers like Frederick Taylor[42] and Frank and Lillian Gilbreth.[43] Thus, by the eve of World War I, when the United States would be faced with the monumental challenge of mobilizing hundreds of thousands of civilians for military jobs, the importance of job analysis was clearly recognized as an approach for gathering facts about jobs.[44]

One of the major job analysis-related products of the war years was the *Index of Occupations*, which was the progenitor of the *DOT*, published since 1939 by the U.S. Department of Labor. The *Index of Occupations* had its beginnings in a survey conducted by Walter Bingham, a psychologist who started the first Department of Applied Psychology at Carnegie Tech in 1915. Bingham's work focused on determining what civilian occupations gave experience of value to different jobs in various branches of military service. This led to the creation of the *Tables of Occupational Needs* in 1918, which outlined the manpower needs and specific skill requirements of different military units. Alvin Dodd, who later became president of the American Management Association, followed with a second edition, which detailed the job requirements (i.e., physical, educational, intellectual, and leadership needs) of every Army organization.[45]

After World War I, the practice of job analysis bumped along through a fallow period. What is most interesting about this time is that so little of consequence was built on so firm and solid a foundation (an observation that, to some extent, still applies today). One notable exception was the work of the Occupational Research Program (ORP) of the U.S. Employment Service headed up by Carroll Shartle, which was charged with developing a dictionary of jobs and a method for analyzing job requirements. The first installment of the *DOT* was a three-volume set prepared by the Job Analysis and Information Section of the Division of Standards and Research (the job analysis work unit of the ORP) and was published in 1939.[46] The *DOT* quickly became an indispensable part of the U.S. recruiting and classification effort during World War II and was referred to in newspapers at the time as "the book that went to war."[47]

In the 30 years subsequent to World War II, most of the individuals who contributed thought leadership to the field of job analysis were linked, in one way or another, to the ORP. To begin with, there was Carroll Shartle, who led the ORP at one point and later worked with John Hemphill at Ohio State, where Ed Fleishman was a graduate student. Ernest Primoff, Sidney Fine, Ernest McCormick, and Jay Otis were all members of the ORP staff. The latter member of this quartet later taught at Case Western Reserve where Erich Prien was a graduate student. Of the job analysis brain trust operating from the late 1940s to the early 1970s, only John Flanagan and Ray Christal were in no way linked to the thinking that evolved at the ORP, although both were influenced by their work and involvement with the military.

Although I personally find the history and development of the specific job analysis approaches fascinating stuff, I suspect this is not a widely held view. Therefore, I will not delve into the topic here. For those who are interested, Gatewood and Feild provide nice overviews,[48] and the contributing authors to Gael's handbook on job analysis provide more detailed reviews for many of the specific approaches.[49]

I do want to mention that the practice of job analysis got a bit of a shot in the arm after the war as the usefulness of the method for developing selection tests was recognized.[50,51] As noted earlier in this chapter, the emphasis has broadened well beyond just test development—to the point where job analysis procedures underlie the development of most HR interventions.[52,53] Concurrent with the broader emphasis that has emerged, there has been a proliferation of job analysis approaches. The myriad of approaches that have evolved differ along a wide range of variables and aspects, although in the broadest terms the variation is primarily in terms of focus and method differences.

Focus Differences Across Approaches

One way in which conventional job analysis approaches differ from one another concerns the focus of the analysis. In other words, what type of information is targeted and collected? What type of descriptive variables are used to characterize the work in question?

On one hand, *worker*-oriented approaches target individual differences, focus on requisite job incumbent characteristics, and may be thought of as competency based. The works of McCormick, Jeanneret, and Mecham;[54] Primoff;[55] and Fleishman and Reilly[56] are in this camp. On the other hand, *work*-oriented approaches target job activities or outcomes, focus on job characteristics, and are typically work activity based. Christal's work at the U.S. Air Force Human Resource Laboratory,[57] Fine's Functional Job Analysis,[58] and Hemphill's[59] work with the Executive Position Description Questionnaire (EPDQ) are all examples of this orientation.

Up until about 1970, the different approaches focused primarily on a single type of information.[60] However, multimethod approaches have begun to emerge. Examples of multifocus or hybrid approaches include Prien's Multi-Domain Job Analysis[61] and Lopez's work with his Threshold Trait Analysis.[62] Because the worker- and work-oriented foci are independent, it is possible to create a table in which each can be high or low (in terms of emphasis) independent of the other. Figure 1.1 provides a basis for comparing some of the more prominent approaches on the focus dimension.

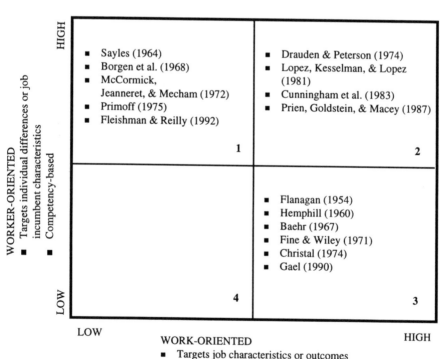

FIG. 1.1 Focus classification grid.

Method Differences Across Approaches

A second way that conventional job analysis approaches differ concerns the method of the analysis. In other words, what procedures are used to collect and analyze the needed descriptor information? Rational approaches rely on interviews, focus groups, and observation to collect information that is then deductively interpreted to create descriptions of the target work domain. Sayles' observation- and interview-based investigations of management work[63] and Flanagan's efforts to gather retrospective accounts of behavioral episodes from managers[64] are examples.

Empirical approaches rely on gathering data, primarily from questionnaires, and use quantitative methods in concert with qualitative procedures to guide the creation of information displays that describe the target domain. Hemphill's work with the EPDQ is an example.[65]

Similar to the blending of worker- and work-oriented approaches we have seen on the *focus* side of the house in the past 25 years, multimethod hybrids have cropped up on the *method* side. Examples of the method blends include the works of Fine and Wiley,[66] Primoff,[67] and Prien, Goldstein, and Macey.[68]

The rational- and empirical-based methods are also independent, making it possible to create another 2 x 2 table. The classification grid in Fig. 1.2 takes the

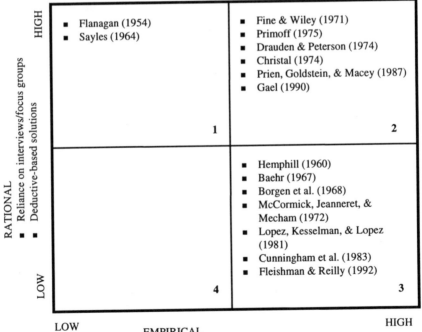

FIG. 1.2. Method classification grid.

same prominent approaches noted in the focus-based grid of Fig. 1.1 and reclassifies them on the basis of method similarity.

Taken together, the focus and method dimensions provide a basis for comparing and contrasting the different job analysis approaches, as Table 1.1 illustrates (where the numbers in the *classification* column refer back to Figs. 1.1 and 1.2). Although typologies are important as a way to facilitate understanding, this is only one reason for doing so here. The other is to make the point that the job modeling approach proposed in this book is an ongoing process that shifts emphases along these key distinguishing dimensions according to the demands and constraints of the situation.

TABLE 1.1

Prominent Job Analysis Approaches and Associated Focus/Method Classifications

Reference	Approach	Classification
• Flanagan (1954)	Critical Incident Technique	F-3, M-1
• Hemphill (1960)	Executive Position Description Questionnaire	F-3, M-3
• Sayles (1964)	Anthropological Method	F-1, M-1
• Baehr (1967)	Work Elements Inventory	F-3, M-3
• Borgen, Weiss, Tinsley, Dawis, & Lofquist (1968)	Minnesota Job Description Questionnaire	F-1, M-3
• Fine & Wiley (1971)	Functional Job Analysis	F-3, M-2
• McCormick, Jeanneret, & Mecham (1972)	Position Analysis Questionnaire	F-1, M-3
• Primoff (1975)	Job Element Method	F-1, M-2
• Drauden & Peterson (1974)	Domain Sampling	F-2, M-2
• Christal (1974)	CODAP Task Inventory	F-3, M-2
• Lopez, Kesselman, & Lopez (1981)	Threshold Traits Analysis	F-2, M-3*
• Cunningham, Boese, Neeb, & Pass (1983)	Occupational Analysis Inventory	F-2, M-3
• Prien, Goldstein, & Macey (1987)	Multidomain Job Analysis	F-2, M-2
• Gael (1990)	Work Performance Survey System	F-3, M-2
• Fleishman & Reilly (1992)	Ability Requirements Scales	F-1, M-3

Note. Thirty-three traits are fixed and built into questionnaires; if a concurrent task analysis is built into the procedure, interviews or focus groups can be employed.
F = Focus, M = Method.

REFERENCES

[1]Asimov, I. (1988). *The relativity of wrong.* New York: Windsor.

[2]Boudreau, J. W. (1991). Utility analysis in human resource management decisions. In M. D. Dunnette & L. M. Hough (Eds.), *Handbook of industrial and organizational psychology* (Vol. 2, pp. 621–745). Palo Alto, CA: Consulting Psychologists Press.

[3]Huselid, M. A. (1993). *Estimates of the impact of human resource management practices on turnover and productivity.* Paper presented at the annual meeting of the Academy of Management, Atlanta.

[4]Huselid, M. A. (1995). The impact of human resource management practices on turnover, productivity, and corporate financial performance. *Academy of Management Journal, 38,* 635–672.

[5]Gerhart, F., & Milkovich, G. T. (1993). Employee compensation: Research and practice. In M. D. Dunnette & L. M. Hough (Eds.), *Handbook of industrial and organizational psychology* (Vol. 3, pp. 481–569). Palo Alto, CA: Consulting Psychologists Press.

[6]Bartel, A. P. (1994). Productivity gains from the implementation of employee training programs. *Industrial Relations, 33,* 411–425.

[7]Knoke, D., & Kalleberg, A. L. (1994). Job training in U.S. organizations. *American Sociological Review, 59,* 537–546.

[8]Terpstra, D. E., & Rozell, E. J. (1993). The relationship of staffing practices to organizational level measures of performance. *Personnel Psychology, 46,* 27–48.

[9]Baird, L., & Meshoulam, I. (1988). Managing two fits of strategic human resource management. *Academy of Management Review, 13,* 116–128.

[10]Lengnick-Hall, C. A., & Lengnick-Hall, M. L. (1988). Strategic human resource management: A review of the literature and a proposed typology. *Academy of Management Review, 13,* 454–470.

[11]Wright, P. M., & McMahan, G. C. (1992). Theoretical perspectives for strategic human resource management. *Journal of Management, 18,* 295–320.

[12]Becker, B., & Gerhart, B. (1996). The impact of human resources management on organizational performance: Progress and prospects. *Academy of Management Journal, 39,* 779–801.

[13]Arthur, J. B. (1994). Effects of human resource systems on manufacturing performance and turnover. *Academy of Management Journal, 37,* 670–687.

[14]Delery, J. E., & Doty, D. H. (1996). Modes of theorizing in strategic human resource management: Tests of universalistic, contingency, and configural performance predictions. *Academy of Management Journal, 39,* 802–835.

[15]MacDuffie, J. P. (1995). Human resource bundles and manufacturing performance: Organizational logic and flexible production systems in the world auto industry. *Industrial and Labor Relations Review, 48,* 197–221.

[16]Youndt, M. A., Snell, S. A., Dean J. W., Jr., & Lepak, D. P. (1996). Human resource management, manufacturing strategy, and firm performance. *Academy of Management Journal, 39,* 836–866.

[17]Davidson, W. N., Worrell, D. L., & Fox, J. B. (1996). Early retirement programs and firm performance. *Academy of Management Journal, 39,* 970–984.

[18]Huselid, M. A., & Becker, B. (1995, August). *High performance work systems and organizational performance.* Paper presented at the annual meeting of the Academy of Management, Vancouver, Canada.

[19]Huselid, M. A., & Becker, B. E. (1996). Methodological issues in cross-sectional and panel estimates of the HR-firm performance link. *Industrial Relations, 35,* 400–422.

[20]Welbourne, T. M., & Andrews, A. O. (1996). Predicting the performance of initial public offerings: Should human resource management be in the equation? *Academy of Management Journal, 39,* 891–919.

[21]Mitchell, T. W. (1991). Comprehensive job analysis: Multipurpose or any purpose? *The Industrial Psychologist, 29,* 69–74.

[22]Mumford, M. D., & Peterson, N. G. (1995). Introduction. In N. G. Peterson, M. D. Mumford, W. C. Borman, P. R. Jeanneret, & E. A. Fleishman (Eds.), *Development of prototype occupational information network content model* (Vol. 1, pp. 1.1–1.16). Utah: Utah Department of Employment Security (Contract No. 94-542).

[23]Fleishman, E. A., & Quaintance, M. K. (1984). *Taxonomies of human performance.* Orlando, FL: Academic Press.

[24]Ash, R. A., Levine, E. L., & Sistrunk, F. (1983). The role of jobs and job-based methods in personnel and human resource management. In K.M. Rowland & G.R. Ferris (Eds.), *Research in personnel and human resources management* (Vol. 1, pp. 45–84). Greenwich, CT: JAI Press.

[25]Title VII of the Civil Rights Act of 1964 (Pub.L. 880352), as amended, 42 U.S.C. 2000e et. seq.

[26]U.S. Department of Labor. (1971). *Equal pay for equal work under the Fair Labor Standards Act.* Washington, DC: Author.

[27]Age Discrimination in Employment Act of 1967 (Pub.L. 90-202)(ADEA), as amended, 29 U.S.C. 621 et. seq.

[28]Civil Rights Act of 1991 (Pub.L. 102-166) (CRA).

[29]Americans with Disabilities Act of 1990 (Pub.L. 101-336) (ADA), as amended, 42 U.S.C. 12101 et. seq.

[30]Sparks, C. P. (1988). Legal basis for job analysis. In S. Gael (Ed.), *The job analysis handbook for business, industry, and government* (Vol. 1, pp. 37–47). New York: Wiley.

[31]Equal Employment Opportunity Commission, Civil Service Commission, Department of Labor, & Department of Justice. (1978). *Uniform guidelines on employee selection procedures.* Federal Register, *43*(166), 38295–38309.

[32]Ibid, p. 38300.

[33]Ibid, p. 38302.

[34]American Psychological Association. (1985). *Standards for educational and psychological testing,* Washington, DC: Author.

[35]Society for Industrial and Organizational Psychology. (1987). *Principles for the validation and use of personnel selection procedures* (3rd ed.). College Park, MD: Author.

[36]Kleiman, L. S., & Faley, R. H. (1985). The implications of professional and legal guidelines for court decisions involving criterion-related validity: A review and analysis. *Personnel Psychology, 38,* 803–831.

[37]Lozada-Larsen, S. R. (1992). *The Americans With Disabilities Act: Using job analysis to meet new challenges.* Presentation at the IPMA Assessment Council Conference, Baltimore, MD.

[38]Sanchez, J. I., & Fraser, S. L. (1992). On the choice of scales for task analysis. *Journal of Applied Psychology, 77,* 545–553.

[39]Werner, J. M., & Bolino, M. C. (1997). Explaining U.S. Courts of Appeals decisions involving performance appraisal: Accuracy, fairness, and validation. *Personnel Psychology, 50,* 1–24.

[40]Plato. (1986). *The republic and other works* (B. Jowitt, Trans.). Buffalo: Prometheus.

[41]Descartes, R. (1960). *Discourse on methods and meditations* (L. J. Lafleur, Trans). Indianapolis, IN: The Liberal Arts Press.

[42]Taylor, F. W. (1911). *The principles of scientific management.* New York: Harper.

[43]Gilbreth, F. B., & Gilbreth, L. E. (1919). *Motion study for the handicapped.* New York: E.P. Dutton.

[44]Primoff, E. S., & Fine, S. A. (1988). A history of job analysis. In S. Gael (Ed.), *The job analysis handbook for business, industry, and government* (Vol. 1, pp. 14–29). New York: Wiley.

[45]Ferguson, L. W. (1963). *Psychology and the army: Classification of personnel.* New York: The Heritage of Industrial Psychology.

[46]Ibid.

[47]Primoff, E. S., & Fine, S. A. (1988). A history of job analysis. In S. Gael (Ed.), *The job analysis handbook for business, industry, and government* (Vol. 1, pp. 14–29). New York: Wiley.

[48]Gatewood, R. D., & Feild, H. S. (1994). *Human resource selection.* Fort Worth, TX: The Dryden Press.

[49]Gael, S. (1988). *The job analysis handbook for business, industry, and government* (Vol. 2). New York: Wiley.

[50]Flanagan, J. C. (1954). The critical incident technique. *Psychological Bulletin, 51,* 327–358.

[51]Super, D. E. (1947). The validity of standard and custom-built inventories in a pilot selection program. *Education and Psychological Measurement, 7,* 735–744.

[52]Butler, S. K., & Harvey, R. J. (1988). A comparison of holistic versus decomposed rating of position analysis questionnaire work dimensions. *Personnel Psychology, 41,* 761–777.

[53]Levine, E. L. (1983). *Everything you wanted to know about job analysis.* Tampa, FL: Mariner Publishing.

[54]McCormick, E. J., Jeanneret, P. R., & Mecham, R. M. (1972). A study of job characteristics and job dimensions as based on the Position Analysis Questionnaire (PAQ). *Journal of Applied Psychology, 56,* 347–368.

[55]Primoff, E. S. (1975). *How to prepare and conduct job-element examinations* (U.S. Civil Service Commission, Technical Study 75-1). Washington, DC: U.S. Government Printing Office.

[56]Fleishman, E. A., & Reilly, M. E. (1992). *Handbook of human abilities.* Palo Alto, CA: Consulting Psychologists Press.

[57]Christal, R. E. (1974). The United States Air Force occupational research project. *Selected Documents in Psychology, 4*(61), 1–66.

[58]Fine, S. A., & Wiley, W. W. (1971). *An introduction to functional job analysis: A scaling of selected tasks from the social welfare field.* Kalamazoo, MI: W.E. Upjohn Institute for Employment Research.

[59]Hemphill, J. K. (1960). *Dimensions of executive positions.* (Research Monography No. 98). Columbus, OH: Ohio State University, Bureau of Business Research.

[60]Prien, E. P., & Ronan, W. W. (1971). Job analysis: A review of research findings. *Personnel Psychology, 24,* 371–396.

[61]Prien, E. P., Goldstein, I. L., & Macey, W. H. (1987). Multi-domain job analysis: Procedures and applications. *Training and Development Journal, 41,* 68–72.

[62]Lopez, F. M., Kesselman, G. A., & Lopez, F. E. (1981). An empirical test of trait-oriented job analysis technique. *Personnel Psychology, 34,* 479–502.

[63]Sayles, L. (1964). *Managerial behavior.* New York: McGraw-Hill.

[64]Flanagan, J. C. (1954). The critical incident technique. *Psychological Bulletin, 51,* 327–358.

[65]Hemphill, J.K. (1960). *Dimensions of executive positions* (Research Monography No. 98). Columbus, OH: Ohio State University, Bureau of Business Research.

[66]Fine, S. A., & Wiley, W. W. (1971). *An introduction to functional job analysis: A scaling of selected tasks from the social welfare field.* Kalamazoo, MI: W. E. Upjohn Institute for Employment Research.

[67]Primoff, E. S. (1975). *How to prepare and conduct job-element examinations* (U.S. Civil Service Commission, Technical Study 75-1). Washington, DC: U.S. Government Printing Office.

[68]Prien, E. P., Goldstein, I. L., & Macey, W. H. (1987). Multi-domain job analysis: Procedures and applications. *Training and Development Journal, 41,* 68–72.

Chapter 2
The Language of Strategic Job Modeling

> ... *Zounds! I was never so bethump'd with words.* ...
> —William Shakespeare's *King John*

Plain speech is a curious and nearly extinct tongue that few people use anymore. Particularly susceptible to the malady of obtuse discourse are technical experts, in any field, whose verbal abilities have been distorted to such an extent that one may wonder if it would ever be possible for them to speak like normal people again. In job modeling, the result has been confusion in terminology, which has created some basic muddles that could have been avoided if terms had simply been defined along the way. I make an honest effort here to define my terms and minimize the use of a specialist dialect. With this in mind, there are a few basic terms and concepts that should be covered before going further. Figure 2.1 provides an illustration of the conceptual building blocks in the field, and Table 2.1 provides a list of brief definitions for each of these key terms.

The building blocks are, to this point, simply concepts in the abstract. We can begin putting a finer point on things once we put the HR function into context. In short, most HR interventions involve making decisions about people based on knowing something about the work being (or to be) performed. Hence, in the simplest terms, there is a *people* component and a *work* component in the HR equation. Elaboration on the job description and situation description variables depicted in Fig. 2.1 can be found in the next three sections of this chapter.

THE PEOPLE SIDE OF THE EQUATION

For a long time, I used the acronym KSAO to refer to the person-related capabilities an individual brought to a job or role (i.e., knowledge, skills, abilities,

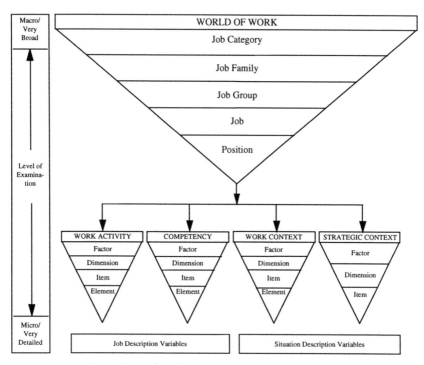

FIG. 2.1. Hierarchy of strategic job modeling building blocks.

and other characteristics). However, beyond the little club of psychologists and behavioral scientists who work extensively in the areas of employee selection, testing, and related personnel research, this term was not broadly used or meaningful. For example, virtually every client I ever worked with refused to use the term when communicating about our work inside his or her organization.

Then for several years, I followed Erich Prien's lead and tried to use the term *job skill* as a generic replacement for KSAO. However, this phrase never really seemed to capture the full meaning of person-related capabilities that were an integral part of many modeling efforts.

Then several years ago, the idea of competencies exploded on the business and HRM world. *Competencies* have been defined in various ways. Fleishman, Wetrogan, Uhlman, and Marshall-Mies noted that the term often refers to a mixture of knowledge, skills, abilities, motivation, beliefs, values, and interests.[1] Spencer, McClelland, and Spencer specifically stated that competencies can be motives, traits, self-concepts, attitudes or values, content knowledge, or cognitive or behavior skills—any individual characteristic that can be reliably measured or counted and that can be shown to differentiate superior from average

TABLE 2.1

Basic Terms

WORLD OF WORK	
Job Category	A grouping of jobs according to broad occupational class or generic job title (e.g., managerial, supervisory, administrative, sales). This grouping is primarily based on job level and might occur within or across job families.
Job Family	A grouping of jobs according to organizational function or work process (e.g., marketing, finance, HR).
Job Track	A grouping of jobs representing a logical hierarchy that may cut across job categories (e.g., administrative to supervisory to managerial), although usually occurs within a single job family.
Job Group	A small cluster of jobs within a job category or job family that represents a fairly homogeneous subset, although the differences from other job groups in a job category or job family are distinct or important enough to warrant breaking out the job cluster as a separate group.
Job	A relatively homogenous grouping of individual positions based on similarity in activities performed, competencies required, and goals or outcomes accomplished. Despite what one might read in the popular HR press, the job concept does not thwart organizational flexibility or crush individual initiative, and it is not responsible for all evil in the world of work today. It is merely a contrivance that exists at the pleasure of an organization and, when properly structured, helps clarify organizational goals.
Position	A grouping of work responsibilities or activities that are performed by one person. There are as many positions in an organization as there are employees.

WORK ACTIVITY DOMAIN: Work activities are tasks that describe the work performed. They are outcome-oriented in that they are performed for the purpose of leading to the accomplishment of some objective required for job performance.	
Work Activity Factor	A grouping of similar activity dimensions or duty areas into a broad key results area (e.g., the key results area of supervisory activities can subsume several dimension-level task categories or duty areas, such as supervise operations and supervise employees).
Work Activity Dimension	A grouping of similar activity items into a fairly broad duty or area of responsibility.
Work Activity Item	A statement that describes a discrete work activity that constitutes a whole unit of work that is a necessary component in the performance of a job.
Work Activity Element	The smallest unit or level of statement detail into which work can be divided without analyzing separate motions and movements.

(continues)

TABLE 2.1 (continued)

COMPETENCY DOMAIN: Competencies are individual capabilities. They represent the surface structure or most observable and occupationally relevant description of the KSAO (knowledge, skill, ability, and other personal characteristics) characterization of individual differences.	
Competency Factor	A grouping of similar competency dimensions into a broad set of occupationally relevant individual difference capabilities (e.g., communication, interpersonal, leadership—each of which subsume a number of more specific competency dimensions).
Competency Dimension	A grouping of similar competency items into a fairly distinct subset of related individual difference categories (e.g., provide direction or influence others—each of which subsume a number of more specific competency items).
Competency Item	A statement that describes a distinct individual difference skill, knowledge, or willingness capability (see later discussion for more detail).
Competency Element	The smallest unit into which individual difference capabilities can be divided without making reference to the specific test or scale(s) used to measure the targeted knowledge, skills, abilities, or other characteristics.

WORK CONTEXT DOMAIN: Job context variables are a broad mix of job characteristics that help define the workplace (e.g., job security, collegiality, opportunities for development, work environment, work stress). These variables indirectly impact work activities performed and ultimately the competencies that are required in a particular job or family of jobs in the organization.	
Work Context Factor	A grouping of similar work context dimensions into a broad set of work characteristics (e.g., work benefits, work itself, work conditions, organizational structure).
Work Context Dimension	A grouping of similar work context items into a fairly distinct subset of work characteristic areas (e.g., work variety, creativity, coaching or mentoring, tools and equipment; these four dimensions subsume a number of more specific items and, as a whole, roll up to define the factor work itself).
Work Context Item	A grouping of work context elements to form distinct work characteristic descriptors (e.g., "Extent to which employees perform many different work activities throughout the day" is one statement defining the work variety dimension).
Work Context Element	The smallest or most detailed work characteristic descriptor. Although job context items are generalizable enough to apply across organizations and work levels and functions, job context elements are so detailed they capture unique characteristics of a particular organization, level, or function.

TABLE 2.1 (continued)

STRATEGIC CONTEXT DOMAIN: Strategic context variables are the array of characteristics that define the environment in which a business operates, describe the collective aspirations for the future, and detail the game plan from the current situation to the envisioned future state.	
Organizational Context Factor	A grouping of similar strategic context dimensions into a broad set of organization characteristics (e.g., macroenvironment and microenvironment).
Organizational Context Dimension	A grouping of similar strategic context elements into a fairly distinct subset of organization context areas (e.g., social, economic, political/legal, and technological; these four dimensions subsume a number of more specific descriptor items and, as a whole, roll up to define the factor macroenvironment.
Organizational Context Item	The smallest or most detailed strategic context descriptor (e.g., "Extent to which there are major movements in an industry sector" is one item-level descriptor for the economic dimension in the macroenvironment factor).

performers.[2] Finally, Boyatzis defined competency simply as any underlying characteristic of an individual that is causally related to effective or superior performance.[3]

In fact, *competency* has become something of a Humpty-Dumpty word that has no meaning beyond the particular definition of the person with whom one is speaking.[4] Everyone has a different definition. Well, I have one, too. What I have done in recent years is appropriate the term *competency* and nail down a definition that I can live with and still talk to my clients without having to use different vocabulary. It really is not just about semantics, however. To my thinking, at least, competencies represent a next-generation concept.

The definitions of competencies tend to be more behavioral and ostensibly linked to meaningful organizational activities and outcomes than their KSAO counterparts. In addition, there often is a level of proficiency implied by the description of a competency, although I shy away from this common feature because I prefer not to commingle competencies with performance standards. Finally, competencies seem to facilitate the inclusion of personality-related aspects in the person-side of the models that are created; this seldom seemed to happen with KSAOs, where the "O" was typically considered to be a catchall that was tacked on as an afterthought.

For purposes here, *competencies* are defined as measurable, occupationally relevant, and behaviorally based characteristics or capabilities of people. In this respect, competencies can be thought of as reflecting the evolution of KSAOs to descriptors that have become more specific, behavioral, and useful.[5] These capabilities can be broken into two broad types:

1. **Can-do Competencies.** These individual capabilities tap into the basic ability to perform a work activity. Can-do competencies include the following:

- Skills: Individual capabilities that have been developed as a result of education, training, or experiences that underlie an individual's capacity to perform a work activity.
- Knowledge: Individual understanding of ideas and concepts that have emerged as a result of education, training, or experience and that serve as a platform for performing a work activity.

2. **Will-do Competencies.** The focus here is on personality and attitudinal characteristics that tap into an individual's willingness to perform a work activity; an aspect of people that has been overlooked in conventional job analysis approaches.[6,7] Will-do competencies may be written as *willingness to* (e.g., "Willingness to persist in the face of obstacles or difficulties").

Some people perform certain work activities better than others, and it is the degree of possession of specific competencies (skill-, knowledge-, and personality-based) that explains different levels of task performance. Competencies may be thought of as being composed of three broad classes of individual characteristics: abilities, traits, and interests/values/motivations. These three classes of individual difference characteristics constitute the deep structure or foundation on which education/training and experience opportunities are laid; these opportunities constitute the middle structure or bricks and mortar that rest on the foundation. Competencies, then, constitute the occupationally relevant surface structure, which is the capstone to the People Pyramid. This model is illustrated in Fig. 2.2.[8]

Starting at the top of the People Pyramid, competencies can be defined in varying degrees of specificity, and this variation impacts the extent to which they are generalizable across jobs and organizations. More on this topic is found in chapter 4, but two examples illustrate the point.

Example 1
(Very Generalizable)   *Skill in persuading others.*

Example 2
(Somewhat Generalizable)   *Skill in persuading potential customers to consider the benefits of a financial product or service.*

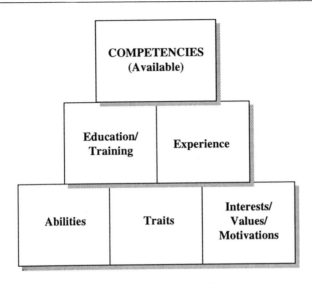

FIG. 2.2. People pyramid.

The formal educational or training opportunities represented in the pyramid can be either general or targeted. These opportunities are designed to build on basic abilities, interests, and so forth and enhance the acquisition of occupationally relevant knowledge or skills. A seminar entitled "Strategic Decisions: Seminar for Analyzing the New World Competition" would be an example of a formal training opportunity.

However, experience is either informal exposure to the ideas and concepts or the opportunity to observe or practice the work activities related to a particular competency over time. Serving on a task force designed to evaluate competitive technologies and identifying opportunities for strategic alliances is an example of a job-related experience.

At the base of the pyramid, abilities may be thought of as basic characteristics or aptitudes of individuals that constitute the present power of an individual to perform a fairly homogeneous set of related work activities. *Abilities* are relatively stable over long periods of time, although they can be developed over time as a result of education, training, or experience. The degree to which an individual possesses some abilities, such as mathematical reasoning, is relatively fixed, whereas other abilities, such as oral expression, are more responsive to exposure to situations.

The next block in the People Pyramid refers to traits. *Traits* are basic characteristics of individuals that are primarily dispositional or personality-like in nature. Traits are similar to abilities in that they are relatively stable over long periods of time, probably even more so than abilities. *Initiative,* defined as the willingness to self-start and take on responsibilities and challenges, is an example of a trait.

Finally, interests, values, and motivations are a fairly broad collection of individual difference characteristics that can be best understood as personal preferences. Interests, values, and motivations are much less stable over time than either abilities or traits; therefore, they are more likely to be influenced by situational events. Nevertheless, they are an important component in the model because it is not enough for people to be *able* to do the work—they must also be *willing* to do the work. *Work variety,* defined as a preference for multiple and varied work activities, is an example.

THE WORK SIDE OF THE EQUATION

As in the people side of the equation, the Work Pyramid in Fig. 2.3 is capped off with a competency block. These competencies are the same competencies defined previously as part of the people side of the job modeling equation. As such, they are occupationally relevant capabilities that underlie an individual's capacity to perform a work activity or set of related work activities. However, there is one small difference. The difference is one of perspective: The competencies referred to here are those required by the job versus those possessed or available on the part of an individual.

Rather than reiterate the characteristics that comprise competencies, the focus here is to describe the underlying *drivers* that underscore certain competencies as being either more or less important in a given context. As Fig. 2.3

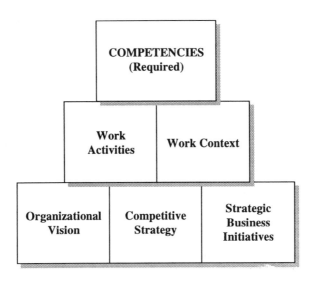

FIG. 2.3. Work pyramid.

illustrates, work activities and work context determine competency requirements, and the organization's vision, strategic objectives, and initiatives form
the basis for the work context and associated work activities.

After competencies, the next building block in the Work Pyramid involves
work activities. *Activities* are the compensable tasks performed as part of a job.
The activity is goal oriented in that it is designed to lead to some outcome or the
accomplishment of some objective, which is required (to some extent) for full
job performance. As with competencies, activities can be defined in varying degrees of specificity. The level of specificity then makes them more or less
generalizable across different jobs and organizations.

Example 1
(Very Generalizable)   *Planning activities.*

Example 2
(Not Very Generalizable)   *Develop a 5-year business plan for the re-
                                search and development unit to guide project
                                expenditure allocations by assimilating in-
                                formation about product readiness, cus-
                                tomer needs, internal resource requirements,
                                expected annualized return on investment,
                                and so on.*

The next building block involves work context variables. These are a broad
mix of work role or job characteristics that help define the workplace. These
characteristics can be broken down into four broad categories: work benefits of
either an intrinsic or extrinsic nature (e.g., compensation, job security, job mobility, collegiality, recognition, development opportunities), the work itself
(which includes work variety, opportunities for creativity, coaching or
mentoring possibilities, tools and equipment used to complete work), work conditions (e.g., the work environment, travel requirements, time flexibility, autonomy, structure, level of work stress), and organizational structure (e.g.,
organization size, hierarchy, degree of centralization, level of performance
tracking). These variables are important for understanding the context in
which work takes place; they indirectly impact work activities performed and
ultimately the competencies required in a particular role, job, or class of jobs in
an organization. For example, *collegiality* is a job context variable and might be
defined as the extent to which job incumbents interact with others and feel a
part of a team.

The organization's vision includes two types of information: the organization's mission and the organization's core values or beliefs. Management can be
more or less specific in articulating this information. Although once it is articu-

lated, it can shed light on the fundamental ideas around which the business is built and guide the firm's overall behavior. This information naturally leads to questions about the organization's competitive strategy and strategic initiatives, which elaborates on and provides an operational definition for the language of the vision and values/beliefs statements. More on this is found in chapter 3.

PERFORMANCE STANDARDS

To this point, the chapter has discussed viewing *the people* side of the job modeling enterprise as a constellation of knowledge, skills, abilities, traits, interests, values, motivations, education/training, and experience components that give rise to *competencies available*. On the other side of the equation, we have the organization's vision, competitive strategy, strategic initiatives, work context, and individual work activities all interacting to give rise to *competencies required*. This process is illustrated in Fig. 2.4, in which the models presented in Figs. 2.2 and 2.3 have been rotated and now appear together. Here, *the people* side of the equation and *the work* side of the equation are now building toward each other.

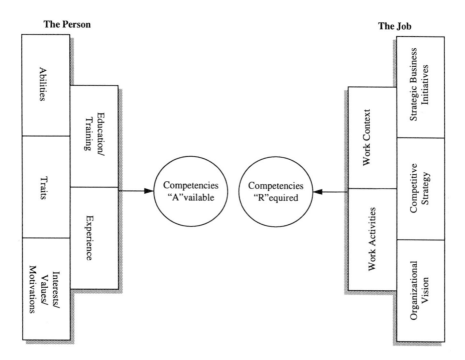

FIG. 2.4. How the person and the job interact to create the domain of job performance.

Figure 2.5 simply extends this illustration a little further by showing the overlap between competencies "A"vailable and competencies "R"equired. The degree of overlap between competencies available and competencies required has performance implications for *the person* performing *the work.* If the available competencies are less than the required competencies, the performance implications are negative. To the degree they match, there are positive implications.

In short, performance standards represent the value-laden aspect of the work domain that results from the intersection of person capabilities (which, according to our model, include knowledge and motivation differences) and job requirements. At a fairly detailed level of specificity (see Example 2), these statements represent critical incidents of effective or ineffective behavior in a manner similar to the ideas proposed by Flanagan,[9] although Flanagan's approach clearly excludes incidents that involve any mention of traits or judgmental inferences.

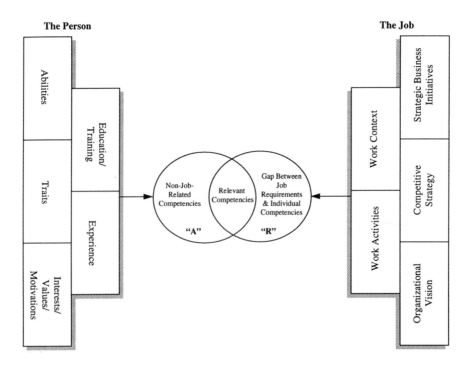

FIG. 2.5. Comparing competencies available
to competencies required.

Example 1
(Most Generalizable)   Demonstrates highly effective thinking capa-
                                                  bility.

Example 2
(Somewhat Generalizable)   Demonstrates highly effective strategic
                                                  thinking capability by explicitly articulating
                                                  how proposals, plans, and day-to-day deci-
                                                  sions and issues relate to broader strategic is-
                                                  sues.

At the level of specificity in Example 2, where there is clarification about
what an individual does that makes the behavior either effective or ineffective
and how the behavior impacts job performance, we have what is traditionally
conceived as a critical incident. In short, performance standards are
value-based examples of behavior that are critical in determining whether performance is good, average, or poor.

A MODEL FOR SJM

Having covered some of the basic concepts and terms, it is now time to present a model for SJM. Unfortunately, heuristic models are seldom pretty
things. They are often unwieldy, complex, and somehow lacking in aesthetic
appeal. Nevertheless, there must be a reason for their popularity. So, without frittering away too much time discussing the value of heuristic models or
theories, let us assume from their popularity that they are a good thing and
move on.

An enduring source of confusion in traditional job analysis research has
been the failure to specify clearly the objectives of one's particular enterprise.
To underscore this issue, let me recount a bit of conversation between Alice and
the Cheshire Cat from Lewis Carroll's *Alice in Wonderland*:

> Alice: "Would you tell me, please, which way I ought to go from here?"
> Cheshire Cat: "That depends a good deal on where you want to get to."

With reference to this quotation, let me offer up for your consideration the
Cheshire Model of SJM in Fig. 2.6. This exhibit is a representation of the key
questions and decision points influencing the typical job modeling effort. As a
heuristic aid, it might be useful to think of each step in the model as a filter
through which information must pass to reach decisions and, subsequently, the
next set of decision points in the model. These filters have the capacity to dramatically alter the perspective, configuration, and ultimately the utility of the
modeling results.

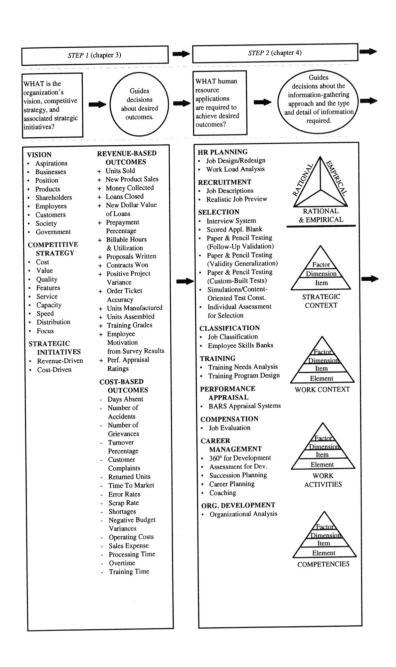

FIG. 2.6 . Cheshire model of strategic job modeling.

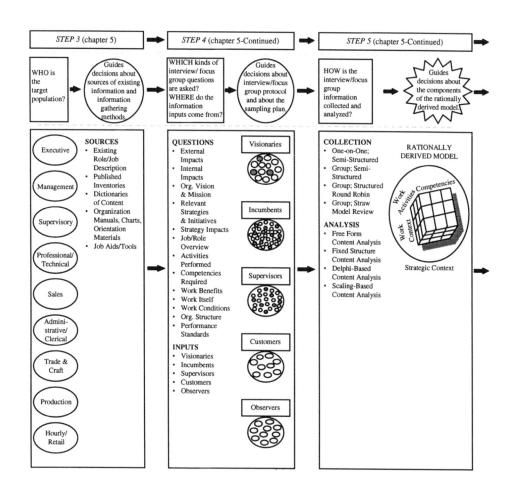

FIG. 2.6 (continued). Cheshire model of strategic job modeling.

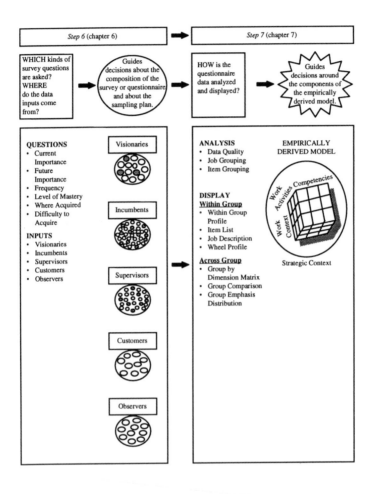

FIG. 2.6 (continued). Cheshire model of strategic job modeling.

Another way to conceptualize the Cheshire Model is as a series of five sets of questions that, when answered, tell you where you need to go in terms of the next step in building a relevant information path. One of the important features of the model is that it requires clear thinking up front about the organizational opportunities or obstacles that precipitate the need for job modeling. In this way, the model helps clarify a criterion for success for the subsequent applications and provides a clear path for cycling back to evaluate success and economic impact. Actually, each of the questions in the model is a key question and decision point. The questions that comprise the Cheshire Model are presented

TABLE 2.2
Key Questions in Job Marketing

The Questions	For More Information
• What is the organization's vision and competitive strategy, and what are the corresponding strategic initiatives? Within this context, what are the desired business outcomes?	See chapter 3
• What human resource application(s) are required to achieve the desired outcome? Given those applications, which job modeling approach is most appropriate, what type of information needs to be built into the information platform, and what degree of detail or precision is required in the descriptor content?	See chapter 4
• Who is the target population? Given the scope of the targeted population, how is existing descriptive information leveraged? How is additional information collected and integrated to close the gaps and create a rationally derived job model?	See chapter 5
• If the research context and target applications require following up on the rationally derived model and collecting data using a job modeling questionnaire, then which questions are asked? Of whom? How many respondents are needed?	See chapter 6
• How should the results from job modeling questionnaires be analyzed, and how should the results be displayed? What kinds of decision rules should be applied to the data for guiding the final components of the empirically based job model?	See chapter 7

in Table 2.2. With some slight consolidation, where Steps 3, 4, and 5 are considered together, they serve as the organizing structure for the next five chapters in the book.

The specific questions are offered in a sequential series that makes the most sense for most applications. However, by nature, the questions are interrelated as a result of the fluid nature of this type of work. This is particularly true for Steps 2 and 3, which are not only interactive, but probably more concurrent versus truly sequential sets of downstream decisions flowing from Step 1. There also may be some variability in the sequence of decisions attributable to the modeling context. Nevertheless, the model in Table 2.2 is useful for conceptualizing the sequence of decision points involved in most job modeling projects. Had enough background? Okay, then roll up your sleeves, spit on your palms, turn the page, and let's get to work.

REFERENCES

[1] Fleishman, E. A., Wetrogan, L. I., Uhlman, C. E., & Marshall-Mies, J. C. (1995). Abilities. In N. G. Peterson, M. D. Mumford, W. C. Borman, P. R. Jeanneret, & E. A. Fleishman (Eds.), *Development of prototype occupational information network content model* (Vol. 1, pp. 10.1–10.39). Utah: Utah Department of Employment Security (Contract No. 94-542).

[2] Spencer, L. M., McClelland, D. C., & Spencer, S. (1994). *Competency assessment methods: History and state of the art.* Boston: Hay McBer Research Press.

[3] Boyatzis, R. E. (1982). *The competent manager: A model for effective performance.* New York: Wiley-Interscience.

[4] Zemke, R. (1982). Job competencies: Can they help you design better training? *Training, 19,* 28–31.

[5] Barrett, R. S. (1996). *Fair employment strategies in human resource management.* Westport, CT: Quorum Books.

[6] Guion, R. M. (1998). *Assessment, measurement and prediction for personnel decisions.* Mahwah, NJ: Lawrence Erlbaum Associates.

[7] Raymark, P. H., Schmit, M. J., & Guion, R. M. (1997). Identifying potentially useful personality constructs for employee selection. *Journal of Applied Psychology, 50,* 723–736.

[8] This conceptualization benefited from input from Elaine Sloan.

[9] Flanagan, J. C. (1954). The critical incident technique. *Psychological Bulletin, 51,* 327–358.

II

THE PRACTICE OF STRATEGIC JOB MODELING

Chapter 3
What Is the Organization's Vision and Competitive Strategy?

> *... I find the great thing in this world is not so much where we stand, as in what direction we are moving....*
>
> —Oliver Wendell Holmes

An organization's vision and competitive strategy is the battle plan for moving into the future and achieving its goals. It is the banner pointing the way for everyone who needs to know what the organization is all about and where it intends to go. It is the marching orders for the subsumed business units, divisions, departments, functional areas, teams, and individuals to follow as they maneuver on the battlefield of business.

These statements are made with some reservation because many people are offended by military metaphors. However, one need only read the daily paper or popular newsprint magazines to get a feel for how the captains of business and industry think about their work:

> ... Christopher Pettit, who served as a captain in Vietnam, is engaged in another uphill conflict as president of Lehman Brothers. ...
> —Shawn Tully, *Fortune* article

> ... Yamaha o tsubuso! ("Annihilate and squash Yamaha!"). ...
> —Honda's local battle cry

> ...The war isn't over but we've definitely landed on the beaches. ...
> —Robert Lutz, vice chairman, Chrysler

D'Aveni suggests that this kill-or-be-killed attitude is the result of strategic maneuvering among increasingly global and innovative combatants. It is just part of the new reality created by hypercompetition.[1] An implication of this new reality is that, without a carefully crafted vision and subsequent set of competitive strategies and initiatives, an organization runs the risk of becoming a victim of the marketplace instead of a victor.[2,3]

Before you stop reading and look at the cover to make sure this is a book on job modeling and not one on strategic planning, I should let you know where I am going with all of this. Although it is the responsibility of management to marshal the resources to achieve the vision and strategy, it is HR's job to guide and support the acquisition, maintenance, development, and application of the human capital. Therefore, it follows that the various HR interventions must be in alignment with the vision and competitive strategy of the organization. The better the fit between these variables, the more clout the specific HR initiatives will have and the more powerful strategy execution is likely to be.

Strategic job modeling focuses on this vertical alignment in two important ways. First, there is an effort to identify the most relevant and impactful interventions. Second, there is a concerted effort to ensure that HR interventions are designed around the content (e.g., work activities, competencies, performance standards) required for individual employee success over the long haul. Many potential customers—either internal or external—are simply not clear about what they want (which does not mean they are not frequently in a headlong rush to find someone who will give it to them). In these situations, working to understand the business context and environment can be illuminating. In these cases, the customer will likely feel as if someone in a dark tunnel has handed them a flashlight.

In other instances, a customer will have a specific request in mind, such as "We need to build a selection system for hourly retail employees" or "We need to make sure our employee performance measurement system is aligned with the business goals, and we want to use the results to drive individual development planning." Once you start probing into the organization's vision and business strategy, you may get some pushback along the lines of, "Wait a minute—I already told you what we need. What makes you think we need to revisit our decision?" Of course, your customer might be quite correct, particularly if the expressed need is clearly articulated and couched in an understanding of the desired outcomes that link back to broader business goals. However, even in these situations, it is often worthwhile to develop a deeper understanding of the organization's broader vision and business strategy. At a minimum, it is a relatively painless way to confirm that the proposed intervention(s) will succeed in doing what is needed (a process on how to actually do this is presented in chap. 4). At the other extreme, it might uncover clues you can use to consult with your customer about developing the most appropriate set of interventions.

In fact, perhaps the most useful thing a strategic job modeler can do is develop his or her own understanding and framework for thinking about the customers' problems. This means not only listening to and probing around the presented problem, but also working to understand the underlying issues and developing working hypotheses about what is important and relevant in a given context. Customers who complain about the additional diagnosis can actually become more loyal once they understand they are working with someone who is trying to maximize the fit between needs and deliverables. Customers want to deal with people who will work to understand their business, understand their needs, and can partner with them to add value beyond responding with stock answers to complex business problems. With this in mind, part of the intent of this chapter is to provide a broad framework for building business context and strategy information into the job modeler's thinking for the purpose of identifying the type of HR interventions that are likely to be most relevant and have the greatest impact.

As noted earlier, there is a second reason for paying attention to vertical alignment issues. Understanding an organization's competitive strategy can give the job modeler a preview of the types of competencies that are likely to maximize organizational fit and differentiate successful from poor performers over the long term. A related issue involves the identification of the critical constellations of competencies (i.e., job groups or job families) within the organization—those sets of competencies that are directly linked to the overall performance and success of the company (a process on how to do this is presented in chap. 5).

The environment in which organizations operate has long been recognized as playing an important role in the way people are supervised, co-workers treat one another, decisions get made, and so on. [4,5,6,7,8,9] To paraphrase Schneider, work roles, job requirements, and organizations do not exist independently.[10] For example, in addition to the job-specific knowledge and skills required to perform effectively as a production manager, individuals who are judged to be truly successful in a cost-driven organization might be characterized somewhat differently from those who are star performers in a speed-driven organization. Based on the business characteristics commonly found in the first type of organization, we might expect to find star performers who are task-oriented, direct, and tough when dealing with employees, customers, and vendors. The business characteristics found in the second type of organization might lead the job modeler to expect competencies associated with creativity, innovation, and a willingness to accept some risk as key individual differentiators. Of course, subsequent steps in the job modeling process are designed to identify and describe the relevant competencies in detail. However, this up-front analysis allows the job modeler to start gathering clues, identifying gaps in information, and testing hypotheses sooner.

Furthermore, in business, change may be the only constant. Any effort to model jobs in the world of work without considering this component would be like Einstein endeavoring to explain relativity without his conversion constant: c. Come on; you remember: $e = mc^2$, where Einstein proposed, to everyone's dismay, that energy (e) and mass (m) are just two different ways of looking at the same thing. As you may recall, e does not quite equal m by itself; in fact, just a little bit of mass equals a whole lot of energy. The key to understanding the relationship between the two is c.

Similarly, for those of us engaged in modeling endeavors, the key to understanding the relationship between the job of today and the job of tomorrow is c, although for us this implies an assessment of the expected degree of change. If there were no changes in the business environment, the models built today would equal the models required for success 3, 5, and 10 years out. However, this is an untenable assumption.[11] As Fig. 3.1 illustrates, jobs do change and these changes impact the work activities performed, the competencies required, the performance standards expected, and so forth. Thus, a second reason for examining vertical alignment is to gain some clarity around expected change in an effort to build thinking about future job requirements into the equation and establish the relevance of the different types of competencies built into the model.

To jump right into a discussion of vision and strategy without first examining some of the important antecedents would be premature. Figure 3.2 illustrates the major types of information that form the basis for the framework presented in this chapter; they are divided into three primary segments.

1. NOW: an environmental scan of where the organization currently sits. Every journey starts with a determination of one's starting point. Whether figuratively going from A to B or concretely from Minneapolis to Dallas, it is not possible to chart a course to a particular destination before understanding

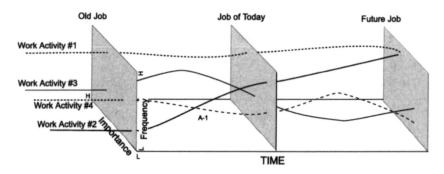

FIG. 3.1. Changing job work activities over time.

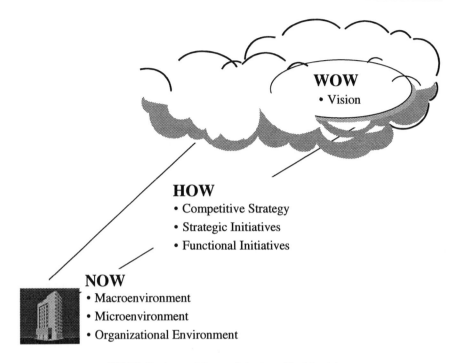

FIG. 3.2. Business vision and strategy: The big picture.

where one is starting from. In business and industry, where the journey might be moving from Number 2 to Number 1 in the car rental business, this assessment of the starting point includes understanding the macroenvironment, microenvironment, and organizational environment.

2. WOW: an articulation of the organization's destination; its aspirations and goals. These are the *blue-sky* possibilities—based on what is known about the business environment today and speculations about the future—filtered through a lens of what is considered valuable, worthwhile, and reasonably attainable.

3. HOW: the game plan for moving from NOW to WOW. Individuals who carefully follow a logical path will go farther than those who move rapidly in the wrong direction. The same is true for organizations. For an organization, this means thinking through the competitive strategy, strategic initiatives, and functional initiatives that lead to the lofty heights captured in the vision.

The NOW, WOW, and HOW segments each have a number of components and subcomponents that need to be understood as part of the process. These components and subcomponents are spelled out in the business strategy map in Fig. 3.3, which is a finer grained description of the business strategy process. The

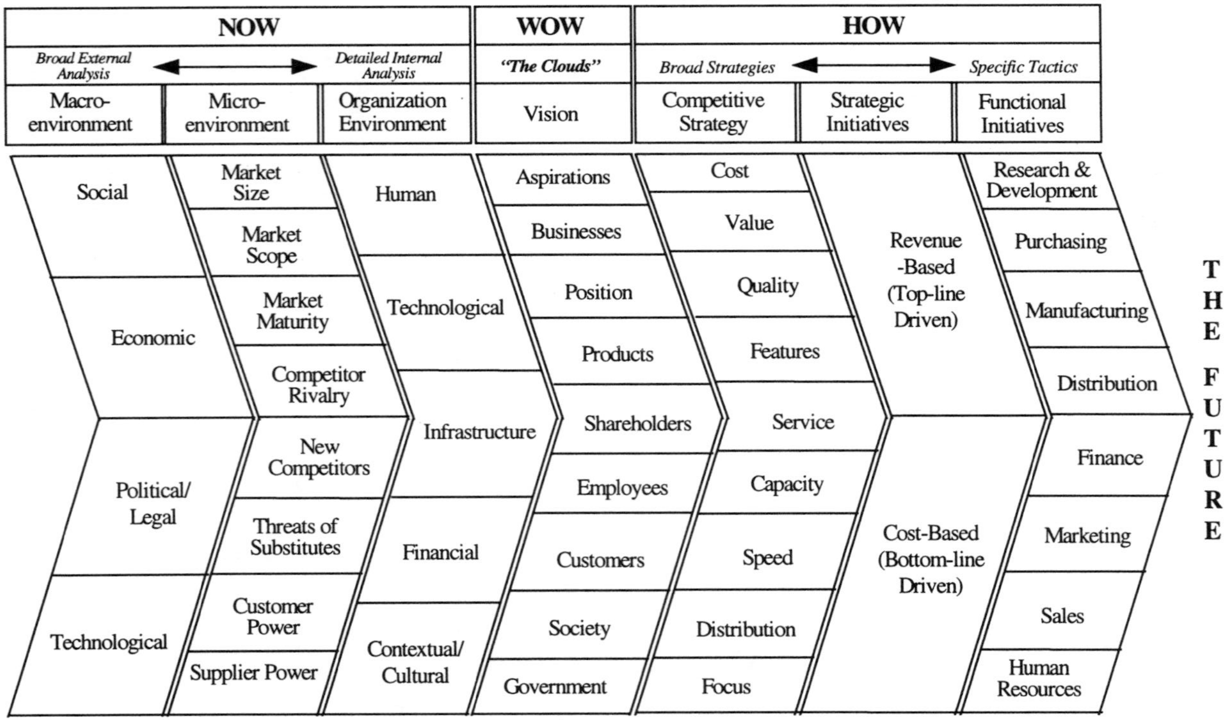

THE FUTURE

NOW			WOW	HOW		
Broad External Analysis	Detailed Internal Analysis		"The Clouds"	Broad Strategies	Specific Tactics	
Macro-environment	Micro-environment	Organization Environment	Vision	Competitive Strategy	Strategic Initiatives	Functional Initiatives
Social	Market Size	Human	Aspirations	Cost	Revenue-Based (Top-line Driven)	Research & Development
	Market Scope		Businesses	Value		Purchasing
Economic	Market Maturity	Technological	Position	Quality		Manufacturing
	Competitor Rivalry		Products	Features		Distribution
	New Competitors	Infrastructure	Shareholders	Service		Finance
Political/Legal	Threats of Substitutes	Financial	Employees	Capacity	Cost-Based (Bottom-line Driven)	Marketing
	Customer Power		Customers	Speed		
Technological		Contextual/Cultural	Society	Distribution		Sales
	Supplier Power		Government	Focus		Human Resources

FIG. 3.3. Business strategy map.

goal is to present a sufficiently comprehensive framework for organizing the broad mix of potential input information that may be generated in a wide range of modeling contexts. It is not being suggested that every job modeling situation requires an in-depth investigation and documentation of all the strategic components noted in Fig. 3.3 or described over the next few pages. One does not want to sink the modeling project at the outset by attempting to collect every scrap of conceivably useful information. Instead, consider this taxonomy as something akin to a crate of potential provisions, and then do a lifeboat analysis and throw overboard everything you do not need.

Furthermore, one might disagree with this conceptualization of the variables that help shape business strategy or one might prefer to use the approach of a particular theorist. That is fine. It is not all that important that everything gets slotted in at the right place. What is important is identifying and understanding the relevant variables so that one can use the information to guide future choices related to the job modeling effort. With this in mind, a brief discussion of each of the potential components of the business strategy process is worthwhile.

NOW

Macroenvironment

It is useful to think of an organization as operating in a larger, general business environment that extends beyond the bounds of the organization's particular industry. This is the *macroenvironment*, which has been described as huge and ponderous where much of what is useful to know is buried under something heavy.[12] For example, the macroenvironment includes events such as demographic shifts, movement toward an integrated global economy, advent of Internet technology, and changes in government, all of which have implications for a wide band of organizations and their respective strategies. Understandably, the line of sight between these events and real-world impacts on a specific organization in a particular industry can be difficult to follow. Nevertheless, the links exist and are important to consider. As Fig. 3.3 indicates, the macroenvironment consists of four broad subcomponents: social environment, economic environment, political environment, and technological environment.

- Social Environment: This subcomponent consists of demographics and social values, including population size, age structure, ethnic mix, income levels, education and skill mix, political values, and societal values in general. For example, what effect is the increasing fervor of the antismoking movement likely to have on the tobacco industry, particularly in the harsh glare of trials like the *State of Minnesota and Blue Cross and Blue*

Shield vs. Philip Morris, Inc. et al., which are attracting international media attention?

■ Economic Environment: This refers to the nature and direction of the economy in which an organization operates. There is a wide range of variables of interest in this segment, including major movements in an industry sector, world economy and investment markets, gross domestic product, interest rates, inflation, producer prices, consumer prices, housing starts, and industrial investment. For example, emboldened by a skyrocketing stock market and greater participation by institutional investors, today's capital markets are friendly toward entrepreneurial startups in software, communications, medical devices, electronics, and biotech. Leading venture capitalists lament that they have more money and interested investors than they do investment opportunities.[13]

■ Political/Legal Environment: This subcomponent includes the major institutions of government, such as the executive branch, the legislatures, the judiciary, and regulatory agencies, as well as informal arenas in which political activity occurs, such as community relations and the media. For example, societal concerns over the negative environmental impacts of commercial and manufacturing activities have led to a sharp increase in environmental regulations throughout the world at multilateral, regional, national, subnational, and municipal levels.[14]

■ Technological Environment: This involves both how knowledge is acquired and how it is practically applied. The technological environment can be segmented into three classes:

• Research: Basic research that seeks to uncover principles and relationships underlying knowledge (i.e., discovery and invention).
• Development: This refers to the utilization of knowledge in some prototype form (i.e., innovation).
• Operations: Operations refers to putting knowledge to practical use in a way that can be adopted by others (i.e., deployment).

For example, research in biotechnology offers the potential to revolutionize the food industry. Enhanced nutritional profiles for existing foods, the creation of entirely new products, and new flavors represent just some initial possibilities and you can bet the big food companies of the world are paying attention.

Macroenvironmental change affects all of the other elements of the strategic management process outlined in Fig. 3.3. Without some understanding of how the future might play out in the social, economic, political, and technological environments, an organization will be ill prepared for adapting and surviving in the future. At this point I can sense the clicks of many minds snapping shut.

This predicting the future stuff is just a little much for some of you to take. Well, take heart. I am one of you! Although occasionally interesting to think about, I also believe it is pointless to try and make business decisions today based on predictions of what will happen 50 years from now in the social, economic, political, or technological environments. However, to paraphrase Peter Drucker, it is possible and fruitful to prepare for the future that has already happened.[15] In other words, there are events taking place today that will continue to play out and have an impact for the next 10 years or so. For the job modeler intent on building a strategic focus into his work, understanding the future of today is the best way to get a heads-up on the broad external factors that are likely to impact the business. These forces, in turn, will impact the business strategies that affect the functional strategies and subsequently play out in changes in the configuration of work activities and requisite competencies.

The commercial banking industry provides a nice case example. With respect to questions about the appropriate type of HR intervention, consider recent developments in the political/legal arena, where deregulation has removed many of the barriers between commercial and investment banks. As a consequence, investment products and mutual funds are a booming part of the business mix for commercial banks, and training programs focusing on product knowledge and specialized sales are both prevalent and relevant. So are selection programs that emphasize the new competencies.

With respect to the type of competencies likely to be important, think about the shift in banking toward automation and electronic service (i.e., technological environment). Banks are striving to remain competitive by staying on the forefront of technology, as illustrated by the introduction of automated banking kiosks and Internet banking. Consequently, the simple order-taking jobs are disappearing or being reengineered, such that the remaining front-line jobs will require especially strong interpersonal, service, and sales competencies.

Microenvironment

The microenvironment includes the relevant markets and competitors of a particular organization. Although we are still talking about the world outside of the organization proper, the variables of interest are now much closer to home. In fact, they are just outside the organization's doors. When business strategists talk about industry analysis, they are really talking about the microenvironment. Along these lines, Porter presented the *Five Forces Theory of Industry Structure*.[16,17] Although Porter's primary focus is on strategy in individual industries, his concepts are designed to be extended to organizations for the purpose of developing customized competitive strategies. The five forces serve as part of the basis for the microenvironment segmentation presented here (the last five subcomponents are variations of Porter's five forces). Porter's books are cornerstones of strategic thinking geared toward helping an organization's senior management team develop strategies for survival in competitive environments. However, he is not known for his brevity. In this way, Porter is following in the footsteps of George Steiner, the strategy guru of the previous decade, whose three-volume, 800-page opus anchors many a manager's bookshelves and whose thinking also contributes to the conceptualization of the microenvironment presented here.[18]

- Market Size: Describes the potential available market in terms of annual sales or unmet need and answers this question: "Is the market growing or shrinking?"
- Market Scope: Describes the geographic dispersion of the current or potential market (i.e., dispersion across global, national, regional, and local boundaries).
- Market Maturity: Describes the stage of the product life cycle for the bulk of products or services competing in the market. For example, is the market in the introduction, growth, mature, or decline phase?
- New Competitors: Refers to the entry barriers that prevent an influx of firms into an industry arena (e.g., proprietary learning curve, economies of scale, government policy, and capital requirements).
- Competitive Rivalry: Describes the type and degree of rivalry in an industry (e.g., number of competitors, competitor strategies, and industry growth).
- Threat of Substitutes: Refers to the existence of potential substitutes that perform the same functions as the products or services being targeted for analysis and is a condition that caps the amount of value an industry can create (e.g., buyer propensity for substitutes and supplier switching costs).
- Customer Power: Characterizes the extent to which customers can squeeze industry margins by pressing competitors to reduce prices or increase the level of service offered without associated price adjustments (e.g., concentration of customers, presence of buyer information, price sensitivity, and degree of brand identity).
- Supplier Power: The flip side of the coin to customer power (e.g., supplier concentration and differentiation of inputs).

The impact of microenvironment variables clearly cascades down to the remaining components of the strategic management processes illustrated in Fig. 3.3. Without a clear understanding of market size, market scope, market maturity, new competitors, competitive rivalry, the threat of substitutes, customer power, and supplier power, the organization is adrift in the tide like a boat loose from its moorings in treacherous waters.

The strategic job modeler needs to be clued in to what is going on in this environment as well. For example, with reference to questions about relevant types of HR interventions, consider the Competitive Rivalry variable in the telecommunications industry, where local telephone, cable TV, wireless, and long-distance telephone providers are all in a frenzied competitive dash to gain ground in a growing market. This frenetic activity (how many solicitation calls have you received at home from a telecommunications provider in the past week?!) is the result of rapid growth in new methods of transmission and products and legislation that lifts many of the regulations that restrict telecommunications carriers from operating in certain markets. As a consequence, many of these organizations have ever-changing work environments where people, work processes, and technology are reconfigured to aggressively push forward various program initiatives. In this environment, the development of employee skill banks designed to keep track of the human talent portfolio and facilitate the allocation of the right technical skills to important projects are being viewed as one particularly relevant form of HR intervention.

Now consider the Market Maturity variable and the question about the type of competencies that are likely to be important. The competency mix for a sales manager who works for an organization that competes in an emerging market where rivalry is intense and everyone is hustling for market share (e.g., AT&T, the Baby Bells, MCI, GTE) is likely to be different from that of a sales manager in an organization that operates in a declining market with shrinking share and reduced resource support (e.g., most defense contractors and, to an extent, freight track railroads). The first role is likely to emphasize the energy and drive for success that characterize volume-based sales,[19] whereas the emphasis in the latter is likely to be centered on the interpersonal competencies that make up long-term relationship-based sales.

Organization Environment

The framework for examining the organization environment is similar to the strengths and weaknesses (S–W) part of the review in the traditional SWOT analysis (i.e., organizational strengths, weaknesses, opportunities, and threats). The purpose of this internal analysis is to see what the organization has to work with as it begins to position itself to deal with the opportunities and threats identified through the analysis of the external environments. Specifically, it helps identify what existing strengths and weaknesses might impact the organization's value creation capabilities.

Despite the infinite range of potential strengths and weaknesses that could characterize a particular organization, the S–W landscape can be broadly described with the following five subcomponents:

- Human: The people portfolio and associated numbers, talents, and characteristics. Specifically, the human side of the organization environment includes:

- Staff size relative to staffing needs.
- Individual competencies, both *soft* and *technical.*
- Leadership from the work team and department level up through the senior management team. Although leadership is certainly an individual-level competency, it is usually important enough to warrant breaking it out separately.
- Morale, in terms of the team spirit and level of employee motivation.
- Commitment, which is slightly different from morale. Specifically refers to the extent individuals in the organization share a collective state of mind and resolve concerning the articulated goals.
- Collaboration or collegiality, which refers to the extent to which individuals interact smoothly with others and feel part of a team both within and across work groups.

■ Technology: The technological assets available to the organization. For example:

- Facilities and heavy equipment, which includes an evaluation of their number, size, capability, state of repair, and safety.
- Tools and office equipment, including computers, software, photocopiers, shredders, and so forth.
- Level of information technology support.

■ Infrastructure: The structure, systems, and decision-making styles or processes that characterize how things get done.

- Structure, in this context, refers to how the organization is organized internally (in terms of subdivided units such as business sectors, business units, and departments and the associated reporting relationships) and how it maps onto relevant external entities (such as customers, suppliers, distributors, strategic partners, and public or community groups) through alliances, partnerships, and networks. Common organizational structures include a functional organization structure, process-oriented structure, decentralized business/division structure, strategic business unit structure, geographic structure, and a matrix organization structure.
- Systems, in this context, refer to how information moves through the structure, how it is monitored, and how it is used by decision makers.
- Decision-making styles and processes refer to the procedures used to make decisions. These procedures could range from large, formal, data-driven meetings to small, informal, viscerally guided get-togethers.

■ Financial: The dollar-based numbers that drive business decisions, including:

  • Assets available, which include cash, inventory, accounts receivable, intellectual capital, equipment, and structures/buildings.
  • Liabilities pending, which include bank debt, accounts payable, taxes owed, wages owed, and prepaid accounts or advances from customers.
  • Financing practices, which refers to how the organization creates operating capital.
  • Prices for products or fees for services (i.e., on what part of the price continuum does the organization compete?).
  • Compensation (pay plus benefits) levels for employees (i.e., on what part of the compensation continuum does the organization compete for employees?).

■ Contextual/Cultural: The variables that comprise the context dimension are more descriptive characteristics that could impact the human capital (and, to a lesser extent, the technological, infrastructure, and financial assets) than they are true sources of competitive advantage in and of themselves. These variables are listed next. A detailed definition of each appears in chapter 5.

  • Job security
  • Job mobility
  • Recognition
  • Development opportunities
  • Work variety
  • Creativity
  • Coaching/mentoring
  • Work environment/safety
  • Travel
  • Time flexibility
  • Autonomy
  • Work standards
  • Work stress

The range of Human, Technology, Infrastructure, Financial, and Contextual/Cultural variables presented above comprises the third and last stage preceding the visioning process. In summary, they are also the key factors to be considered in a detailed, internal environment analysis, which is not what is being suggested. However, there are implications for the job modeling consultant. Thus, what is being suggested is a high-level audit and assessment of these variables.

The meaning and potential modeling impacts of the Human variables are easily grasped, but there are meaningful clues to be found in understanding the other variables that characterize the current organization environment. As an example, consider the Infrastructure class of variables. With respect to the type of HR intervention, a geographic organization structure (e.g., Delta and most other large airlines) creates needs for a larger management staff, particularly general managers. As a result, interventions involving training and development are likely to be relevant.

Now consider the Financial class of variables. With respect to the type of competencies likely to be important, a retail organization that devotes a large part of the budget to compensating employees tends to emphasize a different mix of skills in its sales force. This is evident on entering Saks Fifth Avenue after shopping at a discount department store. In fact, understanding where on the compensation continuum the organization competes for employees is frequently a critical piece of information. Thus, the final components of the model for a job or class of jobs should be critically examined in terms of what kinds of people the organization can hope to attract, and keep, given the compensation model.

WOW

Vision

In personality theory, there is the concept of cardinal traits—those that serve as the primary drivers of behavior and that set one individual apart from another and give one a particular identity. The same concept may be applied to organizations. The idea here is that behind each organization is a mix of some small number of motives that are fundamental drivers around which the business is built and that guide the overall behavior of the firm. So, in one sense, the vision can be thought of as an articulation of the organization's aspirations for its future based on underlying motives. For the most part, these motives can be divided into two segments: those relating to the mission and those relating to the core values.

Mission.   A mission is the stated purpose of an organization; it addresses the question: "Why do we exist?"[20] There are a number of components to this question, but in broad terms the following four provide a nice organizing structure:

- Aspirations: Involves a description of the organization's wishes and hopes for the future (e.g., Where does the organization want to be in 5, 10, or 15 years? What will the future value chain of the industry look like? Where will the organization want to fit in?).
- Businesses: Includes a description of the organization's current core businesses and cash cows and an understanding of the hopes for future busi-

nesses (e.g., What businesses does it want to get into, stay in as a primary player, stay in as a secondary business, or divest? How should the businesses of the organization be interrelated, if at all?).

- Position: Describes the market leadership goals for specific business segments (e.g., What rank or level of leadership is targeted for major business segments? What is the timeframe for reaching these goals?).
- Products: Describes the goals for specific product/service lines (e.g., What is the market share target for specific product/service lines? What types of new customers are targeted? Which competitors will the organization take market share from?).

Core Values.   Beyond the drive to accomplish the mission, what is the organization motivated to achieve for its various constituencies? Although not an exhaustive list, the following five stakeholder groups cover a lot of territory:

- Owners/Shareholders: What level of economic return does the organization strive for? What financial returns are sought on specific investments? What indicators best represent total organization success: dollar profit? percent profit? earnings per share? return on investment? return on gross assets? market share?
- Employees: What type of work experience does the organization want to provide for employees? Are there dramatic differences across levels? What kind of financial return does it want to provide employees at all levels? Does the organization spend resources to grow its own people or does it let them take care of themselves and hire from the outside when there is a demand for talent? Where does the organization stand on employee compensation relative to competitive firms: higher, equal, lower? Relevant examples of how organizations express the value of employees in existing vision statements include "Treating all team members with respect," "Communicating openly and honestly among team members," and "Committed to maintaining a safe work environment for all employees."
- Customers: What degree of customer satisfaction and value does the organization seek to provide its customers? How can the organization help customers achieve their goals? Relevant statements from existing vision statements are "Completely committed to customer satisfaction" and "Driven to be the highest quality producer in the market."
- Society: How, specifically, does the organization demonstrate good corporate citizenship? Does it support social projects through gifts or other contributions? Is the organization a community leader, a middle-of-the-road citizen, or does it see itself as free of community obliga-

tions? A relevant statement from one organization's vision statement is "Committed to protecting the environment."

- Government: How does the organization contribute to the goals of specific agencies? What kinds of contributions does the organization make to good government?

HOW

Competitive Strategy

If the organization's vision, subsumed mission, and core values are motives, the competitive strategy is the array of manifest behaviors. These are the organization's broad actions designed to take advantage of the opportunities and protect against the identified threats in the environment. Furthermore, the competitive strategy can be conceptualized using some of the nine components listed next. This part of the business strategy framework builds on Porter's three generic strategies,[21] introduces some ideas related to D'Aveni's work on hypercompetition,[22] and incorporates the thinking of several other strategists, including Steiner[23] and Hamel and Prahalad.[24]

- Cost: The focus of the organization is on competing on the playing field of price. For example, under legendary founder Sam Walton, Wal-Mart experienced staggering growth in the 1970s and 1980s, with a clear-cut strategy: forget the frills and sell brand-name merchandise at low prices. The no-frills philosophy permeates the company, as anyone who has ever been to the company headquarters in Bentonville, Arkansas can attest. Now one of the United State's largest retailers, the company is going global, but the fundamental strategy is unchanged.
- Value: The focus is on developing innovative, unique, valuable products or services that others in the market cannot offer. Intel is a high-tech company that has had to survive on the value of its ideas and innovative solutions; it does so on a continuous basis because of the incredible pace of change in a market that will not stand still. Not surprisingly, Intel spends an impressive 6% of its total payroll ($160 million in 1996), on its inhouse university and training.
- Quality: The focus is on high-quality, defect-free product. For example, when the Japanese targeted U.S. electronics producers, Motorola was one of the few that not only withstood the challenge, but beat them at their own game. The company launched a wide array of initiatives to improve product quality starting in the late 1970s; during the 1980s, it tripled sales and profits while other U.S.-based manufacturers of electrical components were caving in to overseas competition.

- Service: It concerns the *quality* focus for the service side of business. In these cases, the focus is on providing excellent service, whether in support of a product (e.g., dealer networks, technical assistance, hot lines, education about product use) or in terms of the level of comfort or expertise associated with a service. For example, before Seattle-based specialty retailer Nordstrom's opened their first store on the east coast in 1988, people traveling to the west coast used to make it a point to drop into one of their stores to see if the stories were true. Famous for putting customer service first, Nordstrom employees routinely went the extra mile to give visitors to the store a delightful "shopping experience."

- Capacity: The focus is on delivering a product or service on a large scale. For example, consider Coca-Cola and its stated goal of putting a Coke within arms reach of anyone, anywhere. The company appears well on its way, given that 80% of this beverage and food service giant's profits come from outside North America. Citibank is another example—both in terms of breadth of its financial products and services and due to the omnipresence of its locations.

- Speed: The focus is on how quickly innovative products or services can be introduced to the commercial market at one level and how quickly goods and services can be delivered at another. For example, the Minnesota Mining and Manufacturing company fits here (3M for those of you who live outside Minnesota!). From a stumbling start as a producer of sandpaper, 3M is now a leader in a wide range of markets (e.g., magnetic storage media, fluorochemical products, reflective sheeting) and commands a tremendous portfolio of products (estimated to be more than 50,000). This *get there first* mentality is supported by the management decree that 30% of revenues must come from new products every year.

- Distribution: The focus is on efficient and unique ways of getting product or service to the customers. For example, consider the war that is being waged in bookselling. Traditional bookstore chains are losing ground to upstart electronic retailer Amazon.com. The company operates on the Web, has no physical stores, has a limited inventory, and yet offers an electronic list of 2.5 million titles to anyone with access to a browser. Can Virtual Mall or Web Street be far behind?

- Features: The focus is on offering unique or customizable features, options, or benefits to users ("bells and whistles," style, design, shape and size, flexibility to mix and match options). For example, TenFold Corp. is a 150-employee company in the business of developing software-based business applications for organizations whose needs are not met by packaged software. TenFold Corp.'s designers use object-based tools and components to build customized applications, often using the unusual business tactic of reselling technology developed with other customers, with the original client receiving some form of royalty.

- Focus: This is a hybrid strategy; the focus is on satisfying the needs of a specific category of customers or market niche. For example, Estee Lauder is in the tricky business of selling something that its targeted customers can, if you get right down to it, do without. Yet Estee Lauder cosmetics is a $3.6 billion company, controlling 45% of the market in the U.S. department stores. The company has increased revenue 50% since 1993 in a relatively stagnant industry by, in large part, knowing their customers (i.e., knowing what they want, when they want it, how they like to be sold to, and so on). Another example is the rock group the Grateful Dead, which remained a force in the music business for 30 years and pulled in $95 million a year at its height. Built around the distinctive voice and guitar work of the late Jerry Garcia, the Dead produced an improvisational rock dance beat that not everybody liked. However, those that did like it, *really* liked it. Year after year, the group remained true to the niche of fans that loved them—they never changed their musical style and they stayed close to their customer base by playing countless live shows every year.[25]

Of course, most competitive strategies include, in some degree, all nine of these competitive orientations. Although it might not make sense to consider any one of these strategies as a timeless basis of success for an organization,[26] at any one time it is usually possible to find the one strategy that is mission critical. It is the organization's *raison d'être*. It is the one mode of behavior that is strategically most important and is the lead locomotive that propels the organization along the vision track.

Questions that can shed light on the organization's competitive strategy include: "What is the source of the organization's competitive advantage?" "When evaluating specific business ideas or initiatives for fit with the organization's goals, what questions do the senior management team use as the ultimate litmus test?" "What major factors will contribute to the organization's success over the next 5 years?" "How do customers view the organization in terms of things done well or poorly?" Responses to these questions all link back to competitive strategy. Depending on which of the nine competitive strategies is most important to a given organization, the decisions that the organization makes about how to compete for its share of the future will vary greatly. More is said on this later in this chapter.

Strategic Initiatives

Strategic initiatives are the specific ways in which the goals identified in the vision are to be attained. In other words, the strategic initiatives elaborate on the broad goals in the vision and provide an operational definition. For example, there are a number of ways to gain market share, introduce new products to the marketplace, enter a new geographic market, and so on. Consider a broad goal of increasing market share by 20% in a particular market over a 3-year span. This could be accomplished by increasing the utilization of new distribution channels by a given percent in each of the next 3 years, adding a set number of new products to the product line, restructuring the sales force by assigning sales territories and instituting a new incentive system, and so on. Of course, the various initiatives can vary along a number of meaningful dimensions, including the extent to which they involve risk, the degree of creativity involved, and so forth. For job modeling purposes, simply breaking the initiatives into a revenue-generating and cost-savings dichotomy often proves sufficient.

- Revenue-Based: Top-line driven strategies that include specific initiatives such as:

  - Thirty percent increase in customer satisfaction index.
  - Twenty percent increase in proposal to sales hit rate.
  - Twenty-five percent increase in customer contact hours.
  - Twenty-five percent increase in professional time service utilization rates.
  - Fifty percent increase in the utilization of new distribution channels.

- Cost-Based: Bottom-line driven strategies that include specific initiatives such as:

  - Thirty-three percent reduction in production lead times.
  - Sixty-six percent reduction in defective machine parts.
  - Ten percent reduction in hourly workforce without sacrificing volume.
  - Eighty percent reduction in the number of vendors.
  - Sixty-six percent reduction in inventory levels.
  - Fifty percent reduction in new product development costs.

An investigation of strategic initiatives might start with an outline of the key challenges facing the organization. Follow-up questions might include: "What revenue-based, top-line initiatives are in place to accomplish strategic objectives?" "Are new revenue-based initiatives being considered?" "What cost-based, bottom-line initiatives are in place to accomplish the objectives?" "Are new cost-based initiatives under consideration?"

Functional Initiatives

The competitive strategy and strategic initiatives are the upstream elements that become more concrete and actionable as they course through the specific functions. While the framework for classifying the eventual impacts is represented in Fig. 3.3 in terms of traditional functional areas, such an approach need not always be the case. A municipal government might be organized by purpose functions, such as police, fire, health services, parks and recreation, education, water, and streets. A factory configured according to business processes might be organized by *process* functions, such as foundry and castings, milling and grinding, screw machining, finishing, inspection, shipping, customer service, and accounting. The bottom line is that the last column in Fig. 3.3 should represent the channels of accountability, or *way of life,* in the target organization. The completed cells in Fig. 3.3 are for purposes of illustration only. Together with the identification of the strategic initiatives discussed earlier, this information is important for understanding and defining the strategically driven desired outcomes or expectations of the organization.

PUTTING THE PIECES TOGETHER

How does one begin to build an understanding of the organization's ultimate objectives and factor this information into the job modeling effort? The format for linking HR interventions and individual competencies to the organization's vision and strategy is less important than having a systematic process. That said, the framework set out in Figs. 3.2 and 3.3 provides a broad, and then somewhat more detailed structure for capturing the key information and mapping business strategy. Figure 3.4 provides an applied example of how this works. The Figure presents a high-level business map for a company referred to here as Ecology Partners International. To disguise the client, the information reported here has been modified and recast in the fictitious pollution control industry.

As a second example, Fig. 3.5 presents the more detailed structure for capturing the results of a strategic mapping for the sales organization of a client in the banking industry. Again, the results have been modified and the client is referred to here using the fictitious name of Bank Partners Incorporated (it should be noted that this map does not reflect the strategy of BANK ONE or First Tennessee Bank, whose project work is referred to by name elsewhere in this book).

Where does the industry description and business strategy information for completing these maps come from? Sources like the *Encyclopedia of Careers and Vocational Guidance,*[27] the *Occupational Outlook Handbook,*[28] and specific industry searches in a business library can provide broad information about the relevant business environment and an organization's general marketplace. Closer to home, annual reports, business media searches, Dun & Bradstreet reports, Value Line company surveys, published product information, the organization's home page on the Internet, and books like *Hoover's Handbook of American Business*[29] and the company field guide *Everybody's Business*[30] can all be helpful.

Additionally, it is likely that a wide range of documents exist internal to the organization, which may provide a direct assessment of key external variables and detailed examinations of current strategy. Market research reports, existing

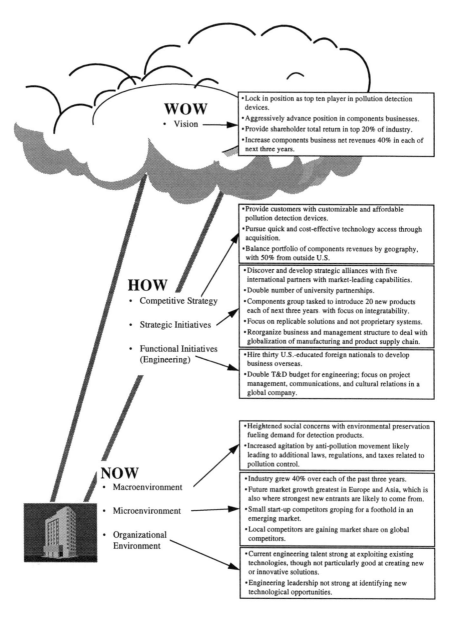

WOW
- Vision

- Lock in position as top ten player in pollution detection devices.
- Aggressively advance position in components businesses.
- Provide shareholder total return in top 20% of industry.
- Increase components business net revenues 40% in each of next three years.

HOW
- Competitive Strategy
- Strategic Initiatives
- Functional Initiatives (Engineering)

- Provide customers with customizable and affordable pollution detection devices.
- Pursue quick and cost-effective technology access through acquisition.
- Balance portfolio of components revenues by geography, with 50% from outside U.S.

- Discover and develop strategic alliances with five international partners with market-leading capabilities.
- Double number of university partnerships.
- Components group tasked to introduce 20 new products each of next three years. with focus on integratability.
- Focus on replicable solutions and not proprietary systems.
- Reorganize business and management structure to deal with globalization of manufacturing and product supply chain.

- Hire thirty U.S.-educated foreign nationals to develop business overseas.
- Double T&D budget for engineering; focus on project management, communications, and cultural relations in a global company.

NOW
- Macroenvironment
- Microenvironment
- Organizational Environment

- Heightened social concerns with environmental preservation fueling demand for detection products.
- Increased agitation by anti-pollution movement likely leading to additional laws, regulations, and taxes related to pollution control.

- Industry grew 40% over each of the past three years.
- Future market growth greatest in Europe and Asia, which is also where strongest new entrants are likely to come from.
- Small start-up competitors groping for a foothold in an emerging market.
- Local competitors are gaining market share on global competitors.

- Current engineering talent strong at exploiting existing technologies, though not particularly good at creating new or innovative solutions.
- Engineering leadership not strong at identifying new technological opportunities.

FIG. 3.4. Big picture business map for Ecology Partners International: Components division (modeling work targeting engineering jobs).

Strategic Job Model

	NOW			WOW	HOW		
	Broad External Analysis ←	*Detailed Internal Analysis* →		*"The Clouds"*	*Broad Strategies* ← →	*Specific Tactics* →	
	Macro-environment	Micro-environment	Organization Environment	Vision	Competitive Strategy	Strategic Initiatives	Functional Initiatives

Macro-environment

- **Social**
- **Economic:** • Unemployment rate less than 5% in most employment markets
- **Political/Legal:** • Deregulation removing many barriers between commercial and investment banks
- **Technological:** • Computing and communications advances have made it possible to increase automation in customer interface (e.g., electronic kiosks and Internet banking)

Micro-environment

- **Market Size:** • Largest U.S. bank only number twenty in world
- **Market Scope:** • Fastest growing customer segment is global markets
- **Market Maturity:** • Business becoming more product and option oriented • Push is on to develop products for retail and corporate markets
- **Competitor Rivalry:** • Pace of banking mergers to reduce number of national banks to less than 12 by year 2000
- **New Competitors:** • Investment firms now competing for same customers
- **Threats of Substitutes:** • Bank products and services increasingly viewed as commodities; and brand name and image more important
- **Customer Power**
- **Supplier Power**

Organization Environment

- **Human:** • Shift from 12.0 FTE branch environment to 9.5 has been difficult and still not there yet • Number of branch teammembers who speak local language continues to be great advantage in cultural niche markets • Too many order takers and not enough proactive sales types on front line
- **Technological:** • Good not great branch locations; incomplete coverage in prestigious towns • Terrific IT support
- **Infrastructure:** • Flat organization and bureaucracy at a minimum
- **Financial:** • Low teammember pay results in bank seldom being viewed as employer of choice
- **Contextual/Cultural:** • Collegial branch environment and strong branch managers who are good mentors

Vision ("The Clouds")

- **Aspirations:** • Establish bank as THE national neighborhood partner devoted to delighting its individual and small business customers, while positioning the enterprise to begin competing internationally
- **Businesses:** • #1 retail banker in markets served and move up to #2 overall within 5 years • #1 corporate banker to small-medium businesses • #1 in self-service banking
- **Position:** • Make strong entry into bank card business
- **Products:** • Double number of asset management products • 50% increase in number of tax-related products • Double self-service options
- **Shareholders**
- **Employees:** • Nurturing work environ. where teammembers treated with respect
- **Customers:** • Bank viewed as accessible and easy to do business with
- **Society:** • Teammembers viewed as community leaders

Competitive Strategy

- **Focus:** • Focus on middle income individual consumers and small to medium size businesses • Technology leadership is key to focus strategy in terms of on-demand customer information for account management purposes
- **Distribution:** • Saturate operating markets with mix of full and self-service branches, electronic kiosks, and Internet banking options • Technology leadership is key to distribution strategy in terms of 24-hour a day, 365 day a year service options

Strategic Initiatives

Revenue-Based (Top-line Driven)
- • Screen For Success Program includes: new employee screening and testing program (20% increase in new money generation and 25% increase in customer partnership service ratings)
- • Develop For Success Program includes: twelve month mentoring program, development planning program, and branch generalist program (20% increase in new money generation and reduction of average branch FTE to < 9.5)
- • Profits Plus Program includes: complete introduction and support of fourteen new financial products and services
- • 100% increase in revenue from self-service offerings

Cost-Based (Bottom-line Driven)
- • Develop For Success; new employee orientation training (bring front-line teammember six month turnover to <15%)
- • Margin Manager Program (5% reduction in branch overhead expenses)

Functional Initiatives

Sales
- • Ten teleconsulting prospecting calls by every branch teammember, every day
- • Up sell or tag on suggestions with every customer contact, every time
- • 100% teammember completion of Branch Generalist Program, all branches
- • 10% increase in personal loans closed per week, all branches
- • 20% increase in real estate loans closed per week, all branches
- • 20% increase in average value of personal loans closed per week, all branches
- • Exceed regional sales targets for expanded line of CD/IRA/Mutual Fund/Annuity products
- • 90% acceptable audits by regional roll-up
- • Monthly service ratings in excess of 90%, all branches
- • 75% teammember participation in incented Neighbor-hood Partners program

FIG. 3.5. Detailed business map for Bank Partners, Inc.: Retail banking (modeling work targeting sales jobs).

strategic plans or other products of internal strategy teams or task forces, recent assessments of potential business partnerships or alliance proposals, department audit reports, and the results of customer and employee surveys are all excellent sources.

Keep in mind that there might be widely held unwritten motives and values that do not end up in formal documents. It may be informative to identify the closely held values of the organization's founders and determine if they are still held by the senior management team. It can be useful to identify and characterize the kind of examples or standards the members of the senior management team set for others to follow.

Of course, interviews with the thought and visionary leaders of the senior management team, key representatives from internal strategy groups or strategic task forces, and so forth can provide rich detail. A word of caution, be sure to do your homework first: Learn as much as possible about the organization's marketplace, key competitors, and strategies before jumping into business context and strategy interviews. These individuals will find going over the basics to be frustrating. Conducted properly, these interviews not only will fill in critical information gaps and provide a useful long-term perspective, they also will have a tremendous relationship-building quality. Always be on the lookout for opportunities to identify and develop internal partners and champions for your project.

Detailed ideas and suggestions for conducting strategic and content-expert interviews and focus groups are presented in chapter 5. For now, it is worth noting that individual interviews typically are preferred when working at this level in the organization. However, small focus groups (i.e., three to five people) can be useful when differences of opinion exist among the leadership team and they need to come to closer agreement about their common fate. In both cases, be careful about introducing a specific theory for understanding business strategy this early in the information-gathering process. Unless the customer is familiar with the specific theory and approach, doing so tends to constrain discussion and decrease the number and richness of customer inputs.

Also, when eliciting information, use open-ended questions to discover facts or clarify issues that are not clear-cut, as is frequently the case at this stage of the modeling process. Closed-ended questions are most appropriate when trying to classify responses precisely, when the issues are clear, or when the interviewee has thought about the topic in detail before the interview.

One way to consolidate and begin to make sense of the information from the external literature review, and/or internal document review, and/or strategic interviews is to reproduce the key ideas on 3 x 5 index cards. These cards may then be organized into piles corresponding to macroenvironmental stuff, microenvironmental stuff, and so on. Identify the themes that repeatedly pop up and investigate major differences of opinion with additional interviews if necessary.

Once the major ideas have been captured and categorized into the appropriate NOW, WOW, and HOW categories (or subcategories), it may prove informative to visually display the interdependence among the variables by creating a business and strategy web. Figure 3.6 illustrates such a web, where the 3 x 5 cards are taped to the wall and colored yarn is used to depict critical linkages (or you can get a 36-inch-wide role of brown wrapping paper from most office supply warehouses, tape huge sections to a wall, and use colored markers to list the variables and draw the linkages). This analysis can also help reveal those clusters of jobs in the organization that are hypercritical in terms of achieving the vision and strategic goals. Of course, unless the job modeling work is building on previous work, the activity and competency dimensions listed in the final two columns will only be broad labels that logically make sense given the particular mix of targeted jobs.

It would be misleading not to mention that the vision and strategy juggernaut has taken some hits in the past few years. Mintzberg has even written the equivalent of an obituary for the discipline called *The Rise and Fall of Strategic Planning.*[31] I suspect Mintzberg was deliberately overstating the case to draw attention to his point that strategic planning frequently separates thinking from doing. For example, the strategists in the organization often lack the detailed business and technical knowledge required to make good business decisions. At the same time, the typical front-line employees who have the technical and functional knowledge and the intimate understanding of customer careabouts are too removed from the strategy process to have any real impact. These are wonderful points that highlight some of the soft spots in typical strategy development efforts.

Although the practice of business strategy development is currently having some of its flaws examined under a microscope, I agree with Micklethwait and Wooldridge that reports of its demise are exaggerated.[32] In fact, Hamel and Prahalad's recent contribution, *Competing for the Future,*[33] may be the most important book impacting strategy to come along in a decade. A central thesis of the book is that the truly important form of competition is the fight to create and then dominate emerging opportunities. As noted earlier in the chapter, the decisions the organization makes about how to compete for its share of the future will vary greatly.

For example, each of the competitive strategies discussed previously under HOW can lead the organization in a different direction and alter its business characteristic profile. Similarly, each of these competitive strategies is implemented and supported in different ways throughout the organization. All of this leads us to Table 3.1, which illustrates some potential effects each competitive strategy may have on the business and the management of human resources. It should be made clear that, although many of the business and human resource impacts noted in Table 3.1 are based on a distillation of the research and observations reported in outlets like the *Sloan Management*

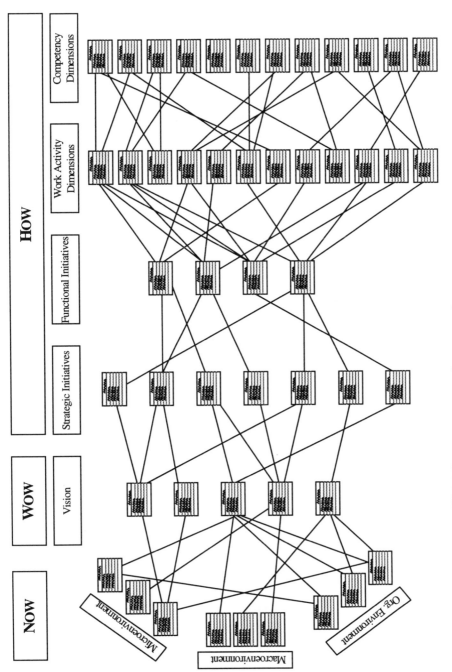

FIG. 3.6. Business context and strategy web.

TABLE 3.1

Competitive Strategy: Business Characteristics and HR Impacts

Cost-Driven Organization
(Focus is on competing on the playing field of price.)

Potential Business Characteristics	Potential HR Impacts
■ Vigorous pursuit of production/delivery efficiencies.	• Redesign work to allow for ease in product/service manufacture/delivery. Creative use of part-time workers and flex schedules.
■ Tight control over cost of inputs in particular (e.g., materials and resources) and close management of overhead in general.	• Minimal entry-level selection requirements for large/unskilled (in relative terms) labor force, beyond basic skills and reliability and dependability.
■ Minimal expenditures in R&D, marketing, service, sales, and training.	• Select and train strong supervisors to monitor and coach a large/low-wage labor force.
■ Emphasis on large accounts, both in terms of procurement of inputs from vendors and delivery of products or services to customers. Economics of scale is key.	• Performance appraisal and incentive systems linked to meeting production/delivery targets and improving processes.
■ Use of low-cost distribution system.	• Job description, classification, and design to capture/articulate clear organization structure and work group/individual responsibilities.

Value-Driven Organization
(Focus is on developing unique, valuable technologies that others in the market cannot offer.)

Potential Business Characteristics	Potential HR Impacts
■ Laser-beam focus on developing *best in class* capabilities in selected activities and knowledge areas.	• Selection tools to identify high-caliber scientists and professionals with necessary creative flair to complement technical skills.
■ Promote reputation for technological leadership and capitalize on brand image.	• Job evaluation and compensation programs designed to motivate and ensure the retention of scientists and professionals with highly sought-after skills.
■ Emphasize product engineering or service integration.	• Skills assessment and training in technical areas to combat knowledge decrements in scientific and professional fields.
■ Maintain an active basic research contingent.	• Simulations and/or assessments to aid scientists in moving successfully from the technical track to the management track (i.e., creating management leaders from technical stars).
■ Partner with industry leaders, universities, or independent research organizations to pool technical resources for mutual benefit.	• Individual development assessment to identify marketing and sales personnel suited to working in complex value-based organization vs. marketing/selling simply on price.

TABLE 3.1 (continued)

Quality-Driven Organization
(Focus is on high-quality, defect-free product or service.)

Potential Business Characteristics	Potential HR Impacts
■ Aggressive pursuit of information on customer careabouts, including the involvement of customers in product/service design. ■ Serious efforts to instill a continuous improvement orientation and a deliberate ongoing improvement agenda throughout the organization. ■ Strict monitoring of franchisee, subcontractor, and supplier screening requirements, performance standards, and consistency metrics. ■ Investment in people and knowledge communities. ■ Somewhat more liberal expenditures in R&D, marketing, service, sales, and training.	• Process consulting on quality management and continuous improvement programs, such as Motorola's Six Sigma, Emerson Electric's Best Cost Analysis, Xerox's Systematic Benchmarking, and various process-mapping techniques. • Organization development work diagnosing learning disabilities and creating a learning organization. • Simulations designed to evaluate and provide feedback on teamwork. • Training programs emphasizing collaboration and teamwork skills and statistical quality control techniques. • Surveys and focus groups with customers to identify needs and solicit performance feedback.

Service-Driven Organization
(Focus is on providing excellent service, whether in support of a product or in terms of the level of comfort or expertise associated with a service.)

Potential Business Characteristics	Potential HR Impacts
■ A value on investments in people as much as, if not more than, investments in machines/technology. ■ Close monitoring of multiple metrics tracking service responsiveness. ■ Relationship-oriented in terms of cultivating good work relations among associates to dealings with partners, franchisees, subcontractors, and suppliers. ■ Creative involvement of R&D and manufacturing groups in after-sales support. ■ Increased customer service *and* sales ranks to increase contact with customers.	• Recruiting, training, and retention issues are equally important for front-line employees and managers. • Select front-line labor force with strong interpersonal skills. • Training programs designed to hone service-related skills, indoctrinate new associates, and drive home the company vision statement. • Training seminars on product knowledge and customer relations and service. • Compensation linked to performance for employees at every level, not just those at the top, with clearly stated standards relating to interpersonal attitude and image.

(continues)

TABLE 3.1 (continued)

Capacity-Driven Organization
(Focus is on delivering a product or service on a large scale.)

Potential Business Characteristics	Potential HR Impacts
■ Aggressively manage production efficiency to eliminate waste or duplication of effort to increase speed and output.	• Attention to detail and a sense of urgency are two competencies that are predominant in many job groups throughout the organization.
■ Continuously monitor status and progress against plans/objectives at all levels of product development or service delivery.	• Training programs for imparting the planning and delegating skills needed by project leaders.
■ Close attention to detail and troubleshooting activities.	• Empowerment training for supervisors and team leads, designed to get associates to manage their own responsibilities.
■ Emphasis on large accounts, both in gaining input from vendors and delivering products or services to customers.	• Process consulting around reengineering work.
■ Frequently slow to respond to new technologies because of high-capital investment (in both things and people) supporting current streamlined procedures.	

Speed-Driven Organization
(Focus is on how quickly a new product or service can be delivered.)

Potential Business Characteristics	Potential HR Impacts
■ Willingness to accept risks associated with delivering product/service to market ahead of competitors.	• Recruit and select associates with strong teamwork skills.
■ Emphasize analysis of market trends to gain insight.	• Performance appraisal and incentive systems linked to measures of teamwork and continuous learning.
■ Aggressive management of new product development cycles.	• Job redesign work to identify overlapping activities and eliminate time-consuming practices.
■ Engage in joint ventures to speed entry and share risks associated with new markets.	• Employee skills banks to facilitate the allocation of the right technical skills to the right projects.
■ Identify and create geographical and technology partnerships to augment organizational capabilities.	• Coaching efforts targeting entry-level managers to create influential and strong project leaders.

(continues)

TABLE 3.1 (continued)

Distribution-Driven Organization
(Focus is on getting products or services to the customers in efficient and unique ways.)

Potential Business Characteristics	Potential HR Impacts
■ Manage ventures and alliances to augment distribution network.	• Recruit and select associates with a strong work efficiency orientation and good planning and teamwork skills.
■ Aggressive and extensive reviews of product or service flows.	• Often more receptive to unique ways of automating standard HR practices (e.g., using in-store scanning or other digital technologies to score preemployment tests).
■ Quick response capabilities at the point of contact with the customer.	
■ Efficient systems for capturing point-of-sale data and using the information to drive replenishment efforts and pricing.	• Reengineering work processes and work flows is "in," and so is an openness to interventions like job design/redesign.

Features-Driven Organization
(Focus is on unique features/options/benefits to users ["bells and whistles," style, design, shape and size, flexibility to mix and match options].)

Potential Business Characteristics	Potential HR Impacts
■ Aggressive pursuit of information on customer careabouts; always on the lookout for what is missing from current market offerings.	• Recruiting and selection programs designed to screen into the organization people who are bright, creative, adaptable, willing to take educated risks, and capable of *listening.*
■ Ever-changing work environment in which people, processes, and technology reconfigure to give customers what they want.	• Performance appraisal and compensation systems focus on rewarding ingenuity and the identification of strategic opportunities.
■ Strong continuous improvement orientation throughout the organization.	• Employee skills banks to keep track of the human talent portfolio and facilitate the allocation of the right technical skills to the right projects.
■ Aggressive pursuit of competitive intelligence about product plans and service enhancements.	
■ Similar to the quality-driven organization in that there are somewhat more liberal funds routed to R&D, marketing, sales, and training.	• Training and individual coaching programs designed to develop conceptual and creative thinking.

(continues)

TABLE 3.1 (continued)

Focus-Driven Organization
(Focus is on satisfying particular needs of a specific market niche.)

Potential Business Characteristics	Potential HR Impacts
■ Strong marketing function and an emphasis on market research data detailing micromarket proclivities.	• Strong customer orientation and listening skill emphasized throughout all HR programs.
■ Risk averse with laser-beam focus on customer careabouts.	• Individual coaching for associates working with customers on encouraging and listening to feedback.
■ Intense management of modifications of product/service offerings, product/service-line extensions, and technical services to needs of profiled customers.	• Conducting focus groups with the organization's front-line people define customer base, customer's expectations and requirements for doing business.
■ Active involvement of targeted customer group in product/service development.	• Performance appraisal and incentive programs linked to the measurement and reward of excellent customer service.
■ More so than other competitive strategy types, the focus-driven strategy often has a twin engine and will also exhibit the business characteristics of the compliment strategy.	

Review, Harvard Business Review, and the *Academy of Management Journal,* just as many derive from personal experiences and those of colleagues. In any event, these potential impacts should be thought of as well-reasoned likelihoods versus research-based facts.

In summary, the purpose of this section has not been to prescribe algorithms linking specific macroenvironment variables to specific microenvironment variables and on down to specific HR interventions and competency requirements. This would have been akin to creating a detailed roadmap showing all possible interconnections between different starting points and destinations. Instead, the approach has been to provide a compass, introduce some key reference points in the business strategy terrain, and let you chart your own course. This approach should prove more useful and satisfying.

PROJECT MANAGEMENT TIPS

Perhaps the best tip I can offer for Step 1 of the Cheshire Strategic Job Modeling Process is to know your limitations. The typical job modeler is not in a position to consult with organizations about what businesses to be in, advise them about business entry or exit strategies, or recommend competitive postures for product lines. If a leadership team questions what business to leave or enter, or what position to seek within a marketplace, the questions should be referred back to the key leadership team members, an internal strategy group, or some other strategy consulting resource.

Next, be aware that the role of the SJM consultant shifts over the life of the project. Figure 3.7 is an effort to illustrate this point. In the beginning stages of a project, such as strategy definition and mapping the business context, the modeler will likely be operating primarily as a process consultant, following a somewhat less structured approach in dealing with the customer and gathering information to guide subsequent choices. Moving toward the end of a project, the modeler will probably be most effective employing more of a technical expert orientation, following a more structured protocol, and offering more concrete interpretations of information to guide subsequent choices. Many HR practitioners and consultants excel in one role or the other and operate in delivery niches that allow them to leverage their strengths. In contrast, the job modeler has to be good at both.

Finally, when researching the organization's competitive strategy, look for ways the strategy drivers manifest themselves in individual behavior. Depending on how clear the organization strategy is, the employees will have developed perceptions about organization careabouts and strategies based on hundreds of work experiences. People do a good job of basing their behavior on the perceptions they have of what the organization wants them to do. For example, the customers and support personnel a job modeler meets at the beginning of a project represent an extension of the entire organization. The behaviors, decision-making styles, competency levels, and so forth that a job modeler observes at the outset will likely be mirrored elsewhere in the organization. Although this observation is particularly relevant for external consultants, it also applies to internal experts who are being tapped to consult with an unfamiliar business unit of the organization. Stay vigilant and learn!

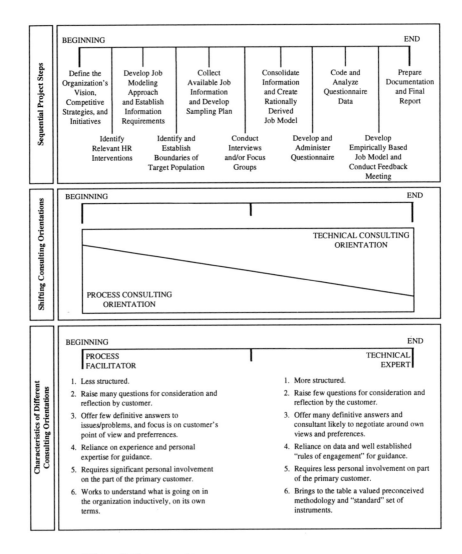

Sequential Project Steps

BEGINNING   END

| Define the Organization's Vision, Competitive Strategies, and Initiatives | Develop Job Modeling Approach and Establish Information Requirements | Collect Available Job Information and Develop Sampling Plan | Consolidate Information and Create Rationally Derived Job Model | Code and Analyze Questionnaire Data | Prepare Documentation and Final Report |

Identify Relevant HR Interventions — Identify and Establish Boundaries of Target Population — Conduct Interviews and/or Focus Groups — Develop and Administer Questionnaire — Develop Empirically Based Job Model and Conduct Feedback Meeting

Shifting Consulting Orientations

BEGINNING   END

TECHNICAL CONSULTING ORIENTATION

PROCESS CONSULTING ORIENTATION

Characteristics of Different Consulting Orientations

BEGINNING   END

PROCESS FACILITATOR   TECHNICAL EXPERT

1. Less structured.

2. Raise many questions for consideration and reflection by customer.

3. Offer few definitive answers to issues/problems, and focus is on customer's point of view and preferrences.

4. Reliance on experience and personal expertise for guidance.

5. Requires significant personal involvement on the part of the primary customer.

6. Works to understand what is going on in the organization inductively, on its own terms.

1. More structured.

2. Raise few questions for consideration and reflection by the customer.

3. Offer many definitive answers and consultant likely to negotiate around own views and preferrences.

4. Reliance on data and well established "rules of engagement" for guidance.

5. Requires less personal involvement on part of the primary customer.

6. Brings to the table a valued preconceived methodology and "standard" set of instruments.

FIG. 3.7. Shift in consulting orientation over time in a strategic job modeling project.

REFERENCES

[1]D'Aveni, D. (1994). *Hypercompetition*. New York: Free Press.

[2]Pearce, J. A., & David F. (1987). Corporate mission statements: The bottom line. *Academy of Management Executive, 1,* 109–116.

[3]McLaughlin, D. J., McLaughlin, B. L., & Lischick, C. W. (1991). Company values: A key to managing in turbulent times. In R. J. Niehus & K. F. Price, (Eds.), *Bottom line results from strategic human resource planning* (pp. 261–274). New York: Plenum.

[4]Burns, T., & Stalker, G. M. (1961). *The management of innovation.* London: Tavistock.

[5]Duncan, R. B. (1972). Characteristics of organizational environments and perceived environmental uncertainty. *Administrative Science Quarterly, 17,* 313–327.

[6]Lawrence, P. R., & Lorsch, J. W. (1967). *Organizations and environments.* Boston: Division of Research, Harvard Business School.

[7]Lawrence, P. R., & Lorsch, J. W. (1986). *Differentiation and integration in complex organizations.* Cambridge, MA: Harvard Graduate School of Business Administration.

[8]Mintzberg, H. (1979). *The structuring of organizations.* Englewood Cliffs, NJ: Prentice-Hall.

[9]Thompson, J. D., & McEwen, W. J. (1958). Organizational goals and environment: Goal setting as an interaction process. *American Sociological Review, 23,* 23–31.

[10]Schneider, B. (1976). *Staffing organizations.* Santa Monica, CA: Goodyear Publishing Company.

[11]Schneider, B., & Konz, A. M. (1989). Strategic job analysis. *Human Resource Management, 28,* 51–63.

[12]Narayanan, V. K., & Fahey, L. (1994). Macroenvironmental analysis: Understanding the environment outside the industry. In L. Fahey & R. M., Randall (Eds.), *The portable MBA in strategy.* New York: Wiley.

[13]Davids, M. (1997). Money, money everywhere. *Journal of Business Strategy, 18,* 49–51.

[14]Rugman, A. M., Kirton, J., & Soloway, J. A. (1997). NAFTA, environmental regulations and Canadian competitiveness. *Journal of World Trade, 31,* 129–144.

[15]Drucker, P. F. (1997, September–October). The future that has already happened. *Harvard Business Review,* pp. 18–32.

[16]Porter, M. E. (1980). *Competitive strategy.* New York: Free Press.

[17]Porter, M. E. (1985). *Competitive advantage.* New York: Free Press.

[18]Steiner, G. (1969). *Top management planning.* London: Macmillan.

[19]Vinchur, A. J., Schippmann, J. S., Switzer, F. S., & Roth, P. L. (1998). A meta-analytic review of predictors of job performance for salespeople. *Journal of Applied Psychology, 83,* 586–597.

[20]Senge, P. M. (1990). *The fifth discipline: The art and practice of the learning organization.* New York: Doubleday.

[21]Porter, M. E. (1980). *Competitive strategy.* New York: Free Press.

[22]D'Aveni, D. (1994). *Hypercompetition.* New York: Free Press.

[23]Steiner, G. (1969). *Top management planning.* London: Macmillan.

[24]Hamel, G., & Prahalad, C. K. (1994). *Competing for the future.* Boston: Harvard Business School Press.

[25]Rifkin, G. (1997). How to "truck" the brand: Lessons from the Grateful Dead. *Strategy & Business, 6,* 51–57.

[26]Ghemawat, P. (1991). *Commitment: The dynamics of strategy.* New York: Free Press.

[27]Cosgrove, H. R. (Ed.). (1997). *Encyclopedia of careers and vocational guidance*. Chicago: J. G. Ferguson.

[28]Department of Labor. (1996).*Occupational outlook handbook*. Washington, DC: U.S. Government Printing Office.

[29]Hoovers Business Press Staff. (1997). *Hoovers handbook of American business*. Austin, TX: Hoovers, Inc.

[30]Moskowitz, M., Levering, R., & Katz, M. (1990). *Everybody's business*. New York: Doubleday.

[31]Mintzberg, H. (1994). *The rise and fall of strategic planning*. New York: Prentice-Hall.

[32]Micklethwait, J., & Wooldridge, A. (1996). *The witch doctors*. New York: Times Books.

[33]Hamel, G., & Prahalad, C. K. (1994). *Competing for the future*. Boston: Harvard Business School Press.

Chapter 4
What Applications are Required to Achieve Desired Outcomes?

> *... human resources in an organization, like a mobile, is a web of interconnections; a change in one area throws a different part off balance....*
>
> —Unknown

I recently had the chance to go watch my 5-year-old nephew play a soccer game. What a spectacle! Twelve girls and boys all doing their own thing, running very fast, often in different directions, spinning around and tripping over each other, and sometimes just striking off alone. The fact that there was a goal on either end of the field and a soccer ball in their midst was incidental. When the game was almost over, I noticed what appeared to be a high school game taking place on the field behind us, and the difference in the game was amazing. These more advanced players, although having no more energy or fervor than their younger counterparts, moved across the field with an interrelated intent and purpose that was fascinating to watch.

Maybe it was just that I was in the middle of writing this chapter at the time, but the similarity to different *levels of play* on the part of different HRM functions stuck with me. To play with the big kids, this same interrelated intent and purpose needs to drive the various aspects of HR. Think of the HR function as a wheel, with the different aspects of HR representing spokes of the wheel. The idea behind Fig. 4.1 is that these spokes do not represent discrete steps as much as they do fairly arbitrary slices of an ongoing process. Each slice of the process rolls into the next in a never-ending cyclical fashion. Recruiting strategies impact selection systems, selection systems ultimately affect training programs, training programs are linked in many ways to performance appraisal systems, compensation and rewards should be linked to good performance, and so it goes until it comes back around.

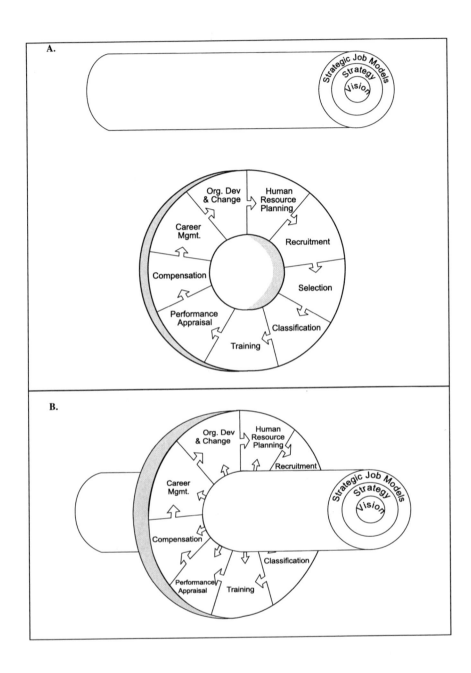

FIG. 4.1. Human resource management process wheel.

In relation to the wheel, the organization's vision, strategies, and resulting strategic job models can be visualized as an axle. If HR is going to be truly impactful, these core components must be considered as the wheel moves along the axle over time (i.e., we must keep the goal in mind).

Each of the slices in the HRM wheel subsumes a variety of specific applications. A sample of some of the primary applications that may be utilized in an organization as part of the effort to achieve specific outcomes appears in Table 4.1. Exactly which applications are likely to be most impactful in a particular situation may be narrowed down in a couple of ways. First, two important concepts need to be introduced.

VALIDITY AND RELEVANCE

Everyone knows what is meant by the concept of *the truth*. Despite this conceptual agreement, things can get convoluted once one gets down to the details. Reality introduces numerous forks in the road. As a result, the truth seldom runs along a nice straight path. "So what!" you say. Well, keep in mind that all HR applications are designed to do something. That *something* serves as the basis for an expectation about the anticipated outcomes. For example, a preemployment test is designed to measure a competency and predict a particular performance outcome. To the extent the test delivers on this expectation it can be considered to truly work, and the inferences about future performance from the test scores are valid. Similarly, an individual coaching program can be designed to measure and develop a specific set of competencies for members of an executive team. If the program produces the expected outcome, it may be thought of as truly effective. Therefore, *validity* can be defined as "the best approximation to the truth or falsity" of inferences and predictions based on some application[1] resulting from the extent to which the application produces the desired outcome. Furthermore, although beyond the scope of this discussion, it should at least be mentioned that there are a number of ways for testing hypotheses regarding application–outcome relationships.[2,3]

Things get fuzzier still when discussing the concept of what is right. How many things are definitively and without question right or wrong? In the latter category, things like cannibalism, plane crashes of any kind, and baseball's designated hitter rule come to mind. In contrast, for parents to love and teach their children must surely always be right. However, beyond a few things, the answers to most questions about rightness and wrongness are value-based and depend on who is asked.

Similarly, decisions about vision and competitive strategy are the value-based decisions of an organization's leadership team. Consequently, strategy development has been described as kind of like climbing a mountain, where individuals are roped together by some common goals; the upward direction is agreed on, but there are multiple paths leading to the top and it is likely there is

TABLE 4.1

Human Resource Management Applications*

Human Resource Planning

1. Job Design/Redesign: Create or reconstitute jobs or work roles in terms of work functions and worker capabilities that are both palatable to individuals and are in alignment with the organization's strategy and vision.[10]

2. Work Load Analysis: Estimate the number of jobs and people requirements needed to accomplish objectives resulting from the organization's vision and strategy, where job analysis procedures might be used to create a structure for estimating the hours per week required for specific work activities.[11,12]

Recruiting

3. Job Descriptions & Minimum Qualifications: Summarize the essential work content and worker capabilities required for full job performance in a target job, derive the worker capability requirements of a job, and specify how the requisite capabilities may be acquired.[13,14]

4. Realistic Job Preview (RJP) Content: Create RJP cards, video content, or other materials that present the basic work content and worker capabilities in conjunction with job opportunities and obstacles for both recruitment and self-selection purposes.

Selection

5. Interview System: Create behaviorally based interview questions, follow-up probes, and evaluative rating scales for a target job.[15,16]

6. Scored Application Blank/Biodata: Develop questions about verifiable aspects of an individual's background, education, training, and experiences, all of which are weighted with reference to the requirements of the target job.[17]

7. Paper-and-Pencil Testing (Using Existing Measures and Follow-up Validation): Select existing tests or scales with known psychometric properties and use to screen new hires into target job.[18,19,20]

8. Paper-and-Pencil Testing (Using Existing Measures and Validity Generalization): Select existing tests or scales with extensive antecedent validation research and known psychometric properties and use to screen new hires into target job.

9. Paper-and-Pencil Testing (Using Custom-Built Measures and Follow-up Validation): Create a test or series of scales from scratch, beginning with the development of new items through the creation of unique scoring keys.[21,22,23]

10. Simulations/Content-Oriented Test Construction: Develop realistic samples of problems faced by incumbents in the target job and build into an interactive preemployment test that includes an evaluative rating scheme with behavioral anchors. [24,25,26]

11. Individual Assessment for Selection: One-on-one individual or psychological assessment for screening candidates into key jobs, where the relative infrequency of the selection question makes the development of a conventional selection system cost-prohibitive. [27]

Classification & Placement

12. Job Classification: Develop job families and subsumed job groups based on functional activities and hierarchy of capability level. [28,29,30]

13. Employee Skills Bank and Corresponding Person-to-Job (or Team) Matching: Develop structure for organizing jobs, create system for maintaining information on worker capabilities, and devise procedures for matching individual capabilities with job or team requirements.

Training

14. Training Needs Analysis: Conduct an audit of employee capabilities to determine whether employees need training and confirm the relevance of a training program. [31,32,33]

15. Training Program Design: Develop training content and procedures designed to enhance individual capabilities that are (a) most important for job performance, (b) most difficult to train, and (c) most likely to be acquired after coming to the target job. [34,35,36]

Performance Appraisal

16. BARS Appraisal Systems: Create instruments and procedures for evaluating employee performance of current work content using behaviorally anchored rating scales. [37,38]

Compensation

17. Job Evaluation: Design systematic method of evaluating the value or worth of a job or group of jobs in relation to other jobs in the organization. [39,40]

(continues)

TABLE 4.1 (continued)

Career Management & Career Building

18. 360° Instruments for Development: Create or modify 360° instruments for individual development purposes, and develop procedures for capturing, maintaining, and using multiperspective information for individuals.

19. Individual Assessment for Development: Individual or psychological assessment to identify strengths and development needs for individual development planning.

20. Career Ladders/Succession Planning: Identify feeder jobs for key positions and create, in terms of planning, a series of stepping stones to move people through the organization to ensure continuous staffing.[41]

21. Career Planning: Develop structure to guide individual career choices that match interests and capabilities with job/career requirements.[42]

22. Coaching: Develop one-on-one coaching programs designed to leverage the strengths and shore up development need areas for an organization's key team members.

Organization Development

23. Organizational Analysis and Change: Investigate how the attributes of a particular organization affect the behavior of organization members and impact overall organization effectiveness.[43,44,45]

Note. The references next to specific applications note articles or book chapters that offer some description as to how job information is used to guide the creation of that particular application.

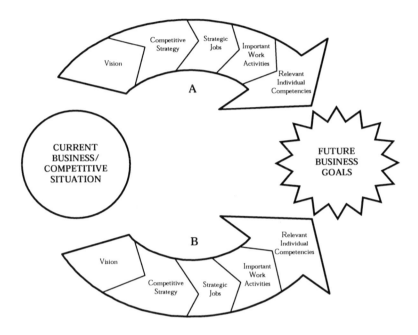

FIG. 4.2. Different paths to the same future goals.

no single right path. As Fig. 4.2 illustrates, there may be multiple paths that could be crafted leading to future business goals. In other words, it is not simply a matter of one being the right path and the other wrong.

In contrast to validity, relevance addresses the question of whether the something produced by the intervention focuses on the right set of stuff and has a meaningful relationship to the higher order aims of an organization's success and goal attainment. For example, the preemployment testing program used in the individual banking department of a recent client, which focused entirely on basic administrative competencies, was producing adequate validities. Therefore, it could be construed, in truth, to be working, and the resulting inferences from test scores could be considered valid. However, to compete in an increasingly deregulated and unprotected market with an influx of new competitors, the strategy of the bank was shifting from a passive service orientation to a proactive sales orientation. In turn, the front-line individual banking jobs were becoming much less administrative in nature and focused more on prospecting and sales. In this case, this same testing program, although apparently working, was not particularly relevant when juxtaposed with an organization's direction and needs, which were, out of necessity, shifting to meet the future.

Figure 4.3 presents validity and relevance within the context of the SJM enterprise. In this representation, a major distinction between these two ideas is based on the chronological sequence in which they are organized. *Validity* examines the proximal relationship between results and performance expectations associated with specific downstream applications, and quality job modeling data increase the likelihood of a positive payoff with this immediate objective. *Relevance,* examines the distal relationship between results and the organization needs associated with upstream superordinate goals. From this perspective, quality SJM data increase the likelihood of a positive payoff associated with these broader ultimate objectives.

WHERE TO START

Granted, the prior discussion was a bit abstract. However, it provides some context for the concrete discussion that follows. Given the range of potential HR applications that might be developed for an organization at any one point in time, a practical question emerges: Where to start? Depending on the situation, there are a number of potential customer responses to this question:

- We think this is our problem. What do you think?
- This is our problem. What is the solution?
- This is our problem and this is the solution we want![4]

Of course, the third situation does not leave much room for diagnosis. Unless your customer is willing to engage in some assessment of the situation, you may wind up simply delivering the stated solution. This is unfortunate because the linkage between the stated problem and the stated solution is often tenuous at best—the product of a knee-jerk reaction resulting from a crisis management situation. An urgent telephone call from a boss, a flurry of e-mails about a previously unnoticed hot topic or volatile issue, an unplanned-for action item resulting from a meeting, and the like often seem to be the driving force behind an expressed need to create a particular application. Given the pace of change in business, there must always be a highly flexible and adaptive component to the process of determining HR priorities. However, there also needs to be some balance. The counterweight here would be some organized, systematic way of determining what is vital versus merely urgent.

An initial, high-level perspective may be gained by identifying the competitive strategy of the organization and then extrapolating from the sample business and HR impacts presented in Fig. 3.7. Using the business and strategy web process, also from chapter 3, is another technique for reducing the size of the inferential leaps involved in linking HR practices to business strategies.

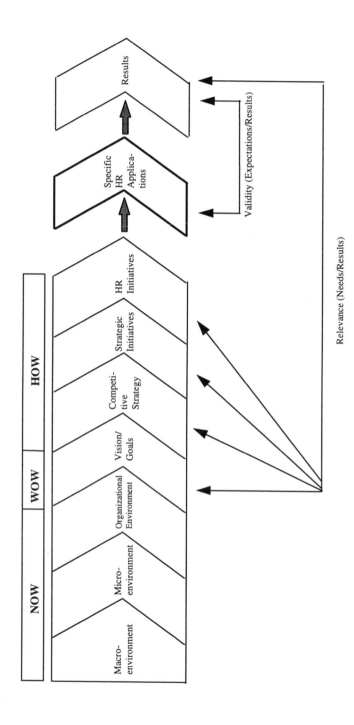

FIG. 4.3. Linking the concepts of validity and relevance to the business context.

A somewhat more systematic process for determining HR priorities is to consider each potential application in terms of the strategic impact criteria listed here:

- Relevance to business strategies and goals (i.e., the linkage or level of fit with strategies and the anticipated contribution to achieving goals).
- Management interest (i.e., the extent to which the application has captured the imagination of the organization's decision makers or the degree to which the collective view of the application is worthwhile and doable). Unfortunately, the relevance of an application and the level of management interest are often two distinct concepts.
- Available resources (i.e., the extent to which the money and/or people necessary to build or redesign the application are readily available).
- Organizational readiness (i.e., the degree to which the organization's people [e.g., level of training, values, commitment], technology, and systems are ready to tackle the issues involved in building, or implementing and supporting, the envisioned application).
- Synergy with current work in progress (i.e., the extent to which the application makes possible, or makes better, other important interventions).

One technique for proactively establishing priorities is to start by developing an Application Relevance Matrix (see Table 4.2). This matrix displays a short list of potentially important applications along the vertical axis of the exhibit. The organizations' identified strategic initiatives are listed along the horizontal axis. In this case, the resulting matrix crosses six applications by four initiatives creating 24 unique cells.

It then becomes possible to judge the degree of relevance for each of the listed HR applications for each strategic initiative. For example, I have used the 5-point rating scale in Fig. 4.4 to help identify the relative importance of some subset of possible HR applications across an organization's specified goals (simply insert the word *relevance* in the blank spaces of the scale). The completed matrix, which would have numbers from 1 to 5 in each cell, provides a visual summary of how a previously undifferentiated basket of potential applications link up with business strategic plans. Summing the numbers by row to get an Overall Relevance value is a nice way to arrive at a rank ordered listing of applications based on strategic relevance.

However, as the previous criteria suggest, true strategic impact is multifaceted and not fully captured using only the perspective of relevance. Consider developing a second matrix—a Strategic Application Matrix, which also lists applications along the vertical axis, but in this case lists the other criteria important for determining strategic impact (see Table 4.3). Simply enter the Overall Relevance value for each application from Table 4.2 in the Relevance column of the Strategic Application Matrix.

TABLE 4.2
Application Relevance Matrix

Strategic Initiatives

Short List of Potential Applications	20% Increase in New Money Generation	25% Increase in Customer Service Ratings	100% Increase in Revenue From Self-Service Offerings	Bring Front-Line Team Member 6-Month Turnover to Below 15%	Overall Relevance
1. 360° instruments for development					
2. Career ladders/succession planning					
3. Job evaluation/compensation					
4. Interview system for selection					
5. Individual assessment for selection					
6. Training program design					

☐ **EXPRESSION OF AMOUNT**

Use the "Expression of Amount" scale to indicate your answer concerning the degree to which a particular strategic impact criterion applies, or is present, in this context.

1 – A trivial amount of_____.

2 – Some limited amount of_____.

3 – A moderate amount of_____.

4 – Quite a bit of_____.

5 – An extraordinary amount of_____.

FIG. 4.4. Expressions of amount rating scale.

The values for the other cells in the matrix may be arrived at by applying the Expressions of Amount Rating Scale (see Fig. 4.4) to the criteria in Columns 2, 3, 4, and 5 for each application. For example, what is the level of management interest in 360° instruments for development? If the judgment is "Quite a Bit," then enter a "4" in the first cell of Column 2. Similarly, to what extent is there money in the budget to conduct the modeling work and create (or purchase) and implement a multiperspective feedback tool like a 360° instrument? If the answer is "A Moderate Amount," then enter a "3" in the first cell of Column 3 and so on.

These five criteria listed across the top of Table 4.3, when taken together, help determine the relative strategic impact of each application under consideration. It should be noted that this technique is not limited to use at the organization level. In fact, most recently I taught the technique to a group of internal HR consultants with an automobile parts manufacturer so they could partner with line managers and develop tailored Strategic Application Matrices for specific business segments. In summary, this process offers an approach for determining where to focus attention and limited resources.

JOB MODELING METHODS

Decisions about the application(s) to be developed affect a number of decisions about how to proceed with the modeling work. The first decision of this type concerns the choice of job modeling method. Table 4.4 offers some suggestions concerning the appropriate job modeling method for different applications. Be-

TABLE 4.3

Strategic Application Matrix

Strategic Impact Criteria

Short List of Potential Applications	Relevance	Management Interest	Available Resources	Organizational Readiness	Synergy	Relative Strategic Impact
1. 360° instruments for development						
2. Career ladders/succession planning						
3. Job evaluation/compensation						
4. Interview system for selection						
5. Individual assessment for selection						
6. Training program design						

TABLE 4.4

Appropriate Job Modeling Method for Different Applications

Application	Rational Analysis Using Interviews/Focus Groups	Empirical Analysis
Human Resource Planning		
1. Job design/redesign	★★★	★★
2. Work load analysis	★★	★★
Recruitment		
3. Job description and minimum qualifications	★★	★★
4. Realistic job preview content	★★★	★
Selection		
5. Interview system	★★	★★
6. Scored application blank/ biodata	★★	★★★
7. Paper-and-pencil testing (follow-up validation)	★★	★★★
8. Paper-and-pencil testing (validity generalization)	★	★★★
9. Paper-and-pencil testing (custom built)	★★★	★★★
10. Simulations/content-oriented test construction	★★★	★★★
11. Individual assessment for selection	★★★	★★
Classification Placement		
12. Job classification	★★	★★★
13. Employee skills bank & matching	★★	★★★

	Column 1	Column 2
Training		
14. Training needs analysis	★★★	★★
15. Training program design	★★★	★★
Performance Appraisal		
16. BARS appraisal systems	★★	★★
Compensation		
17. Job evaluation	★★	★★★
Career Management		
18. 360° instruments for development	★★	★★
19. Individual assessment for development	★★★	★
20. Career ladders/succession planning	★★	★★
21. Career planning	★★	★★
22. Coaching	★★★	★
Organization Development and Change		
23. Organizational analysis and change	★★★	★★

★★★ = Essential information for most applications of this type.

★★ = Important information for many applications of this type.

★ = Nice to have this information, but not essential for most applications of this type.

fore we jump to this table, a brief elaboration on the different methods of job modeling introduced in chapter 2 is in order.

Different methods for collecting job modeling information are more or less appropriate for collecting information to support different (or a different mix of) HR applications. The three methods introduced in chapter 1—rational, empirical, and combined rational and empirical—represent fairly distinct approaches, each with different advantages and disadvantages. A case example of each method will highlight some of the more important similarities and differences and advantages and disadvantages.

Rational Method

In this job modeling approach, interviews and/or focus groups are used to investigate the major aspects of a job and rationally create descriptive content. In other words, interviews or focus groups with subject matter experts (job incumbents, supervisors, organizational visionaries, or other content experts) are required to: (a) gain a comprehensive understanding of the unique work activities, competency requirements, and other elements that exist for a job or job group in a particular organization; (b) investigate the impact that new challenges, technology, changes in business strategy, and so on, are likely to have on the requirements for a job or job group; and (c) create custom descriptive content for defining the target job or jobs.

In summary, this approach requires the job modeler to deductively formulate a scheme to explain the work in question. This approach is particularly useful for gaining a detailed understanding of the business strategy and new challenges that form the context for a new or dramatically changing job.

Some work with a semiconductor manufacturing company makes a good case in point. The result of a joint venture, this third entity company was building a new $500 million facility to build state-of-the-art microchips. However, the facility and technology were not the only things new and state-of-the-art. The configuration of the work for the engineering staff and technicians was also unique, representing a blend of the work structures and cultures from the two parent organizations.

This is exciting, but challenging stuff when one gets to the point of designing work roles and creating selection specifications to guide staffing efforts for these critical job groups. Given that there were no job incumbents to study, that no one person or group of people had the complete picture of the envisioned jobs in their head, and that the inferential leap from the most similar constellations of job groups from the parent companies were too great to put much faith in efforts to extrapolate research results targeting those jobs, the decision was made to use a purely rational approach for modeling the work to be performed and deriving the initial selection specifications.

Based on a combination of interviews and focus groups with the management team and work group team leaders who had literally spent years crafting the vision of the workplace, and who were now responsible for launching the business, a detailed model composed of work activities and competencies was deductively derived. This rationally based metamodel, and the subsumed models for specific job clusters, now serves as the platform for several recruiting and selection initiatives designed to identify and screen engineering staff and technicians with the correct mix of general and technical competencies.

The challenge for these kinds of studies is that the results are qualitatively based. Thus, they require the end user of the information to place a great deal of faith in the job modeler's ability to capture and conceptualize information from a not necessarily generalizable set of inputs. Also, the purely rational approach makes it difficult to link resulting information with other information sets or databases and limits the kinds of analysis that might be conducted. For example, information from a rational-based approach would not readily permit a comparison of how the possession of certain competencies is related to performance outcomes in different job families. These concerns can be best answered by aggregating information across other databases and rolling this information up to some general level of specificity that allows comparisons across occupational groups.

Empirical Method

A second approach for conducting job modeling research involves conducting some form of empirical analysis using data generated from questionnaire results. This approach uses a fixed set of descriptors built into a questionnaire format, which is then used to: (a) obtain the input from a larger group of SMEs, (b) provide an empirical base for evaluating the psychometric soundness of SME judgments, (c) check for group differences in the results, (d) classify jobs, and (e) collect data, quantify the obtained information, and build necessary paper-trail documentation.

A recent project with PETsMART provides a good illustration. This pet service and supply company has experienced tremendous growth over the last several years, growing from five employees operating out of a garage in Phoenix in 1987 to more than 250 stores throughout the United States in 1998. Although the organization is dynamic and built around some unique operating concepts, the composition of the store team is similar to that of many other retailers. Hence, when the company decided it needed to enhance its screening procedure for entry-level store associates, it was not necessary to start at ground zero to build descriptive content for the entry-level store associate job.

Instead, previous work with other hourly retail jobs was leveraged to build a job modeling questionnaire covering the already well-understood aspects of work, such as handling and stocking supplies, cleaning and maintenance, cash register operations, and receiving and ordering supplies. Thus, the job modeling questionnaire that was built was a 90% solution before the client saw it the first time to review it for coverage and applicability to PETsMART. With minor revisions, the resulting questionnaire was finalized and administered to a broad sample of incumbents and supervisors to help identify and prioritize the specific competencies that should be emphasized in the multilayered screening process that is now in place.

Keep in mind that certain job targets (job group, job track, or jobs in a value chain) and certain organizations are more amenable to this process than others. Collecting poor-quality or unreliable quantitative information from a large number of respondents is no substitute for capturing high-quality qualitative information (i.e., detailed, comprehensive, and reliable) from a smaller number of true SMEs.

Keep in mind, too, that data may be generated from other sources than questionnaires. Direct observation and videotaping, work diaries, electronic performance monitoring, and records of activity–outcome combinations are some of the possibilities. However, I have found opportunities to use these methods few and far between. For this reason, I have chosen to focus and elaborate on questionnaire methodology. Nevertheless, opportunities to do things differently do crop up, so do not put blinders on.

Combined Rational and Empirical Methods

The two tactics for collecting job modeling information described earlier are not mutually exclusive. Although these two approaches can be used singly, in many cases it makes sense to use them in combination. Thus, a third approach to conducting job modeling research involves combining the rational and empirical approaches. The combined approach involves methodology composed of three broad steps:

- First, interviews and/or focus groups are used to identify and create a comprehensive set of descriptors for covering the job content domain being studied. This step is the equivalent to the rational approach to job modeling, although in this case the resulting model is only an initial solution.
- Second, the initial solution of descriptive content is built into a questionnaire and administered in survey format to a sample of experts, with directions to rate each statement with regard to *Current Importance, Level of Mastery, Difficulty to Learn,* or some other characteristic. Thus, the combined approach extends the thinking of the rational approach to the point of collecting quantitative information and empirically investigating judgments about job requirements.
- Finally, a data-reduction technique is used to aggregate sets of related statements to compose more precise descriptions of work activities, competencies, or whatever. This more precise set of statements is then used as a set of building blocks for creating a final job model.

Recent work with a major financial services organization provides the basis for an operational example. This company provides consumer loan products through a network of more than 2,200 branches. A couple of years ago, they were interested in performing job modeling work to accomplish a variety of objectives. One of the primary objectives was to formalize its understanding of the key competencies needed by individuals in the branch offices given the strategic objectives of the company. As a whole, the company was becoming more sales focused, individual offices were expected to function more autonomously, and a promote-from-within emphasis was emerging. All of this impacted the competency requirements of entry-level jobs. Furthermore, there was pressure for the different business subsidiaries to incorporate a common set of operating precepts and drive toward common performance metrics across the operating organizations.

These factors all pointed toward the need to employ a combined rational and empirical approach to job modeling. No one group of individuals in any one place in the organization had all the information from all the different perspectives required to accomplish the broad objectives of the project. Consequently, a series of interviews, focus groups, and feedback sessions were conducted across the country as the initial job model was built. Then a questionnaire was built based on this input and administered to an even larger set of SMEs. Clearly the combined approach allows one to take advantage of the best of both approaches. However, there are cost and time implications that need to be considered.

Which Method Is Best?

The discussion of which method works best is something of a turning point in the book. Table 4.4 is the first of a series of guideline-type tables that are presented over the next several chapters. Although the hope is that these tables will provide useful suggestions, it is at this juncture that I am reminded of a young grade school student who, when asked to write a report on Socrates over the weekend, turned in his paper on Monday with just two sentences on it:

Socrates was a man who traveled a lot and gave people good advice.
They made him drink poison.

A little brief perhaps, as far as over-the-weekend reports go, but it is hard to quibble with the fact that the basic highlights are there. With this piece of history in mind, I want to be clear that what follows is not a prescription for conducting job modeling research.

In other words, I am not advocating the equivalent of a paint-by-numbers approach to job modeling. This point is so important that I am not above begging: please, Please, PLEASE, *PLEASE* do not view information in Table 4.4 (or the subsequent tables with similar guidelines) as concrete advice or a set of fixed decision rules. Rather, think of them as nonstrict guidelines to be considered in the mix of the unique complexities associated with a particular job modeling situation.

That caveat behind us, the information in Table 4.4 is based on a research study investigating the thinking of 12 job modeling experts to identify and weight the important variables they use when planning for a modeling project.[5] Eleven of the experts have doctorates in industrial-organizational psychology, and all have a number of years of experience collecting job modeling information to create a wide range of HR applications. These content experts responded to a series of questionnaires designed to capture their thinking about best practices in job modeling research. They represent more than 200 years of job modeling experience, and their accumulated judgments serve as a basis for several of the tables in the book. For example, in Table 4.4, our experts indicated which job modeling method—other things being equal—is typically best suited for capturing information for each of a wide range of possible HR applications. In many cases, a combined approach is recommended.

However, because the rational and empirical approaches can be independent, we can create a table in which it is possible to be either high, medium, or low on one axis independent of the other. Figure 4.5 recasts the information from Table 4.4 and categorizes the various human capital management applications into the appropriate cells of the resulting 3 x 3 table (where three stars in Table 4.4 equal a high need in Fig. 4.5, and so on).

Thus, Table 4.4 and Fig. 4.5 present some ideas for preferred methods used to support different applications, other things being equal. However, when was project work ever that simple? Things are never equal. The 13 job modeling research impact variables described as the *Baker's Dozen* in Table 4.5 offer some additional precision to these general guidelines. Here are 13 variables that could impact decisions about the method that might work best for collecting the information one needs to support a particular application in a particular situation. The array of questions in Tables 4.6 and 4.7, which are based on the Baker's Dozen impact variables, can be thought of as situation assessment worksheets. These worksheets enable one to evaluate the extent to which some important undercurrents are swirling around in a given job modeling situation. Identifying potentially tricky waters and using the information to guide adjustments to the suggested course of action offered in Table 4.4 is the whole purpose of these worksheets.

For example, a job modeling effort might be undertaken to support the development of a paper-and-pencil testing procedure (with follow-up validation) used to screen entry-level management and sales associates into a bank. On the surface, Table 4.4 indicates that, for the development of this type of HR intervention (No. 7 in the table), the empirical analysis method is essential and it may be important to use interviews or focus groups to collect initial information (i.e., three stars in the Empirical Analysis column and two stars for the Rational Analysis column). However, if one knows more about the business situation and the job modeling research setting, it is possible to get an even better feel for a preferred method.

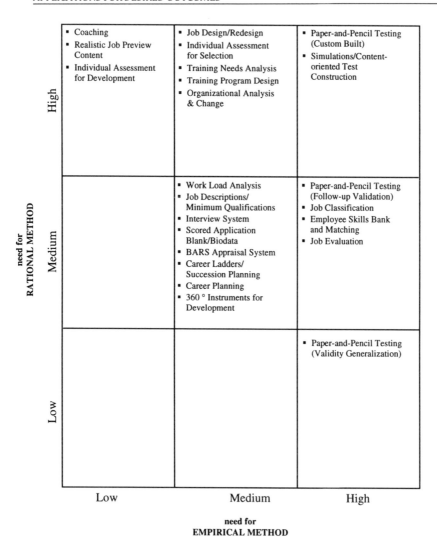

		Low	Medium	High
need for RATIONAL METHOD	**High**	▪ Coaching ▪ Realistic Job Preview Content ▪ Individual Assessment for Development	▪ Job Design/Redesign ▪ Individual Assessment for Selection ▪ Training Needs Analysis ▪ Training Program Design ▪ Organizational Analysis & Change	▪ Paper-and-Pencil Testing (Custom Built) ▪ Simulations/Content-oriented Test Construction
	Medium		▪ Work Load Analysis ▪ Job Descriptions/ Minimum Qualifications ▪ Interview System ▪ Scored Application Blank/Biodata ▪ BARS Appraisal System ▪ Career Ladders/ Succession Planning ▪ Career Planning ▪ 360 ° Instruments for Development	▪ Paper-and-Pencil Testing (Follow-up Validation) ▪ Job Classification ▪ Employee Skills Bank and Matching ▪ Job Evaluation
	Low			▪ Paper-and-Pencil Testing (Validity Generalization)

need for
EMPIRICAL METHOD

FIG. 4.5. A 3 X 3 table of job modeling supported interventions.

To help drive this point home, take a few moments to review the fictional case study presented in Fig. 4.6. Then take a few more minutes to complete the rational method and empirical method worksheets in Tables 4.6 and 4.7, respectively. Although your assessment of the situation might be slightly different, the results of my assessment of the situation appear in Fig. 4.7. As you can see, the impact variables described up to this point can serve as the basis for a situation profile to help guide thinking about the preferred modeling method. In this case, a combined rational and empirical approach makes the most sense. Any time the average of the impact variables for either the rational or empirical method are close to 3, one might consider bumping up the recommendations regarding the appropriate job modeling method for different applications in Table 4.4 by one star. Similarly, when the impact variable assessment suggests one

---

BANK PARTNERS, INC.

Organization Overview

Bank Partners, Inc. is an international company providing individual bank services and consumer loan products through a branch network consisting of 1,600 branch offices nationwide. The company has experienced tremendous growth in the past 5 years primarily through acquisition of smaller, regional-based banks with experienced management and service representative (i.e., sales) staffs. Although the expansion efforts are slowing down, the company is bracing for significant industry change, primarily in the form of changing regulations that will dramatically increase the number of competitors and complicate the consumer loan process. However, the change is not unexpected, and everyone included in BPI's senior management team has a fairly clear idea of what looms on the horizon.

Typical Branch

Although each of the 1,600 branches has a branch manager, assistant manager, and a wide array of service representative jobs, there really is no typical branch. Because of the rapid acquisition growth and the run-and-gun mentality of the company, there has been little effort to assimilate and standardize the various jobs, products, and services across the system. In fact, it is likely that job incumbents with the same job title perform different functions depending on the size of the branch and whether it serves an urban or rural location, although it is unclear to what extent these differences exist because there has been no concerted effort to document who does what where.

Business Need

The service representative job is central for the continued success of the company for two main reasons. First, these 3,400 representatives hold the primary sales and revenue-generating role in the branch system. Second, the position is the entry point on the management track in the company, which has a strong promote-from-within policy. However, there has been a marked increase in turnover in this job over the past couple of years, most of it within the first 6 months on the job and most of it involuntary due to performance-related problems. The company has never used formal testing procedures to screen new hires before, and the rank and file in this decentralized organization are fairly suspicious of new ideas and initiatives introduced by the folks at corporate. However, the senior management team has decided that something needs to be done.

Service Representative Job

The service representative job was originally a service and passive/responsive sales job, which is increasingly becoming a more proactive sales-oriented job in which there is a definite emphasis on pushing certain services and loan products. Job incumbents operate independently to identify and qualify potential customers, generate loan applications, and make collection calls on overdue accounts. Actually, a number of different titles make up the service representative job (Service Rep I, Service Rep II, Senior Service Rep). The job has a frenetic pace; every day is different, and each Service Rep has his or her monthly performance evaluated by a supervisor using a wide range of objective sales performance measures.

Assumptions

For the sake of this case study, assume that (a) the something that needs to get done is the development of a paper-and-pencil testing procedure (with follow-up validation) for screening new service representatives, that (b) the legal environment is fairly contentious, and (c) as the consultant, you have had some previous experience conducting job modeling work with this job group.

FIG. 4.6. Case study.

TABLE 4.5

Baker's Dozen: Job Modeling Research Impact Variables

Rational Impact Variables

- *Envisioned Changes in the Organization Affecting the Job Over Next 3 Years.* As a result of changes in the work process, the introduction of new technology to the workplace, job redesign efforts, or other changes, will there be corresponding changes to job requirements?

- *Existence of Job Description Information for Titles in Job Group.* Are the requirements of the target job(s) already well understood? Is there detailed descriptive information within the organization or in the published literature that provides a rich understanding of work activities and required competencies?

- *Breadth of Expertise and Depth of Knowledge of SMEs About Titles in Job Group.* Do the SMEs (whether incumbents or supervisors) have a comprehensive understanding of the components of the job (i.e., important activities and/or strategic competencies and/or work environment) being investigated?

- *Extent to Which Results of Work Are Observable.* Are the outputs or results of work observable or are work products primarily unobservable and hard to define?

- *Extent to Which Work Content is Relatively Fixed/Routine versus Dynamic.* Are work activities fixed or do the tasks and competencies needed to successfully perform the job change from day to day and week to week in response to shifting demands of the job?

- *Extent to Which It is Important to Create Buy-in on the Part of End Users of the Target Application.* Will the resulting HR application being constructed be accepted and used, no questions asked? Or is it necessary to allow multiple constituents to have input to help foster internal acceptance?

- *Extent to Which the Job Modeling Team Has Experience Working With the Target Jobs.* Do the project leader and others conducting major portions of the job modeling work have the benefit of having worked with similar jobs in other organizations, and are they familiar with the major work activities, work products or outcomes, and terminology?

(continues)

TABLE 4.5 (continued)

Empirical Impact Variables

- *Number of Incumbents in Target Job(s).* Is the application being designed for a job or job group with several incumbents or thousands?

- *Number of Work Locations.* Are all the incumbents in the job(s) targeted by the intervention in one location, are they spread out across dozens, or are they spread out across hundreds or even thousands of locations?

- *Number of Different Work Functions, Grade Levels, or Business Units Involved.* Does the planned application involve jobs that cut across organization business units, work functions, or grade levels?

- *Extent to Which Work Content is Expected to be the Same in a Job or Job Title Across Locations/Business Units.* Is a customer service rep job in a rural branch of the bank the same as a CSR job in a large metropolitan branch? Is a CSR job in Consumer Branch Operations the same as a job with the same title in Commercial Lending Operations?

- *Number of Specific Job Titles Included in Scope of Proposed Application.* If a project targets the customer service rep job, is this the only job title that exists or does the target really include CSRI, CSRII, CSRIII, Associate CSR, Senior CSR, etc.?

- *Extent to Which Resulting HR Application is Expected to Be Free from Legal or Union Review.* Is the target application being built in a litigious environment or do you expect the resulting program to be free from legal scrutiny? Similarly, is the application being constructed within a contentious union environment?

TABLE 4.6
Rational Method Impact Variables

	1	1.5	2	2.5	3
	★		★★		★★★
1. Envisioned Changes in the Organization Affecting the Job Over Next 3 Years	No anticipated changes in the organization that are likely to impact job requirements in target group (e.g., introduction of new technology or job redesign efforts).		Might be some changes in the organization to impact job requirements in target group (e.g., introduction of new technology or job re-design efforts).		Great changes in the organization are planned that will impact job requirements in target group.
	★		★★		★★★
2. Existence of Job Description Information for Titles in Job Group	There is a great deal of high-quality and up-to-date descriptive information in the organization and published literature.		There is some fairly high-quality and reasonably current descriptive information in the organization and published literature.	.	There is no descriptive information in the organization or published literature, or the information that exists is of poor quality and/or old and of questionable value.
	★		★★		★★★
3. Breadth of Expertise and Depth of Knowledge of SMEs About Titles in Job Group	Very few, if any, SMEs really have a comprehensive understanding of the components of the jobs being investigated.		Some SMEs have a fairly broad and fairly deep understanding of the components of the jobs being investigated.		Many SMEs have both great breadth and depth of understanding of the components of the jobs being investigated.

(continues)

94

TABLE 4.6 (continued)

	1 ★	1.5	2 ★★	2.5	3 ★★★
4. Extent to Which Results of Work Are Observable	The outputs or results of work are observable and clearly understood.		The outputs of work are a mix of observable and unobservable components; some results may be clearly defined and others are more difficult to clearly describe.		The outputs or results of work are not observable and are hard to define.
5. Extent to Which Work Content Is Relatively Fixed/Routine vs. Dynamic	Work activities and required competencies are fixed and do not change over time or across projects.		Work activities and required competencies are somewhat fixed, and there is a fair amount of change to the composition of work over time and across projects.		Work activities and required competencies are not fixed and change a great deal over time and across projects.
6. Extent to Which it Is Important to Create Buy-in on Part of End Users	Not important; end users will use the resulting HR application, no questions asked.		Somewhat important; end users will likely use the resulting HR application.		Critically important; unless the job modeling team creates buy-in and builds education in as part of the project, the resulting HR application will not be used.
7. Extent to Which the Job Modeling Team Has Experience Working With the Target Jobs	Job modeling team has conducted work with some jobs on numerous occasions and can leverage significant archival information.		Job modeling team has conducted some work with these jobs and can leverage some archival information.		Job modeling team has conducted no work with these jobs and cannot leverage any archival information.

TABLE 4.7

Empirical Method Impact Variables

	1	1.5	2	2.5	3
1. Number of Incumbents in the Target Jobs	★ Few (N = 1 to 5)		★★ Some (N = 50 to 250)		★★★ Many (N = 500+)
2. Number of Work Locations	★ Few Incumbents in the target job are all in one or two locations.		★★ Some Incumbents in the target job are spread out across dozens of locations.		★★★ Many Incumbents in the target job are spread out across hundreds of locations.
3. Number of Different Work Functions, Grade Levels, or Business Units Involved	★ One The job modeling work is focused on a single work function, in a single grade level, in one business unit.		★★ Several The job modeling work targets a limited range of work functions or grade levels or business units.		★★★ Many The job modeling work targets a wide range of work functions, grade levels, and business units.

(continues)

TABLE 4.7 (continued)

4. Extent to Which Work Content is Expected to be the Same in a Job or Job Title Across Locations/Business Units

1 ★	1.5	2 ★★	2.5	3 ★★★
The same; expect no variation in job content across locations/business units.		Expect some variation in job content across locations/business units.		Not the same; expect great variation in job content across locations/business units.

5. Number of Specific Job Titles Included in Scope of Proposed Intervention

1 ★	1.5	2 ★★	2.5	3 ★★★
One (N = 1)		Several (N = 2-10)		Many (N = 11+)

6. Extent to Which Resulting Human Resource Intervention is Expected to be Free From Legal or Union Review

1 ★	1.5	2 ★★	2.5	3 ★★★
Great Extent. Very unlikely resulting application would ever come under legal or union scrutiny.		Some Extent. Fairly unlikely resulting application would ever come under legal or union scrutiny.		Not Free. Very likely the resulting application would eventually come under legal or union scrutiny.

Rational

1. Envisioned changes in the organization affecting the job over next 3 years
2. Existence of job description information for titles in job group
3. Breadth of expertise and depth of knowledge of SMEs about titles in job group
4. Extent to which results of work are observable
5. Extent to which work content is relatively fixed/routine versus dynamic
6. Extent to which it is important to create buy-in on part of end users
7. Extent to which the job modeling team has experience working with target jobs

| **Total Rational Score** | 2.4 |

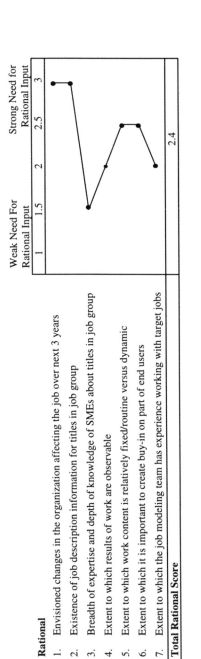

Weak Need For Rational Input			Strong Need for Rational Input
1	1.5	2	2.5	3

Empirical

1. Number of incumbents in the target jobs
2. Number of work locations
3. Number of different work functions, grade levels, or business units involved
4. Extent to which work content is expected to be the same in a job or job title across locations/business units
5. Number of specific job titles included in scope of proposed application
6. Extent to which resulting HR application is expected to be free from legal review

| **Total Empirical Score** | 2.4 |

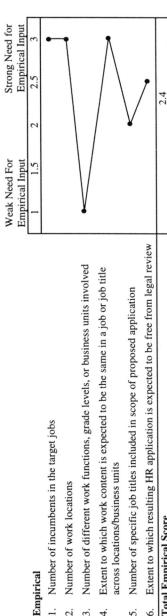

Weak Need For Empirical Input			Strong Need for Empirical Input
1	1.5	2	2.5	3

FIG. 4.7. Situation profile for case study.

97

method over another in contradiction to the recommendations in Table 4.4, then it might make sense to think strongly about using both methods.

A practical question that could prove to have controlling influence over the job modeling approach (but is not listed as part of the situational assessment scoping questions because it is not directly related to the quality of the solution) is organization receptivity to one approach or another. For example, in support of another initiative, relevant groups of employees may have participated in a number of focus groups over the past 6 months. In this context, proposing more interviews and focus groups as part of the job modeling enterprise might be a tough sell and, from a practical standpoint, the option to conduct numerous focus group sessions simply is not in the cards. Concerns such as these should not drive decisions about methodology, but it is also unwise to proceed as if they did not exist.

TYPE OF INFORMATION REQUIRED

To repeat a point made before, choices made earlier in the modeling process guide and constrain later choices. For example, decisions concerning the customer's desired outcomes, which cascade down from the organization's vision and competitive strategy, drive decisions about particular interventions. Choices about target interventions, in turn, guide decisions about the type of information required for building or supporting a particular intervention.

As outlined in chapter 2, there are two broad classes of information types: job description and situation description. Job description variables include the work activities that comprise a job and the competencies required to perform requisite activities. Situation description variables can be expressed in terms of the organizational vision and strategy that serve as a platform for the job, and the work context in which a person carries out his or her job, which could have implications for how the job is designed in the long term. Although there are other types of data that can be used to characterize jobs, such as performance standards or relevant work experience, these four classes of information, used singly or in combination, are appropriate for developing most applications that impact an organization's human capital.

Once the application or system of applications for which information is being generated is clearly articulated, decisions about the type of job modeling information required will logically follow. Without this grounding to the customer's desired outcomes and the HR applications needed to achieve them, it becomes virtually impossible to develop a clear plan for capturing the necessary information, and things can quickly become confusing. With respect to specific applications, then, different types of information could be essential, frequently important, simply nice to have or occasionally useful, or completely unnecessary. Table 4.8 offers some guidance as to the type of information that should be considered grist for the job modeling mill for our core set of 23 HR applications.

TABLE 4.8
Type of Information and Level of Detail Required for Different Interventions

Application		LOW SDS 0–30	MEDIUM SDS 31–90	HIGH SDS 91+
Human Resource Planning				
1. Job design/redesign	Work Activity			★★★
	Competency		★★★	
	Str. Context		★★★	
	Work Context			★★★
2. Workload analysis	Work Activity		★★★	
	Competency	★★		
	Str. Context		★★★	
	Work Context		★★★	
Recruitment				
3. Job description & minimum qualifications	Work Activity		★★★	
	Competency		★★★	
	Str. Context	★		
	Work Context		★★★	
4. Realistic job preview content	Work Activity		★★★	
	Competency		★★★	
	Str. Context	★★		
	Work Context		★★★	
Selection				
5. Interview system	Work Activity	★★		
	Competency		★★★	
	Str. Context	★		
	Work Context		★★★	
6. Scored application blank/biodata	Work Activity	★★		
	Competency	★★★		
	Str. Context	★		
	Work Context	★★		
7. Paper-and-pencil testing (follow-up validation)	Work Activity		★★	
	Competency		★★★	
	Str. Context	★		
	Work Context		★★	

Level of Detail

(continues)

TABLE 4.8 (continued)

8. Paper-and-pencil testing (validation generalization)	Work Activity			★★	
	Competency			★★★	
	Str. Context		★		
	Work Context			★★	
9. Paper-and-pencil testing (custom built)	Work Activity			★★★	
	Competency			★★★	
	Str. Context		★		
	Work Context			★★★	
10. Simulations/content-oriented test construction	Work Activity				★★★
	Competency			★★★	
	Str. Context		★★		
	Work Context				★★
11. Individual assessment for selection	Work Activity		★★★		
	Competency			★★★	
	Str. Context		★★		
	Work Context			★★★	
Classification/Placement					
12. Job classification	Work Activity			★★★	
	Competency			★★★	
	Str. Context		★		
	Work Context		★		
13. Employee skills bank & matching	Work Activity			★★★	
	Competency				★★★
	Str. Context		★		
	Work Context		★★		
Training					
14. Training needs analysis	Work Activity			★★★	
	Competency			★★★	
	Str. Context		★		
	Work Context		★★		

(continues)

TABLE 4.8 (continued)

15. Training program design	Work Activity		★★★	
	Competency			★★★
	Str. Context	★		
	Work Context		★★	
Performance Appraisal				
16. BARS appraisal systems[1]	Work Activity	★★★		
	Competency		★★	
	Str. Context	★		
	Work Context	★★		
Compensation				
17. Job evaluation[1]	Work Activity			★★★
	Competency		★★★	
	Str. Context	★★		
	Work Context		★★★	
Career Management				
18. 360° instruments for development	Work Activity	★		
	Competency		★★★	
	Str. Context	★★		
	Work Context		★★	
19. Individual assessment for development	Work Activity	★★		
	Competency		★★★	
	Str. Context	★★		
	Work Context		★★	
20. Career ladders/succession planning	Work Activity		★★★	
	Competency		★★★	
	Str. Context	★★		
	Work Context	★★		
21. Career planning	Work Activity	★★		
	Competency		★★★	
	Str. Context	★★		
	Work Context		★★	

(continues)

TABLE 4.8 (continued)

22. Coaching	Work Activity	★★		
	Competency		★★★	
	Str. Context	★★		
	Work Context		★★	
Organization Development & Change				
23.Organizational analysis & change	Work Activity	★		
	Competency	★★		
	Str. Context			★★★
	Work Context		★★★	

★★★ = Essential information for most applications of this type.

★★ = Important information for many applications of this type.

★ = Nice to have this information, but not essential for most applications of this type.

Blank = Unnecessary information for most applications of this type.

1 = Typically either work activity content or competency content is used to build this intervention, but not both.

DETAIL OF INFORMATION REQUIRED

A nice metaphor for thinking about job modeling is photography—an art form in which the creation of an image can be likened to developing a clear picture of the requisite work activities, competencies, and so on required to successfully perform a target job. For example, in Fig. 4.8A, the picture of important work activities and information about requisite competencies is vague, leaving the door open for misinterpretation about what is required to successfully perform in a job or set of jobs. As the modeling effort moves through Fig. 4.8B and 4.8C, the clarity improves and the picture of what is truly critical job information becomes sharper and more distinct. Concurrently, the usefulness of the modeling information becomes sharper and more valuable.

However, in job modeling, there are definite costs associated with increasing the resolution and adding detail to the picture. Furthermore, the same level of detail is not required for all types of information or to support all possible HR applications. Despite this generally accepted belief, there are no specific rules to guide practice other than that a set of descriptor statements should contain information pertinent for the intended application and in a degree of detail that proves useful for the intended purpose.

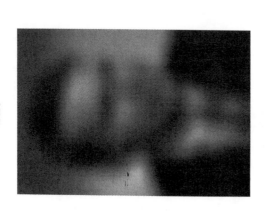

FIG. 4.8. The image resolution issue in job modeling.

103

For example, an activity statement that reads "Types material for use by others" might be sufficiently detailed to drive certain applications, such as the creation of content for recruiting materials. However, for other applications, the reader of this statement (who is of vital interest to a job modeler because he or she will be making inferences from—or be providing judgments about—each of these statements later on in the job modeling process) is left wondering about, among other things, how material is typed (from dictation or hard copy), what is typed (straight text or charts, graphs, and numbers), and what equipment is used (electric typewriter or a personal computer using a specific word processing package).

The reverse can also occur, in which the level of detail is carried to unrealistic extremes. For example, in the area of job modeling to support the development of selection tools, frequent misinterpretation of the *Uniform Guidelines*[6] has led to the creation of huge, leviathanlike inventories of descriptors that go well beyond the point of diminishing returns for creating better instruments.[7]

Although the level-of-detail issue is pertinent to some degree for all four types of descriptor information noted previously in this chapter, it is of supreme importance for the job description of class information (i.e., work activity and competency domains). For this reason, the text and examples in this section are specifically designed to clarify thinking about descriptor detail in activity and competency statements, although the basic ideas also apply to the descriptor domains for work and organizational context.

The question regarding the degree of detail or specificity of a statement has a number of associated implications for subsequent steps in the job modeling process.[8] To meaningfully compare and contrast different levels of specificity in job modeling statements, a means for making these comparisons must first be available. One measure that I have developed in an effort to evaluate the level of specificity in job modeling statements is the Statement Detail Scale (SDS). Application of the SDS to work activity and competency statements are addressed in turn.

SDS and Work Activity Statements

The SDS index is calculated using two components: (a) the number of questions addressed by the descriptor statement, and (b) the number of words in the statement. For any work activity statement, four questions are of potential interest:

- WHAT: What is done or what action is being performed?
- WHO/WHAT: Who or what is being acted on?
- WHY: Why is the action occurring (what is the intended outcome)?
- HOW: How is the action being accomplished?

Thus, if the WHAT and WHO/WHAT questions are both defined, the first component for the SDS calculation is 2. The second component of the

SDS is simply a count of the number of words in the statement. These two values are multiplied and the product is the SDS. The higher the value of the SDS index, the more information is conveyed by the statement and the more the statement moves from being a generalizable statement to having detail that makes it much more organization- and function-specific. Of course, poor writing and the inclusion of unnecessary words in a statement can lead to spuriously high SDS indexes. Working to keep the statement word count low is an important aspect of good item writing. Other guidelines for evaluating well-written items are covered in chapter 5. For now, several examples of how the SDS value changes as the degree of detail of a statement changes appear in Table 4.9.

SDS and Competency Statements

The SDS index for competency statements is similar to that used for work activities, although the questions are slightly different:

- WHAT: What is required?
- WHO/WHAT: Who or what is involved?
- WHY: Why is the skill/knowledge/orientation necessary?
- HOW: How is the skill/knowledge accomplished?

Beyond this, the SDS calculation is the same. Several examples of how the SDS value changes as a function of different degrees of detail in competency statements appear in Table 4.10. Additional scaled examples of work activity and competency statements appear in Fig. 4.9.

Although each situation is different, 12 job modeling experts showed a good deal of agreement in their judgment of the level of descriptor statement detail required to support different applications.[9] Figures 4.10 and 4.11 display the degree of specificity typically needed for work activity and competency statements used as building materials for the different applications.

Although the SDS index has been used successfully to guide project work and consult with customers around the level of detail required in different modeling situations, it is still an evolving concept. As such, the suggestions about the level of detail needed to support different interventions should be considered just that—initial suggestions for a modeler to consider. The hope is that continued work along these lines will eventually make it possible to offer more definitive recommendations.

PROJECT MANAGEMENT TIPS

The most important tip I can offer for Step 2 of the Cheshire Strategic Job Modeling Process is to reach a clear agreement with your customer early on regarding the purpose of the project and expected deliverables. These decisions

TABLE 4.9

Work Activity Statement Composition

WHAT is being done or what action is being performed?	WHO/WHAT is being acted on?	WHY is the action occurring? or WHAT is the outcome/objective?	HOW is the action being accomplished?	SDS VALUE
1A. INSPECTS	engine parts. *			1 x 3 = 3
1B. INSPECTS	polished engine valves.			2 x 4 = 8
1C. INSPECTS	polished engine valve	to detect ragged edges, burrs, nicks, or other irregularities in finished edge.		3 x 16 = 48
1D. INSPECTS	polished engine valves	to detect ragged edges, burrs, nicks, or other irregularities in finished edge	by removing from feeder coil and placing first and second finger on valve head and sliding fingertips across machined edge.	4 x 36 = 144
2A. CALCULATES	financial analyses. *			1 x 3 = 3
2B. CALCULATES	cost-volume-profit ratios.			2 x 5 = 10
2C. CALCULATES	cost-volume-profit ratios	to guide business unit planning.		3 x 10 = 30
2D. CALCULATES	cost-volume-profit ratios	to guide business unit planning	using information provided by the cost accounting department and solving for unknowns, such as finding the average contribution margin per unit required to cover fixed costs and provide operating profits.	4 x 40 = 160

* = Not clear what exactly is being acted on, so no credit.

TABLE 4.10
Competency Statement Composition

WHAT is required?	WHO/WHAT is involved?	WHY is the skill/knowledge necessary?	HOW is the skill/knowledge accomplished (e.g., performance standards)?	SDS VALUE
1A. SKILL	in persuading others. *			1 x 4 = 4
1B. SKILL	in persuading potential customers.			2 x 5 = 10
1C. SKILL	in persuading potential customers	to consider the benefits of a financial product or service.		3 x 15 = 45
1D. SKILL	in persuading potential customers	to consider the benefits of a financial product or service	by anticipating objections and responding succinctly to concerns.	4 x 23 = 92
2A. SKILL	in thinking. *			1 x 3 = 3
2B. SKILL	in evaluating strategies.			2 x 4 = 8
2C. SKILL	in evaluating strategies	that support the organization's business plan.		3 x 10 = 30
2D. SKILL	in evaluating strategies	that support the organization's business plan	by anticipating how various political, economic, and business events will play out and impact proposed research and development alliances with other organizations.	4 x 32 = 128

* = Not clear what exactly is being acted upon, so no credit.

Activity Statements

	Scale
H	175
	70
I	65
	60
G	55
H	**150**
	45
	40
	35
	30
	125
	20
	15
	10
	05
	100
M	95
	90
E	85
	80
D	**75**
	70
I	65
	60
U	55
M	**50**
	45
	40
	35
	30
	25
L	20
	15
O	10
	05
W	04
	03
	02
	0

144 — Inspects polished engine valves to detect ragged edges, burrs, nicks, or other irregularities in finished edge by removing from feeder coil and placing first and second fingers on valve head and sliding fingertips across machined edge. (WHAT, WHO/WHAT, WHY, and HOW answered, thus 4x36 words, or SDS=144)

48 — Inspects polished engine valves to detect ragged edges, burrs, nicks, or other irregularities in finished edge. (WHAT, WHO/WHAT, and WHY answered, thus 3x16 words, or SDS=48)

8 — Inspects polished engine valves. (WHAT and WHO/WHAT answered, thus 2x4 words, or SDS=8)

2 — Inspecting tasks. (WHAT answered, or 1x2 words, or SDS=2)

Competency Statements

	Scale
H	175
	70
I	65
	60
G	55
H	**150**
	45
	40
	35
	30
	125
	20
	15
	10
	05
	100
M	95
	90
E	85
	80
D	**75**
	70
I	65
	60
U	55
M	**50**
	45
	40
	35
	30
	25
L	20
	15
O	10
	05
W	04
	03
	02
	0

128 — Skill in evaluating strategies that support the organization's business plan by anticipating how various political, economic, and business events will "play out" and impact proposed research and development alliances with other organizations. (WHAT, WHO/WHAT, WHY, and HOW answered, thus 4x32 words, or SDS=128)

30 — Skill in evaluating strategies that support the organization's business plan. (WHAT, WHO/WHAT, and WHY answered, thus 3x10 words, or SDS=30)

8 — Skill in evaluating strategies. (WHAT and WHO/WHAT answered, thus 2x4 words, or SDS=8)

3 — Skill in thinking. (WHAT answered, or 1x3 words, or SDS=3)

FIG. 4.9. Statement detail scale example.

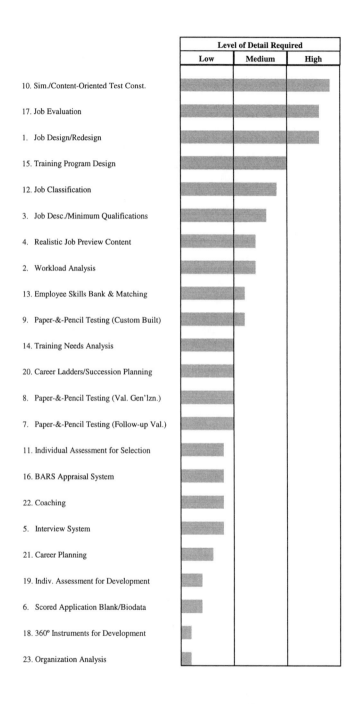

FIG. 4.10. Activity statement detail required for different interventions.

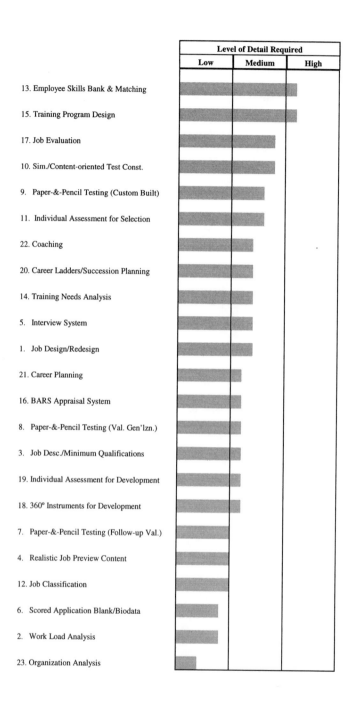

FIG. 4.11. Competency detail required for different interventions.

directly influence the amount of time and effort required on your part to create a model of work that has the appropriate breadth and level of detail. In addition, a job modeler must protect him or herself against *scope creep*, which occurs when a customer pushes the boundaries further away from what was contracted to be accomplished toward what could be done and thereby expands the scope of the project. This happens with internal as well as external customers.

Then there is the reality that customer priorities change, sometimes mid-stream. Carefully documenting enhancements or changes and being able to juxtapose these variances with a clearly worded statement of work gives you a leg to stand on when explaining later impacts on schedule and cost. Keep good notes and records throughout the course of the project and, inevitably, one day you'll find they keep you.

Next, be sure to articulate the roles and responsibilities of individuals and teams for project implementation. Figure 4.12 lays out the roles and relation-ships that characterize most job modeling projects involving outside consul-tants. If you are running a project inhouse, the Customer Project Team essentially becomes the Consultant Project Team and moves from the left of the vertical dotted line to the right. Once the project roles have been clarified and individuals have been identified, insert names and associated voice–fax–e-mail numbers in the appropriate boxes and distribute to project team members.

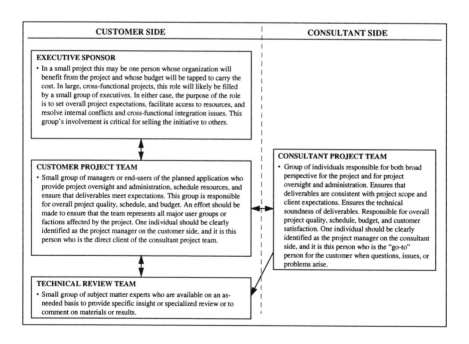

FIG. 4.12. Project roles and responsibilities.

In terms of fleshing out the project plan, avoid the seductive trap of proposing overly elegant solutions to the issues inherent in each project step. Not every customer will be able to swallow the ideal solution, although they might be able to accommodate and buy into a methodology that is perhaps a little short of the state-of-the-art. Find out what is workable for them and you will save time and professional relationships. Once the project plan has been finalized, circulate copies to members of the project team and your executive sponsors. At a minimum, the project plan should include the following:

- Project Context. This includes a broad, high-level description of the organization's vision and strategies driving the need for a particular application and a clear description of desired outcomes.
- Overall Project Steps. This includes not only a brief description of each project activity and associated deliverables, but also an assignment of responsibility for who will conduct or manage the various pieces of subsumed work.
- Timelines. Each major project step should have an associated deadline, with some best- and worst-case scenario boundaries. Although each project is unique, the sample timeline in Fig. 4.13 provides an idea of the time frames frequently associated with each step in a modeling project of average scope and complexity. Probably the most frequent cause for delay in large modeling projects is due to an underestimate of the time required to develop a mutual understanding and alignment of the modeling process and goals across major customer constituents. Having to work to develop consensus across different parts of the organization can significantly expand the time required to complete any of the nine steps in the figure. Try to build a little slack time into two or three steps of the project to give you some flexibility and a chance to recover schedule in the event you do run into obstacles.
- Expected Project Costs. Include both one-time development costs (time, money, resources) and ongoing costs (if any).

Next, set a date for the project kick-off meeting. This meeting should include a broad mix of potential owners of the applications being built and a sample of high-visibility users of the eventual applications. Part of the purpose of this meeting is to inform, setting clear expectations for next steps in the development process, describing the purpose of the resulting application, and so forth. However, an equally important purpose of this meeting is to gain the buy-in and commitment of individuals who will use the application being constructed. Do not underestimate the importance of this part of the equation. Strive to clearly describe the expected payoff and return of the successful system in terms that

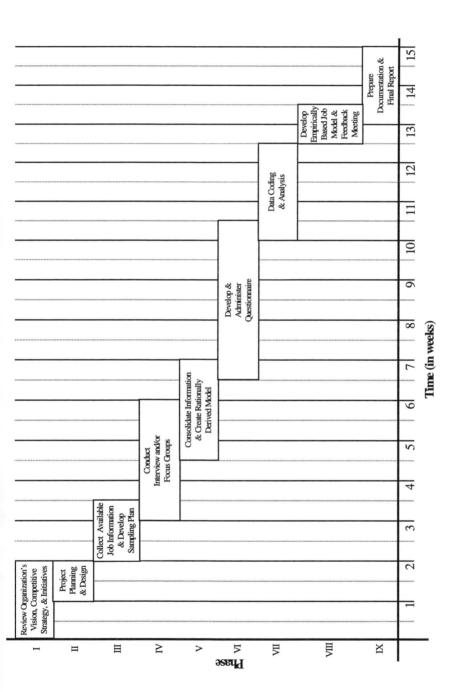

FIG. 4.13. Sample timeline for strategic job modeling project.

113

are meaningful to the target audience. Depending on the scope of the project, this is likely to be a 2- to 4-hour meeting.

Finally, make sure to identify and contact the individuals responsible for supporting other organizational initiatives that must mesh with the target application being constructed. For example:

- If the intent is to build a selection system, be sure to talk about how this effort fits with existing recruiting practices, classification and placement practices, and training initiatives.
- If the intent is to build a performance appraisal system, contact the people who head up training and compensation to discuss linkages with development and pay programs.

REFERENCES

[1]Cook, T. D., & Campbell, D. T. (1979). *Quasi-experimentation: Design and analysis issues for field settings.* Chicago: Rand McNally.

[2]Guion, R. M. (1998). *Assessment, measurement and prediction for personnel decisions.* Hillsdale, NJ: Lawrence Erlbaum Associates.

[3]Schmitt, N., & Landy, F. J. (1993). The concept of validity. In N. Schmitt & W. C. Borman (Eds.), *Personnel selection in organizations* (pp. 275–309). San Francisco: Jossey-Bass.

[4]Paraphrasing from Swanson, R. A. (1994). *Analysis for improving performance.* San Francisco, CA: Berrett-Koehler.

[5]Schippmann, J. S. (1996). *Key decision points in job modeling.* Unpublished manuscript.

[6]Equal Employment Opportunity Commission, Civil Service Commission, Department of Labor, & Department of Justice. (1978). *Uniform guidelines on employee selection procedures.* Federal Register, 43(166), 38295–38309.

[7]Barrett, R. S. (1996). *Fair employment strategies in human resource management.* Westport, CT: Quorum.

[8]Harvey, R. J. (1991). Job Analysis. In M. D. Dunnette & L. M. Hough (Eds.), *Handbook of industrial and organizational psychology* (Vol. 2, pp. 71–163). Palo Alto, CA: Consulting Psychologists Press.

[9]Schippmann, J. S. (1996). *Key decision points in job modeling.* Unpublished manuscript.

[10]Davis, L. E. & Wacker, G. J. (1988). Job design. In S. Gael (Ed.), *The job analysis handbook for business, industry, and government* (Vol. 1, pp. 157–172). New York. Wiley.

[11]Beatty, R. W., Coleman, S. C., & Schneier, C. E. (1988). Human resources planning and staffing. In S. Gael (Ed.), *The job analysis handbook for business, industry, and government* (Vol. 1, pp. 138–156). New York: Wiley.

[12]Page, R. C. & van De Vroot, D. M. (1989). Job analysis and HR planning. In W. F. Cascio (Ed.), *Human resource planning employment and placement.* Washington, DC: Bureau of National Affairs, Inc.

[13]Gael, S. (1988). Job descriptions. In S. Gael (Ed.), *The job analysis handbook for business, industry, and government* (Vol. 1, pp. 71–89). New York: Wiley.

[14]Prien, E. P., & Schippmann, J. S. (1987). Hiring—Screening and selecting staff for the nonprofit organization. In E. W. Anthes & J. Cronin (Eds.), *Personnel matters in the*

nonprofit organization (pp. 151–182). West Memphis, AR: Independent Community Consultants.

[15]Feild, H. S. & Gatewood, R. D. (1989). Development of a selection interview: A job content strategy. In R. W. Eder & G. R. Ferris (Eds.), *The employment interview* (pp. 145–157). Newbury Park, CA: Sage.

[16]Bloom, R., & Prien, E. P. (1983). A guide to job-related employment interviewing. *Personnel Administrator, 28,* 81–86.

[17]Fine, S. A., & Cronshaw, S. (1994). The role of job analysis in establishing the validity of biodata. In G. S. Stockes, M. D. Mumford, & W. A. Owens (Eds.), *Biodata handbook* (pp. 39–64). Palo Alto, CA: CCP Books.

[18]Morgan, R. B., & Smith, J. E. (1996). *Staffing the new workplace.* Milwaukee, WS: ASQC Quality Press.

[19]Gatewood, R. D., & Feild, H. S. (1994). *Human resource selection.* Fort Worth, TX: The Dryden Press.

[20]Kleiman, L. S., & Biderman, M. (1989). Job analysis for managerial selection: A guidelines-based approach. *Journal of Business and Psychology, 3,* 353–359.

[21]Landy, F. J. (1988). Selection procedure development and usage. In S. Gael (Ed.), *The job analysis handbook for business, industry, and government* (Vol. 1, pp. 271–287). New York: Wiley.

[22]Lopez, F. M., Kesselman, G. A., & Lopez, F. E. (1981). An empirical test of a trait-oriented job analysis technique. *Personnel Psychology, 34,* 479–502.

[23]Kane, M. T., Kingsbury C., Colton, D., & Estes, C. (1989). Combining data on criticality and frequency in developing test plans for licensure and certification examinations. *Journal of Educational Measurement, 26,* 17–27.

[24]Schippmann, J. S., Hughes, G. L., & Prien, E. P. (1987). The use of structured multi-domain job analysis for the construction of assessment center methods and procedures. *Journal of Business and Psychology, 4,* 353–366.

[25]Arthur, W., Doverspike, D., & Barrett, G. V. (1996). Development of a job analysis-based procedure for weighting and combining content-related tests into a single battery score. *Personnel Psychology, 49,* 971–985.

[26]Schmitt, N., & Ostroff, C. (1986). Operationalizing the "behavioral consistency approach": Selection test development based on content-oriented strategy. *Personnel Psychology, 39,* 91–108.

[27]Schippmann, J. S., & Vrazo, G. J. (1995). Individual assessment for key jobs. *Performance & Instruction, 35,* 10–15.

[28]Colihan, J., & Burger, G. K. (1995). Constructing job families: An analysis of quantitative techniques used for grouping jobs. *Personnel Psychology, 48,* 563–586.

[29]Harvey, R. J. (1986). Quantitative approaches to job classification: A review and critique. *Personnel Psychology, 39,* 267–289.

[30]See also chapter 7 and Appendix B of this book.

[31]Goldstein, I. L. (1993). *Training in organizations* (3rd ed.). Monterey, CA: Brooks/Cole.

[32]United States Civil Service Commission. (1976). *Job analysis for improved job-related employee development.* Washington, DC: Author.

[33]DeCotiis, T. A., & Morano, R. A. (1977). Applying job analysis to training. *Training and Development Journal, 31,* 20–24.

[34]Ammerman, H. L. (1977). *Performance content for job training: Vol. II. Stating the tasks of the job* (R&D Series No. 122). Columbus, OH: The Ohio State University, The Center for Vocational Education.

[35]Goldstein, I. L. (1993). *Training in organizations* (3rd ed.) Monterey, CA: Brooks/Cole.

[36]Schippmann, J. S., Vinchur, A. J., Smalley, M. D., & Prien, E. P. (1988). Using structured multi-domain job analysis to develop training and evaluation specifications for clinical psychologists. *Professional Psychology: Research and Practice, 19,* 141–147.

[37]Latham, G. P., & Fry, L. W. (1988). Measuring and appraising employee performance. In S. Gael (Ed.), *The job analysis handbook for business, industry, and government* (Vol. 1, pp. 216–233). New York: Wiley.

[38]Bernardin, H. J., & Beatty, R. W. (1984). *Performance appraisal: Assessing human behavior at work.* Boston: Kent.

[39]Henderson, R. I. (1988). Job evaluation, classification and pay. In S. Gael (Ed.), *The job analysis handbook for business, industry, and government* (Vol. 1, pp. 90–118). New York: Wiley.

[40]Hughes, G. L., Prien, E. P., & Hicks, J. (1987). Compensation and benefit plans in nonprofit organizations. In E. W. Anthes & J. Cronin (Eds.), *Personnel matters in the nonprofit organization* (pp. 279–312). West Memphis, AR: Independent Community Consultants.

[41]London, M. (1988). Career planning and development. In S. Gael (Ed.), *The job analysis handbook for business, industry, and government* (Vol. 1, pp. 234–242). New York: Wiley.

[42]Wooten, W. (1993). Using knowledge, skill, and ability (KSA) data to identify career pathing opportunities: An application of job analysis to internal manpower planning. *Public Personnel Management, 22,* 551–562.

[43]See chapter 6 of this book.

[44]Carson, K. P., & Stewart, G. L. (1996). Job analysis and the sociotechnical approach to quality: A critical examination. *Journal of Quality Management, 1,* 49–64.

[45]Langeland, K. L., Johnson, C. M., & Mawhinney, T. C. (1998). Improving staff performance in a community health setting: Job analysis, training, goal setting, feedback, and years of data. *Journal of Organizational Behavior Management, 18,* 21–43.

Chapter 5
Who is the Target Population?

> ... *Wars start at borders.* ...
> —Napoleon

It is unpopular these days in business, and in HRM in particular, to talk about boundaries. Ashkenas and crew wrote about *The Boundaryless Organization.*[1] Voss discussed the emergence of virtual organizations.[2] Hip companies have internal debates about the evils of management structure. There is reengineering, beyond reengineering, and then there is bio reengineering. There is the Third Wave, followed by the Fourth Wave, and do not forget the Second Curve. Then there is Bridges,[3] Aronowitz and DiFazio,[4] and Rifkin[5] writing about the disappearing job as if they were referring to a vanishing species that has simply been unable to keep up with the evolutionary pace.

Well, we will see. For one, I hesitate to join the veritable army of people who view boundaries as a set of leg irons that restrict an organization's agility and ability to succeed as a competitor into the year 2000 and beyond. To the contrary, the borders of things, although often a source of contention and hard to define, convey useful information. The fact of the matter is that the size and shape of things form an outline that helps tell us what they are. Pick up a coffee mug, a book, or your child and the contours of these things will tell you what you are dealing with. This is not to say companies, careers, and jobs are not changing—they are. My point is that the boundaries, and the way we measure and define them, need to change as well, as opposed to being discounted and ignored.

WHERE TO START

The prior discussion is pertinent because, at this stage in the modeling endeavor, it now becomes necessary to (a) get a handle on the scope of the target population, and (b) collect as much currently available information as possible for the jobs involved. However, first things first. In any one organization, there are a number of different kinds of jobs. These jobs may be grouped according to work function, level or hierarchy, position in a business process, and any number of other ways. Where should one start?

Of course, your customer may have a definite starting place in mind: "We want you to model the work of our front-line sales associates so we can use the results to build an XYZ application." However, there are instances where the question of where to start is either open or ill-defined. In these cases, and actually even in the former case for the purpose of helping to establish the relevance of the modeling effort, it may prove useful to employ a systematic process for evaluating potential job group starting points. Similar to the strategic impact criteria for evaluating potential applications discussed in chapter 4, the impact criteria listed next can help guide one to those groups of people in the organization who have the most direct link to the ultimate goals and overall performance of the organization.

- *Relevance of the job or job group.* Given the vision and competitive strategy of the organization and the expected outcomes associated with key strategic initiatives, which groups of people hold jobs that are dead center in the critical path? If you have worked through a business context and strategy web, which envisioned work activity and competency dimensions are linked to major strategic initiatives? What functions, work processes, or outcomes justify the existence of the organization? Given the strategic intent of the firm, what must the organization excel at (or, the reverse, where do errors and poor performance cost the most)? Why do or why should customers choose to do business with the organization? The answers to these questions should lead one to the hyperrelevant jobs or job groups in the organizations.
- *Size of the job group* (i.e., the number of people affected). Which job titles have the most incumbents? Are there obvious instances where people with different job titles are basically performing the same work and should be pooled together to form a larger job group? Financial and political constraints within the organization notwithstanding, it makes sense to work in an area where there is likely to be the greatest amount of impact for the greatest number of people.
- *Degree to which the work and associated worker requirements are currently understood.* For which jobs is there the most confusion about work activities and the associated competency requirements? Are there job groups where there are envisioned changes to the work process or the workplace that will make the current understanding obsolete? Are there job groups where the outputs of work are largely unobservable and hard to define? Does the organization need to develop a future-oriented picture for a job

group that is being redesigned or that does not yet exist? The answers to these questions should provide additional perspective on the broader question of where to start with a modeling effort.

- *Job groups characterized by performance-related problems.* Are there job groups where individual productivity (i.e., revenue-based outcomes like units sold, billable hours, ideas generated, units assembled) is inordinately low? Are there groups where cost-based outcomes like turnover, accidents, customer complaints, budget variances, processing time, grievances, time to market timelines, shortages, error rates, and training time are inordinately high? The jobs that surface after questions like these are often the same as those identified by the third set of questions earlier, but not always, so it often makes sense to apply these as well.

- *Entry-level and feeder jobs in the organization.* Which jobs constitute the primary points of entry for the different job tracks in the organization? Once inside the organization, are there jobs that are widely considered to be grooming spots or hubs in the pipeline to higher level jobs? There may be some duplication in the list of jobs identified by these questions and those identified by questions focusing on the size of job groups.

- *Legal, union, and organizational environment that forms the context for a job or job group.* Are there incumbent groups that operate in a contentious legal or union environment? Are there groups within the organization who simply have to be a part of the development and implementation of any new management practice or human resource initiative to accept or use the result? The answers to these questions should help spotlight job groups where the lack of sound information may have negative consequences.

Now, back to the broader question of which target group to focus on first. As you can see, there is no single criterion that may be applied to arrive at a reasoned response. However, the previous paragraphs contain a good repertoire of questions that can be used to prioritize potential modeling starting points. One way to proceed is to list, in rank order of importance, the top five jobs under each of the six criteria. Look for jobs that crop up in multiple places.

Of course, the six sets of questions are not equally important. It is likely that the first two sets of questions will be considered preeminent, with some drop off in overall value occurring with the third and fourth question sets and then another value drop for the final two sets of questions. Regardless of whether you buy into this ranking, you may wish to differentially weight the six sets of questions to help develop a logical basis for prioritizing potential starting points. Even if you do not formally complete this process, simply posing the questions to your customer will likely lead to thoughtful dialogue that can only help to ensure that strategic business and human resource practices are more tightly linked.

INITIAL INFORMATION GATHERING

One way or another, at this point you should have a pretty good idea of the population being targeted by the modeling effort. Further, you will probably be pleased to learn that there is so much information readily available about most jobs that it is rarely necessary to start a job modeling project from scratch. However, a clear definition of the target job group and the associated boundaries will help focus attention on previous work in the area that can be leveraged. As soon as possible, work with your customer to clearly define the target jobs, job levels, and business units and locations involved.

Descriptions of work content and inventories of items exist for a wide range of job families and jobs. For example, fairly generic inventories are available for broad job families like sales,[6] management,[7,8] and clerical and administrative.[9] In addition, more focused descriptions of content exist for specific job groups, such as police officer,[10,11,12] municipal transit operator,[13] computer programmer,[14] and many others.[15] Although these solutions are excellent sources of information, keep in mind that frequently they are specific solutions designed to support a particular application and often for a particular organization.

When scavenging job information from published inventories, or even from inventories previously constructed within your organization or your customer's organization, a couple of cautions are in order. First, carefully modify existing descriptive content so that it accurately fits and describes the work in the current setting. For example, some job modeling inventories are generic and the general nature of the work activity and competency items might not provide enough detailed information to suit the application in mind. Furthermore, it is possible that an inventory of items constructed for a specific organization or application will contain language or examples that are inappropriate for another. Also, an existing inventory of items might contain voids in coverage and not be comprehensive for the current setting. It is enticing to conclude that a particular set of items is complete and sufficient without critically examining the comprehensive coverage of these items to your application or organization. However, even with these factors to consider and overcome, it is still useful to scavenge from existing sources when constructing an initial job model.

Furthermore, in most settings, some information is available about the content of the jobs in the organization in question. It is possible to learn a great deal from materials or information that exist internally and use them to structure thinking about the work activities and competencies required to perform the target jobs. See Fig. 5.1 for a source material checklist.

JOB MODELING INTERVIEWS AND FOCUS GROUPS

Typically, it is also useful to collect information from various perspectives through one-on-one interviews or focus groups. The specific groups of individ-

---

☐ Organization's annual report (it is crucial to know something about the client's business).

☐ Organization's mission statement or published set of guiding values and principles (to give some idea of the context in which the jobs exist).

☐ Organizational charts starting several layers above the target job or job group and moving a layer or two lower in the organization.

☐ New employee orientation materials (these can be leaflets, workbooks, audiotapes, videos, or other materials).

☐ Organization's training manuals.

☐ Instructional materials relating to the occupational area (this includes manuals relating to equipment used).

☐ Materials used by incumbents in performing the job, such as forms completed or job aids.

☐ Performance appraisal forms used for the jobs in the target job group.

☐ Existing job descriptions (don't get your hopes up too high—often the content can be more misleading than helpful as a consequence of misleading or outdated information).

☐ Previously constructed inventories or job analysis work relating to the occupational area (see the caveat above).

☐ Tests and/or standard interview protocol used to screen candidates in the target job group.

FIG. 5.1. Pre-interview/focus group checklist.

uals you should include as SMEs or focus group participants depend on the questions you plan to ask, which in turn depends on, you guessed it, the intended use and application of the job modeling information. Specific questions are addressed later in the book. For now, bear in mind that, to the extent it is necessary to collect information from SMEs to supplement an existing inventory of items or pool of information, it is important to collect information from a representative group of individuals. These people will provide the descriptive and prescriptive information used to create the rationally derived job model. If you do not ensure that all possible variations and job compositions within the target occupation are included when you collect the interview or focus group information, the resulting inventory of information will contain voids in representation, will not be complete and comprehensive, and will be deficient in the information produced for the intended application.

Whom to Interview or Invite to a Focus Group

As Fig. 5.2 indicates, different individuals in the organization can provide you with the necessary information in different degrees. For most interventions, you will likely be choosing from among five information holders: job incumbents,

❑ **Job Incumbents**

Use job incumbents when collecting information about current job demands, challenges, and competency requirements. Nobody knows what it takes to succeed in a particular job like somebody who does it. Job incumbents should:

- Be current job holders in the area for which the targeted application is being designed.

- Have been in the job long enough to gain a complete picture of job scope and performance expectations and understand the intricacies and subtleties associated with the work. Of course, depending on the job, this may be 3 months or even a matter of years.

❑ **Supervisors/Managers**

Use supervisors or managers to gather information about current job demands and requirements, but particularly to gain information about the difficulty of work activities and the level of mastery required in certain competency areas to perform work activities. Supervisors and managers should also have a good basis for giving you information about anticipated changes in job requirements resulting from the introduction of new equipment, revisions to the work process, the introduction of new work systems, or other systemic changes. Supervisors and managers should:

- Be one level up from individuals in the jobs targeted by the applications.

- Have a comprehensive understanding of the target job.

- Have a broad frame of reference gained by having seen a number of people perform the job.

- Have some understanding of emerging trends and challenges that are likely to impact the content and worker requirements. Try to include people who serve on the organization's strategy or technology teams.

❑ **Organizational Visionaries**

Use visionaries when the target job is changing significantly or when the anticipated change is a long-term enterprise or is understood by only a few key individuals in the organization. Such situations might include dramatically redesigning the jobs in the organization to include more cross-functional work, increasing spans of control for individuals, changing performance expectations, or creating new jobs or new organizations where there is no previous frame of reference (e.g., new plant start-ups with newly designed jobs). Visionaries should:

- Be at least two levels above the job targeted by the application.

- Have a feel for emerging business trends and the implications of these changes for organizational functioning and job requirements.

❑ **Customers**

Use customers when building an information base for how work should be accomplished or redesigned. Customers can help highlight work activities and competencies that are important, but not currently demonstrated or understood by job incumbents. Customers should:

- Include both internal and external customers as appropriate. The group can be broadened to include strategic partners.

- Work closely with and depend on the work and results of work performed by individuals in the target job.

❑ **Observers**

Use observers when you have reason to believe that people's responses on a questionnaire might conflict with actual job demands (e.g., respondents inflating job requirements when the job modeling is being done primarily for job evaluation or the creation of pay grades) or when you are unable to collect data from organization employees (e.g., due to an adversarial union environment or when work is being conducted amidst the constraints of some form of legal challenge). Of course, the use of observers is limited to situations in which the targeted behaviors are observable and measurable tasks; observers are less useful for providing information about unobservable competencies, such as thinking or planning. Observers should:

- Calibrate their use of the rating scale with other observers.

- Be clear on whether they are focusing only on description, or if there are also inferential hypotheses testing objectives (e.g., making judgments about the differences between high and low performers).

- Be sensitive to job incumbent reactivity and demand characteristics that can crop up as a result of being observed.

FIG. 5.2. Potential interview/focus group participants.

supervisors or manager of job incumbents, organizational visionaries, customers, and observers. Of these five groups, you will likely find that most of your modeling work involves incumbents and supervisors of incumbents. Generalizing somewhat liberally from the research involving these two groups, the individuals you choose to include at this step should have the following characteristics:

Be Among the Brightest	There is some evidence to suggest that individuals with higher cognitive ability provide more accurate information.[16,17,18,19,20,21]
Be Among the Most Experienced	Similarly, there is evidence to suggest that individuals with greater tenure in their role provide more accurate information.[22,23,24,25,26]
Be Among the Better Performers	In general, there is converging evidence that indicates better performers provide higher quality information.[27,28,29,30] A note of caution: Your client might be tempted to first offer you access to the worst performers because they are most expendable. Demand the best!

Although I do not want to veer off into a discussion of the potential fallibility of human judgment, I would be remiss if I did not at least make the point that SMEs bring to the modeling situation their own sources of error. Different values, perspectives, experiences, cognitive capability, and so forth all may introduce some unknown amount of error to the information that is collected. For those who wish to research this topic further, Morgeson and Campion recently published a useful article that reviews the literature relevant to the psychological processes that underlie inaccuracy in job analysis data.[31]

Interview/Focus Group Sampling Plan

The quality of the job modeling information obtained is directly related to the representativeness of the information collected in the initial information-gathering phase. The individuals interviewed, or the subject matter experts included in the job modeling focus groups, should represent each of the key groups or areas of potential difference in the organization. As Fig. 5.3 indicates, these sources of potential difference include major job titles in the job group or job family (i.e., titles with many incumbents), different locations, different functions or business units, and different gender, age, and ethnic groups.

❑ **Job Titles**

Job titles with large numbers of incumbents need to be represented accordingly in greater number in interviews or focus group meetings.

❑ **Geographic Location**

Whether across town, on the other side of the country, or in a different country, jobs with the same job title often have differences in content and worker requirements as well. The differences in locale need to be sampled accordingly.

❑ **Functions/Business Units**

Although the same job can be represented in different pieces of the business, different segments of the organization by definition can have different markets, product lines, work processes, or other differences, any of which have the potential to impact the way work is performed.

❑ **Ethnic, Gender, Age Groups**

Different groups often have different perspectives and orientations. Although it is unclear to what extent these differences can have on the job modeling information collected, it is a good idea to sample these groups accordingly. In the event a human resource intervention built from the job modeling work faces a legal challenge, the courts often look at representativeness here as an index of the thoroughness, quality, and objectivity of the information platform. Further, sampling these groups accordingly can facilitate buy-in on the part of eventual users of the intended intervention.

FIG. 5.3. Interview/focus group representation checklist.

Size of Interview or Focus Group Sample

There are no widely accepted guidelines for how many interviews need to be conducted or how many individuals need to be included in focus groups. However, there are a number of variables to keep in mind. For example, if one is starting from scratch without prior research or existing job descriptions versus starting from a solid base (e.g., drawing on published inventories for similar jobs and existing job descriptions that are fairly comprehensive, up to date, and available), it is necessary to conduct more interviews to ensure all the necessary information has been captured. Also, the knowledge and experience of the job modeling team can affect the number of interviews or focus groups required. An individual with little job modeling experience and limited exposure to the type of work being modeled will take longer to collect the necessary information in each interview and will require more interviews to capture and integrate the necessary information. As a general rule, the interviewing process should continue until the interviewers are collecting only redundant information at the level of detail required to understand the work involved for creating the planned application(s). This is an important point because, to the extent the job modeling information is incomplete or faulty, subsequent judgments based on this information in the applications that follow will also be incorrect.

Although each job modeling situation is unique, and thus has its own requirements and variables to consider, Table 5.1 provides some general guide-

TABLE 5.1

Interview/Focus Group Sample Determination Table

								# of Interviews/ Focus Group Participants
1. Number of Incumbents in Target Job(s)	1-5 **(1)**	6-25 **(2)**	26-50 **(3)**	51-250 **(4)**	251-500 **(5)**	501-1000 **(8)**	1000-5000 **(10)** →	

2. What is the Target Application?
1 Job design/redesign **(150%)**
2 Work load analysis **(25%)**
3 Job description & min. qualifications **(50%)**
4 Realistic job preview content **(50%)**
5 Interview system **(50%)**
6 Scored application blank/biodata **(25%)**
7 Paper-&-pencil testing (follow-up val.) **(50%)**
8 Paper-&-pencil testing (val. gen.) **(0%)**
9 Paper-&-pencil testing (custom) **(100%)**
10 Sim./content-oriented test const. **(150%)**

11 Individual assessment for selection **(25%)**
12 Job classification **(50%)**
13 Employee skills bank & matching **(50%)**
14 Training needs analysis **(100%)**
15 Training program design **(150%)**
16 BARS appraisal systems **(25%)**
17 Job evaluation **(50%)**
18 360 instruments for development **(25%)**
19 Individual assmt. for dev. **(0%)**

20 Career ladders/succession planning **(50%)**
21 Career planning **(50%)**
22 Coaching **(50%)**
23 Org. analysis & change **(0%)**

3. Breadth of Expertise and Depth of Knowledge of SMEs About Titles in Job	Great Breadth **(0%)**	Some **(25%)**	Very Little **(50%)**	No Breadth **(75%)**			→	
4. Existence of Job Description Information	Great Amount **(0%)**	Some **(25%)**	Very Little **(50%)**	None At All **(100%)**			→	
5. Extent to which the Job Analysis Team has Exp. Working w/the Job(s) Targeted by the Application	Great Amount **(0%)**	Some **(25%)**	Very Little **50%**	None At All **75%**			→	
6. Extent to Which Results of Work Are Observable	Great Amount **(0%)**	Some **(25%)**	Very Little **50%**	Not Observ. **75%**			→	
7. Extent to Which Work Content is Relatively Fixed/Routine (vs. Dynamic)	Great Amount **(0%)**	Some **(25%)**	Very Little **100%**	Not Fixed **150%**			→	
8. Envisioned Changes in the Organization Affecting the Job Over Next 3 Years	No Changes **(0%)**	Very Little **(25%)**	Some **100%**	Great Amount **150%**			→	
9. Number of Work Locations	1 **(0%)**	2-5 **(10%)**	6-25 **20%**	26-100 **40%**	101-500 **60%**	501-1500 **80%**	1501+ **100%** →	
10. Number of Different Business Units, Work Functions, or Grade Levels	One **(0%)**	Several **(25%)**	Many **50%**				→	
11. Extent to Which Expect Work Content to be the Same in a Job Title Across Locations/ Business Units/Work Functions/Grade Levels	Great Extent **(0%)**	Some **(10%)**	Very Little **30%**	Not the Same **50%**			→	
12. Number of Specific Job Titles Included in Scope of Proposed Application	1 **(0%)**	2-10 **(10%)**	11-50 **20%**	51-100 **25%**	101-250 **30%**	251-500 **40%**	500+ **50%** →	
13. Extent to Which Expect Resulting Application to be Free from Legal Review	Great Extent **(0%)**	Some **(25%)**	Very Little **50%**	Not At All **100%**			→	
14. Extent to Which It is Important to Create Buy-in on the Part of End-users of the Target Application	Not At All **(0%)**	Very Little **(50%)**	Some **100%**	Great Extent **150%**			→	

TOTAL NUMBER OF SUGGESTED INTERVIEWS OR FOCUS GROUP MEMBERS = →

lines for determining the number of individuals to be included in the interviewing or focus group process. The idea behind this determination table is to vary the number of interview and focus group participants based on the demands of the job modeling situation, as represented by the impact variables (1–14) in the far left column. These impact variables and the associated weights are based primarily on the research designed to investigate the key decision points in job modeling projects described in chapter 4.[32]

To use the table, first answer this question: How many incumbents are in the target job(s)? The number in parentheses and bold print associated with a particular incumbent size breakout is the base number of required interviewees or focus group participants; this number gets entered in the top cell in the far right column. This number is then multiplied by the appropriate percentages associated with the response category for each of the remaining 13 impact variables. In each case, the resulting number represents the additional number of individuals added to the interview/focus group sample. In other words, the starting or base number of interviewees/participants is added to the number resulting from the product of base x percentage in Question 2, plus the product of base x percentage in Question 3, and so on.

For example, if there are 3,400 incumbents in the target job group, the base (or starting) number of required interview and/or focus group participants is 10. Second, if the goal of the job modeling work is to create an information platform for supporting a new employee selection program—paper-and-pencil testing with follow-up validation—then multiply the base of $N = 10$ by 50% and enter the product (i.e., 5) in the cell in the far right column. Then proceed to do the same for Questions 3 to 14. Once all the impact variables have been addressed, add the numbers in the 14 cells on the right-hand side of the page to get an approximation of an appropriate sample size.

Take a few minutes to review the Bank Partners, Inc. case study presented in chapter 4. Then complete the interview/focus group determination table in Table 5.1. Although your assessment of the important variables in the case study may differ slightly from mine, I'll bet we are fairly close. The number of people added to the sample as a result of each impact variable, based on my assessment of the situation, appears below:

Q1   10 people
Q2   5 people
Q3   5 people
Q4   10 people
Q5   2.5 people
Q6   2.5 people
Q7   10 people
Q8   15 people
Q9   10 people

Q10	0 people
Q11	5 people
Q12	1 person
Q13	5 people
Q14	10 people

The number of suggested interviews or focus group members in this case is 91. Although this number should not be considered a fixed value, you should find it to be a reasonably good starting point estimate.

Conducting Interviews

The guidelines for conducting job modeling interviews are fairly straightforward. The interviewer should attempt to create a comfortable and relaxed atmosphere to facilitate interviewee comfort with the process. A *heads up* letter goes a long way toward setting the stage in this regard. For example, before individuals are interviewed, they might receive an explanatory memo like the one following, which is from a high-level internal sponsor.

Dear [INCUMBENT, SUPERVISOR, ORGANIZATIONAL VISIONARY, OR CUSTOMER]:

As you may be aware, we have contracted with [YOUR DEPARTMENT OR ORGANIZATION] to develop [NAME OF TARGET INTERVENTION]. The major phases of this project are outlined below.

1.   Conduct job modeling interviews (or focus groups) with key individuals.
2.   Develop a questionnaire to collect ratings about the work activities (and/or competencies) important for the job.
3.   Construct a competency profile of the targeted jobs.
4–6. [SEVERAL DESCRIPTIVE STEPS ASSOCIATED WITH THE DEVELOPMENT OF THE TARGET APPLICATION.]

In the first phase of this project, we will conduct a series of interviews (or focus groups) to collect information about the activities and/or competencies that contribute to success. You have been selected because you are familiar with the duties and responsibilities of [NAME OF TARGET JOB] with [NAME OF TARGET DEPARTMENT OR CUSTOMER ORGANIZATION]. The purpose of the interview is to collect information about the job listed on this memo. We are not interested in the performance of specific individuals. The interviewer will ask a number of questions designed to collect information about the activities and competencies that contribute to job success. The interview results are confidential, so please feel free to speak openly and frankly.

To help you prepare for the interview, please review the questions you are likely to be asked, which are outlined on the next page [NOTE: THIS STEP IS OPTIONAL]. Please note that not all interviews will cover all of the questions listed. The interview (or focus group) will require approximately [AMOUNT OF TIME

ALLOTTED]. Thank you in advance for your participation and cooperation in getting this important project off to a good start.

Sincerely,

[PROJECT SPONSOR]

To actually begin an interview session with a subject matter expert, you might say:

My name is [YOUR NAME], and I work for [YOUR DEPARTMENT OR YOUR ORGANIZATION]. I am collecting information to determine the kinds of work performed by [NAME OF TARGET JOB] and the types of competencies or skills people need in order to perform this work. I will be asking a number of people who work as [NAME OF TARGET JOB] to describe their jobs, and I will combine this information with the information that you provide to come up with a description of the activities performed and competencies required for success as a [NAME OF TARGET JOB].

The information gathered from these interviews (or focus groups) will be used to develop a questionnaire that will then be used to collect information from a larger group of [NAME OF TARGET JOB]. The purpose of all this work is to capture information from experts who know the job well, such as yourself, in order to guide our efforts to develop [NAME OF TARGET APPLICATION]. It is my understanding that we have [AMOUNT OF TIME ALLOTTED] for this interview; is that correct? Do you have any questions for me before we begin?

This introduction should set the interviewee at ease, provide him or her with the necessary information, and encourage him or her to ask any questions. View this contact as an opportunity to build rapport with an important member of the customer organization (this is just as important for internal as external consultants), underscore the importance of capturing quality information, and sell the value of the intended target application. You will find that most people enjoy talking about their jobs. Thus, getting started is typically not a problem. Actually, the trick is to keep the interviewees on track so they give you information that is useful for your purpose.

One approach for keeping interviewees on track is to have the them begin by talking about the general work activities performed and then progressively go into more detail or more abstract information (collecting information about observable work activities is typically an easier process than capturing good information from interviewees about often unobservable competencies or individual worker requirements). For example, it might be useful to have the interviewee group the kinds of activities he or she performs each day into a few categories. An illustration or two from another area of work can be useful to interviewees. If you are interviewing heavy equipment operators, you might wish to use as an example the general duty areas performed by individuals in some of the clerical positions in the organization (such as file and retrieve documents and type and process written materials).

It is easier to get specific examples of tasks performed once the interviewee has grouped his or her work activities into some general areas. Compartmentalizing the work in this way also helps facilitate getting information about the more abstract competencies required to perform the work. Keep in mind that you are interested in trying to discover what actions comprise the work being performed, who or what is at the focus of the action, why the action is occurring and if necessary, and how the action is being accomplished. Once this information has been collected for the various activity areas of the work, it is then appropriate to question the interviewee about the competencies required to perform the identified work activities (if this information is required for your intended intervention).

It is always a good idea to close the interview by reaffirming the purpose of the meeting and intended use of the information. If possible, leave time to provide a high-level summary of the conclusions coming from the interview and give the interviewee a chance to confirm and ask a follow-up question or two. Then thank the person for his or her help and cooperation.

The bottom line is this: Your interviewee is the smartest person in the room. Hence, if as job modelers we do not ask the wrong questions, our interviwees are capable of teaching us everything we need to know. Summaries of the statements, questions, and probes to consider using to solicit information from your job experts appear in Figures 5.4 to 5.8. These are just examples. Each job modeling situation will likely require a different number and configuration of questions.

- For basic documentation needs and introductory statements, see Fig. 5.4.
- For questions designed to tap information about work activities performed and competencies required, see Fig. 5.5.
- For questions used to clarify the organization's business context, vision, and strategic focus, see Fig. 5.6. Of course, given the specific demands of a particular modeling context, one should reorganize the structure for the questions and introduce a different mix of questions or follow-up probes (drawing from the content in chap. 3) as appropriate.
- For organization context questions designed to tap information about work rewards, the work, work conditions that form the environment in which jobs or roles are embedded, and organizational structure, see Fig. 5.7.
- For questions designed to tap information that can be used to create operational definitions of highly effective, satisfactory or solid, and unsatisfactory performance, see Fig. 5.8.

❑ **Documentation**
  • Date of the interview/focus group.
  • Name of the interviewer/focus group leader.
  • Name and title of the interviewee/focus group participant.
  • Interviewee/participant's work group or business unit, work location, and telephone number.
  • Interviewee/focus group participant's tenure in job and with the company.

❑ **Structuring Statement**
  • Your name and affiliation.
  • Purpose of the interview/focus group.
  • Description of how the resulting information will be used.
  • Activities to occur in the interview/focus group and time frames.

FIG. 5.4. Job modeling interview/focus group introduction checklist.

❑ **Purpose of Job/Overview**
  • Can you summarize the target job in one sentence?
  • What is the purpose of the job; what are the major outputs?
  • What happens during a typical day, from the time you arrive to the time you leave?
  • What goals are incumbents held accountable to meet?

❑ **Work Activities Performed**
  • What are the five or six major duties or groups of work activities performed in the job?
  • Describe each of these activity areas in more detail:
    ■ What is done or what action is performed?
    ■ Who or what is being acted on?
    ■ Why is the action important?
    ■ How is the action accomplished?
    ■ What are the most challenging or difficult activities of the job?
    ■ What types of problems or issues do incumbents routinely face?

❑ **Competencies Required**
  • What are the important knowledge, skills, abilities, or personal characteristics needed to perform the work activities we've just discussed?
  • What differentiates a top performer in this job from a marginal or poor performer?
  • If you were hiring someone into this job, what capabilities would you look for?
  • What technical expertise is required?
  • What people skills are critical?
  • What personal characteristics—such as drive or patience—are essential?
  • Where do major work or job pressures come from? Is there a lot of burnout? Why?

FIG. 5.5. Job modeling interview/focus group 'work activity and competency investigation' checklist.

❑ **Factors External to the Organization that are Likely to Impact the Business in the Future (NOW Part 1)**
- What are the external factors or macro- and microenvironmental trends that seem particularly significant for the organization over the next 5 years?
- What emerging opportunities and obstacles will the organization need to contend with over the next 5 years? These may arise from changes in a number of potentially relevant arenas, including:
  - Social
  - Economic
  - Political/Legal
  - Technological
  - Markets (size, scope, maturity)
  - Competitors (new entrants, changes in competitive posture)
  - Customers
  - Suppliers

❑ **Factors Internal to the Organization That are Likely to Impact the Business, or the Way Business is Conducted, in the Future (NOW Part 2)**
- What are the internal factors or organization-level competencies that will be significant variables for the organization to contend with over the next 5 years?
- What are the core strengths and weaknesses of the organization that will impact the organization's value creation capabilities over the next 5 years? These include assets and liabilities in several segments of the organizational landscape, including:
  - Human
  - Technological
  - Infrastructure
  - Financial
  - Contextual/Cultural

❑ **Defining Features of the Organization's Vision and Mission (WOW)**
- Given the external and internal context of the organization, what is the mission?
  - What will the future value chain of the industry look like and where will the organization want to fit in?
  - Where is the organization today versus where it wants to be?
  - What are the current and future cash cows of the business?
  - What are the intermediate and long-range financial goals for the organization?
  - What are the market leadership goals for specific business segments and major product/service lines?
- Given the external and internal context of the organization, what are the core values and beliefs?
  - What level of economic return does the organization hope to provide owners/shareholders? Employees?
  - What were the defining values of the organizational founders? Are these values still held by the senior leadership team? How can one tell?

❑ **Strategies and Initiatives Designed to Prepare the Organization for Future Competitiveness (HOW Part 1)**
- What is the organization's competitive strategy?
  - What is the source of the organization's competitive advantage?
  - What major factors will contribute to the organization's success over the next 5 years?
  - How do customers view the organization in terms of things done well or poorly?
- What strategic initiatives are in place to leverage organizational strengths? Shore up weaknesses? Capitalize on emerging business opportunities? Respond to potential threats? These initiatives may impact the organization's human talent, technological capabilities, infrastructure, financial capital, or culture.

❑ **Impact of Strategies and Initiatives on Jobs and the Job Model (HOW Part 2)**
- Given the strategies and initiatives of the organization, what will be the impact on jobs targeted by the modeling work?
  - What changes will occur in the work activities comprising the jobs? Will there be any changes in reporting relationships?

FIG. 5.6. Job modeling interview/focus group 'vision & strategy review' checklist.

❏ Work Benefits (Intrinsic And Extrinsic)

- Compensation: What is the pay compared to similar jobs in the relevant labor market, and what is the compensation potential over the next several years? What is the perceived linkage between pay to value and between performance and pay?
- Job Security: What level of security do people have in their jobs now? Four to five years out?
- Job Mobility: To what extent are incumbents able to move laterally and vertically into other jobs in the organization?
- Collegiality: To what extent do incumbents interact with others and feel part of a team?
- Recognition: Do incumbents receive recognition for their work efforts within the work group? Across the organization? Outside the organization?
- Development: What opportunities are there to learn new work activities, ideas, work approaches? How do incumbents receive intellectual stimulation in everyday job activities? What kinds of organizational support exist for individual development?

❏ Work Itself

- Work Variety: How many different work activities do incumbents perform throughout the day? What opportunities exist to participate in different work activities or projects throughout the year?
- Creativity: What opportunities are there for individuals to try out new ideas, do things differently, or be creative in terms of how work activities are performed?
- Coaching or Mentoring: To what extent are job incumbents responsible for teaching, mentoring, or developing the skills of others?
- Tools and Equipment: What kinds of general office equipment (fax machines, computers, photocopiers, paper shredders), recording devices (tape recorders, VCRs, security cameras), vehicles (cars, trucks, forklifts), and hand tools or safety equipment are used on the job?

❏ Work Conditions

- Environment: Describe the everyday work environment. Are there safety issues? Does the job involve working outside? What kind of technical and staff supports are available? What kinds of interactions with customers are required?
- Travel: What kind (local, regional, intercontinental) and amount of travel is required to fulfill job duties?
- Time Flexibility: What is the balance between job demands and personal life? Is it possible to adjust schedule or work at home as opposed to at the office on occasion?
- Autonomy: To what extent are job incumbents able to set own goals and work direction? How much discretion do individuals have for deciding on methods for carrying out the job?
- Structure: What kinds of behavioral norms (explicit and implicit) exist in the workplace? In what ways do job incumbents set their own standards governing the appropriateness of workplace behavior? Is the organization rule-driven and by-the-book?
- Work Stress: In what ways do job incumbents have control over the overall number of work activities required during the day? Are there ways to adjust schedules to ease time pressure? Has burnout been a problem? If so, why?

❏ Organizational Structure

- Organization Size: How does the size of this organization compare to others operating in the same market, in terms of number of employees, revenue, geographic dispersion, or any other relevant factor?
- Hierarchy: How many levels are there for a particular job class in the organization? How many pay grades?
- Centralization: To what extent are employees located in one or relatively few locations versus widely dispersed? To what extent are key decisions made in one versus many locations?
- Level of Performance Tracking: Who gets evaluated—individuals? teams? business units? How is performance measured and tracked?

FIG. 5.7. Work context interview/focus group question checklist.

❑   **Highly Effective Anchors**

- For each major work activity or competency category, relate a specific situation or incident that had very successful consequences.
- What led up to the situation and what was it about the job incumbent's behavior that was so effective?
- What were the consequences of the behavior?
- What opportunities were realized as a result of the behavior?
- What potential obstacles were avoided because of the behavior?

❑   **Satisfactory or Solid Anchors**

- For each major work activity or competency category, relate a specific situation or incident that had satisfactory consequences. In other words, think of a time when the job incumbent's behavior did not make the situation worse, nor capitalize on an opportunity to have a more dramatic and positive impact.
- What led up to the situation? What was it about the job incumbent's behavior that kept the consequences in the solid range?
- What were the consequences of the behavior?
- What opportunities were missed?
- What potential obstacles were not completely laid to rest or avoided?

❑   **Unsatisfactory Anchors**

- For each major work activity or competency category, relate a specific situation or incident that had very unsuccessful consequences.
- What led up to the situation? What was it about the job incumbent's behavior that was so ineffective?
- What were the consequences of the behavior?
- What potential obstacles were introduced as a result of the behavior?

FIG. 5.8. Performance standard interview/focus group question checklist.

Conducting Focus Groups

Focus groups can be a lot of fun because you never know what is going to happen when you get a group of people together. They are a little more difficult to manage than one-on-one interviews for the same reason. The facilitation aspect can be tricky; it requires a bit of a balancing act between being supportive and directive as one puts the spotlight on others to learn and understand what they already know.

Keep in mind that the job modeling focus group is not an opportunity for people to come together for a *blue sky* discussion. To the contrary, a good modeling focus group is deliverable oriented, where the deliverable may be the development of a content structure and/or populating the structure with item-level descriptors, or it may be a comprehensive review and enhancement of a straw model, and so forth. Be clear up front about the expected result, and the process for getting there, when dealing with a group of subject experts.

Similar to the approach used for one-on-one interviews, always begin a modeling focus group with a complete introduction of yourself, state the purpose and goal of the meeting, and confirm the time allocation. In addition, in a group setting, it is often useful to drop a name or two of the executive sponsors of the initiative just to drive home its importance and lend some credibility to the work. If you can get an executive sponsor or local representative to kick off the meeting, that is even better.

Next, work your way around the table and have the participants introduce themselves, their titles, and where they work. In part, the purpose of these introductions is to serve as an ice breaker. Once a participant has said something, it is easier for him or her to speak up again. More important, even if people in the group know each other by sight, they often do not recall each other's names or work locations.

You can have a little fun with the introductions, too. For example, in addition to name, title, and work location, ask people to name their favorite movie or tell the group something unique about themselves. When people work as intensely as they do in a modeling focus group, they can burn out if they are not given some relief or opportunities to reenergize themselves by having a little fun. As the facilitator taking careful mental notes about the interesting and unique things you hear about your group participants, you are creating openings for referring back to their comments and introducing a little levity at various points throughout the course of the meeting (e.g., "Okay, I feel as if we've been making progress up the mountain until this point and now we seem to be stuck. Sandy, you're the rock climber in the group, what do your instincts tell you?"). Look for ways to connect and share a few laughs with the group.

Now you are ready to establish whatever ground rules you want to use. For example:

- Only one person speaking at a time.
- Everyone has equal voice in making decisions (this might be a good place to point out that eight people in a 3½-hour meeting have only 22.5 minutes each of air time [minus two 15-minute breaks], and that everyone needs to be considerate of others' right to speak).
- Stick to facts and be specific.

Post the ground rules in a prominent place throughout the meeting (e.g., record the list on a flip chart page, tear it off, and tape it to the wall). You will find most groups do a pretty good job of policing themselves.

However, there will be occasions when, as the facilitator, you will need to step forward to ensure that all voices are heard and represented in the final product. The following are examples of participant types that can interfere with a productive focus group meeting, along with some possible solutions:

Rambler:	Has a difficult time focusing his thinking. Thank the Rambler for his input, then refocus his and the group's attention by restating the goals of the meeting. If the difficulty persists, say "I'm not sure that what you are saying is on target given the intent of the discussion." Then turn to the group and ask, "Can someone help us here?"
Mummy:	Either chooses not to participate in the discussion or participates in a halting and ineffectual way. Do not ignore this person. Her input and perspective may be very valuable. Be sure to maximize eye contact with the Mummy because this provides encouragement to speak. Also, use open-ended probes like "Tell me about your views on this issue" to provide an invitation to talk. Another less direct approach is to ask this person to provide follow-up perspectives on the input of others. If you are still having trouble, consider having the Mummy simply paraphrase the input of another member of the group and ask if she agrees.
Eager Beaver:	Goes overboard in his efforts to contribute. Do not embarrass the individual. Simply saying "That's an interesting point; now let's hear from someone else" once or twice can help reign him in. Another tactic is to ask the Eager Beaver to summarize the points made by others at discrete points in the meeting and try to pull him out of the role of individual contributor.
Provocateur:	The complete opposite of the Eager Beaver, the Provocateur is confrontative and combative. Maybe she is just having a bad day, month, or year. Maybe it is just her normal style of expressing herself. Whatever. Take a breath and ask for examples or details to get all potential concerns or issues to the surface. Do not let this person draw you into an argument or put you on the defensive. You might consider throwing the Provocateur's views back to the group for their evaluation and asking, "What do you think?" If you really get boxed in, there is nothing wrong with turning to the group and saying, "We're stuck. Who can help us here?" Do what you can to identify the issues of her argument, document them, and move on. In extreme cases, you may want to check in with this person directly by saying, "You are very argumentative this morning. What's wrong?" This should be

done outside the group session (e.g., on break) and on a one-on-one basis.

Conversationalist: Precipitates and perpetuates sideline conversations that are distracting to the group. To begin, address the Conversationalist by name and remind him of the ground rules for the meeting. Be sure to tell him that you will get to his concerns momentarily. If that does not work, walk over to the Conversationalist and touch the back of his chair as you redirect the efforts of the group.

Approach 1: Semistructured Open Discussion

One approach for collecting information in a focus group follows the same method used to facilitate the one-on-one interview, where the group would begin an open discussion about the general work activities performed. The discussion would be led into more detail around the emerging broad categories of activities and then, if required, into a discussion of the requisite competencies. In addition to the suggestions for conducting focus groups covered in the preceding pages, it may prove useful to further clarify the game plan or ground rules for this kind of meeting.[33] For example:

- Quantity is desirable. The more descriptor statements generated by the group, the better.
- Redundancy is okay. It is much better to have several statements that are similar and that may be consolidated later than to miss something important.
- Do not wordsmith as you go. Get the gist of the idea out so that it may be recorded and let the modeling team worry about phrasing the perfect statement.
- No editing or criticizing someone else's input. It often helps to keep the process moving if efforts by the group to edit or criticize a group member's input is limited, if not outright disallowed. If a group member wants to build on or restate someone's input and suggest another descriptor item to be added to the pool, great, but no going back to tweak somebody else's ideas.
- State ideas quickly and concisely. Do not encourage group members to provide a rationale for their input. However, as the group leader, you should probe for detail or clarify the meaning of a suggestion as appropriate.

The make-up of this kind of focus group is an important factor in its success. As with the interviews, you want the brightest, most experienced, and best performers available to be your SMEs. Also, unless there is a clear reason for doing so, it is not a good idea to include persons from different levels in the organization in the same group. The presence of one or two bosses can dampen the spontaneity of the meeting, which is a potential strength of the approach.

Approach 2: Structured Round Robin

A second approach involves a round robin collection of ideas. Ask participants to create their own list of major work activity areas (after prompting them with several examples). Then work around the table and ask each person to read one category label from his or her list. At each juncture, document the response on a transparency or flip chart sheet for everyone to see. As a category makes it onto your list, ask the other participants to mark off the same, or similar, categories from their lists. Do not permit discussion or evaluation of categories as they are contributed and recorded. Keep going around the table until a complete list of categories is generated (i.e., all lists have been exhausted). Then go back and, as a group, evaluate the complete set of categories, consolidating or expanding where the group thinks it is necessary.

Once the structure of work activity categories is complete, the same procedure can be used to generate the most important four or five item-level descriptors for each category. The advantage of this approach is that it keeps participants focused and makes it difficult for one or two people to dominate the discussion and results. Also, it helps create the sense that the product is jointly owned. On the downside, it can be time-consuming. Part of this difficulty may be circumvented if it is possible to have participants create category and item lists as prework.

Approach 3: Straw Model Review

Yet another approach is to walk into the meeting with a straw model based on previous work with other customers, edited compilations of published inventories with similar job groups, results of previous interviews or focus groups conducted as part of the current project, and so forth. Select a method for displaying the model, using transparencies, flip chart sheets, handouts, projected displays from a laptop, or other means as appropriate. Start the review at the highest or broadest level of content organization (e.g., factors or dimensions) and then move into a review of the item content.

The obvious advantage of this approach is that it provides a starting point for analysis and saves time from having to build from scratch. A potential liability is that it is terribly easy for participants to lock into a particular way of looking at the world and overlook more meaningful configurations of the content. Also, it can be difficult for participants to recognize oversights or gaps in the straw model when presented with this fairly fleshed-out solution.

A somewhat less frequent difficulty, which makes it no less challenging when it does happen, is to have the participants react negatively to the straw model

based on seemingly minute wording that is inconsistent with the way the organization does business. In this case, it can come across as if you are trying to force
fit a solution rather than trying to build up from a 50% solution. Obviously introducing and positioning the straw model is key. However, despite the best introduction possible, if you choose to use this approach, there will come a day
when you hit this wall. When it happens, be ready to put your well thought-out
straw model aside and build from scratch if the participants demand to start
over.

Wrapping Up

When you are finished with the meeting and are ready to conclude, remember
that a simple "Thank you" and "Good-bye" is never enough. Leave enough time
at the end of the session to review the major decisions or products of the group.
In doing so, tell the group, "If you hear something you believe the group did not
agree to, please say so." You want the group members to feel that they have been
listened to and understood. Then take several minutes to reiterate how the results will be used to enhance future work products. You also want these folks to
feel invested in an important initiative.

Finally, take a couple of minutes to do a meeting critique. You might divide a
flip chart sheet into two vertical columns: "What We Did Well" and "What We
Should Have Done Differently." This gives the facilitator a chance to check in
and identify things to do differently in future focus groups. Just as important, it
gives the participants a chance to reflect a bit and evaluate how well they accomplished the goal. Of course, the hope is that they end up sharing positive reactions to the process and outcome. However, these types of focus groups can be
a bit frustrating, so the critique also offers them a chance to vent and you a
chance to assuage some of this frustration.

You are still not quite done. Several days after the focus group, it often makes
sense for you, or someone from the modeling team, to call the participants and
ask if they have any additional input or contributions they would like to make
and thank them again for their time. You might pick up some additional information, but the time is well spent if for no other reason than you continue to
build rapport with star performers in the organization and solidify commitment
for the project. It is worth saying again: You want these people to feel they have
an ownership interest in the outcome.

CREATING MODEL CONTENT

Translating the results of job modeling interviews and focus groups, reviews of
prior modeling work, and other material into descriptor content is a fairly
straightforward activity, but there are some tricks of the trade that facilitate the
process.

Developing Work Activity Descriptors

When developing work activity descriptors, keep in mind that the overarching goal is to create a set of statements that includes all of the target job's critical activities and excludes the trivial ones. The best statements are simple declarative sentences. Furthermore, one way to get a handle on the thorny level of detail issue is to compartmentalize the different parts of the typical activity statement.

From chapter 4's discussion of the Item Detail Scale, you can recall that activity statements can be configured to address up to four questions of potential interest:

- WHAT: What is done or what action is being performed?
- WHO/WHAT: Who or what is being acted on?
- WHY: Why is the action occurring or what is the intended outcome?
- HOW: How is the action being accomplished?

With respect to WHAT is done, you should begin the statement with a clear and unambiguous action verb (e.g., *persuades, interviews, adjusts, tells, corrects, plans*). Avoid verbs that have multiple meanings (*assists, supports, determines*). Also, refrain from using multiple action verbs in the same statement (e.g., "Advises and instructs ... " or "Weighs and adjusts ... "). Although this might seem to be a good way to consolidate and condense the total set of descriptions, you will merely introduce some unknown amount of imprecision into the final product. The exception is when you are dealing with actions that invariably go together. Terrific starter lists of action verbs are available.[34,35,36,37,38]

With reference to WHO/WHAT is being acted on, the goal is to clearly state the object of the verb. Everything each of us does in our own sphere of work is done to or for someone or something. The purpose of this part of the statement is to be clear about the who or what. Clarity is also essential here, but the consequences of complexity or ambiguity are not as dire. Thus, statements that have multiple meanings because they are overly broad (e.g., "Advises *people* ... ") or actually have multiple objects (e.g., "Attaches *cable* and *switchboxes* ... ") are seldom preferred for customized solutions, but there are occasions in which the additional precision is not critical.

We live in a world that revolves around cause-and-effect relationships. The intent of the third potential component of an activity statement is to explain WHY the action is occurring and outline the intended effect or outcome. If this level of detail is necessary to support your planned application, this question should be phrased in a way that clarifies the purpose of the activity and its relationship to the objective.

Finally, there are a number of ways a particular work activity can be accomplished. In certain situations, job modelers might need to understand and document HOW it is done. For example, if different training activities and learning objectives could not be derived from less detailed statements, it might make sense to drive the definition of the activity domain down one more level. However, as noted in chapter 4, this degree of resolution in the modeling picture is not necessary for most HR interventions.

To recap, keep the following points in mind as you write activity statements:

- Keep each statement as brief as possible (yet maintain the level of detail you need to support a particular application).
- Address the WHAT and WHO/WHAT questions as clearly as possible. If using WHY and HOW questions, address them equally clearly.
- Keep statements on activities that are unimportant to performing a major part of the job, are performed infrequently, or apply to only a few jobs targeted by the research out of your descriptor pool.

The following suggestions should also prove useful in keeping you out of statement-writing traps:

- Use language and words that are meaningful to the people who perform the work (at the same time, it is a good idea to avoid abbreviations and any jargon that is completely meaningless to everyone but subject matter experts).
- There is some evidence that the reading level of statements in an inventory might impact the reliability of subsequent responses by subject matter experts.[39] It makes sense to keep the reading level as low as possible (e.g., keep total word count low, reduce the average number of syllables per word in the sentences, steer clear of technical terminology unless completely familiar to all respondents). However, because of the unique construction of activity statements, it is not clear whether traditional reading level scales such as the Flesch,[40] FOG,[41] and SMOG[42] indexes are appropriate.
- Try to keep the level of detail across statements roughly the same. In other words, it typically confuses things to build a set of descriptors that contain a mix of detailed and general items.
- Because they imply performance standards, avoid using adverbs and adjectives in the statements (e.g., "Coaches employees on the *proper* use of hand tools"). This distinction is important because it shifts the focus to an examination of proficiency, which can cloud the view of activities and results.
- Keep descriptions of worker requirements—such as aptitude, skill, and knowledge—out of the inventory of work activity descriptors. Competencies are somewhat different animals and deserve their own distinct descriptions, as outlined in the next section.

Developing Competency Descriptors

The approach for writing good competency descriptors is similar to that for creating quality work activity descriptors. In addition, the job modeler must be careful not to fall into the trap of simply adding "Skill in" or "Knowledge of" on the front of a work activity and calling this a competency. Although there is some overlap between the domain of work activities and the domain of competencies, this blurring of the boundaries occurs primarily at lower levels on the job complexity ladder. For example, a work activity for a copy typist might be "Types drafts of legal documents using standard word processing software packages." A competency item for the same job might include "Skill in typing from draft copies or dictation."

The fact of the matter is this: As work activities become more complex or abstract (e.g., long-range planning activities versus typing activities), the competencies required for successful performance also become more complex and intangible. In addition, successful performance in more complex work activities seems to be contingent on a greater number of interrelated competencies. Consequently, the causal relation to work activity performance becomes more difficult to identify, although being able to identify this relationship is the primary goal. That said, some basic guidelines for writing competency statements follow:

- Each statement should constitute a unique individual difference capability.
- Each competency should contain enough detail to capture the essence of the individual difference variation.
- Keep the use of trait or psychological construct references out of the competency description.
- Keep statements that refer to trivial competencies out of your inventory. This is obviously a judgment call, but one that you will be in a position to reliably make. For example, although "Knowledge of standard purchasing and supply requisition procedures" might be an important component of a supply officer's role, it probably would not show up in an inventory for most department managers, despite the fact these individuals may make use of this knowledge on an infrequent basis.

Beyond this point, the suggestions for developing quality competency descriptors mirror the recommendations found in the last five bullets for creating work activity descriptors.

DEVELOPING A RATIONALLY DERIVED MODEL

After the interviews and/or focus groups have been completed and after the work activity, competency, or other descriptor statements have been written following the standards described earlier, it is time to refine the descriptor content and create an organizing structure or model to display the results of the modeling effort. By *refine the descriptor content,* I mean examining the statements within each content domain to:

- eliminate redundant items;
- merge or flesh out similar items that, on their own, are a little skimpy in their description;
- identify and smooth out unevenness in item detail;
- clarify cumbersome or ambiguous language;
- identify coverage gaps in the model (i.e., what appear to be important content categories that seem light in descriptor definition); and
- otherwise highlight deficiencies in the descriptor content that are difficult to discern when the statements are reviewed individually.

By *create an organizing structure or model to display the results,* I mean creating a:

- classification of content,
- taxonomy of work descriptors,
- configuration of components,
- representation of facts, and
- partitioning of reality into a conceptual system that has explanatory power.

Explanatory power, you say. Sounds nice, but what exactly does this mean? Well, in part, it means the resulting classification, taxonomy, system, and so on should:

- serve as a basis for understanding variability in individual job performance;
- guide decisions about jobs or people that require having knowledge about the relationships among classes of descriptor content or between classes of descriptor content and other business or work performance variables;
- facilitate communication about important aspects of jobs and work-related individual differences using a common language for talking about jobs and work-related people capabilities;
- ease the storage, manipulation, and retrieval of work- and person-related information by providing a means for chunking related bits of information;
- make it possible to make efficient comparisons of work- and person-related information across job groups, organization levels, business units; and
- otherwise clarify the scope, configuration, and definition of jobs targeted by the modeling effort for the purpose of designing or modifying a wide range of HR interventions.

So, how does one start? Well, depending on the scope of the modeling project, whether descriptor content is being created independently by interviewer/focus group leaders or as a team, the degree of item detail required to support the application, and so forth, the entire pool of item-level descriptors for any one content domain may range from several dozen to several hundred. In either case, it is frequently useful to begin by printing each descriptor statement from the first content domain (e.g., work activities) on a separate 3 x 5 index card. Then sort the cards into piles based on their similarity or relatedness of content. The idea is to reduce the entire pool of items to meaningful dimensions without losing the essential complexity and power of information they represent. Beyond this point, there is considerable variation in the way a modeler may choose to rationally build a model. Several approaches are described next.

Approach 1: Free-Form Content Analysis

This procedure starts by having a subgroup of the modeling team sort the cards into meaningful and relatively homogenous subgroupings with the instruction that: (a) each descriptor or card can be placed in only one pile, (b) all descriptor statements cannot be placed in a single megapile, and (c) the preponderance of items cannot be placed in their own stand-alone pile (although some items can be sorted by themselves). The result is an initial set of dimensions that groups related items together. The group then reviews the descriptor items within a category to eliminate redundancies, create new items that combine minor variations in two or more items, and otherwise refine the content of the dimensions as described earlier.

During this rewriting process, the group needs to be careful not to eliminate or combine items in a way that creates a void in domain representation. Also, during this step, voids in the existing descriptor content may become apparent; these voids necessitate conducting additional interviews or focus groups to gather more information (i.e., lots of stand-alone items or categories that contain only a couple of items).

Assuming that the pool of content is comprehensive and that additional interviews or focus groups are unnecessary, the second step would be for a second subgroup of the job modeling team to take the revised set of descriptor items, printed on a new set of 3 x 5 index cards, and independently conduct a second sorting task applying the same rules of engagement noted earlier. This second sorting activity may reveal some different ways for dividing up the content that needs to be discussed and reconciled with group one. Although the primary purpose of this second sorting effort is to develop the final structure for configuring the item content, additional areas for refining items may also become evident. It often makes sense to have a person or two from the customer project team as part of this second content analysis effort.

Once the second sorting is finished, and after differences between the first and second sorting solutions have been discussed and a preferred view achieved, a potential third step is to sequentially merge the dimensions. This is accomplished by merging the two dimensions that are considered to be the most similar and proceeding with this process until the final dimension or composite dimensions (i.e., a previously merged group of two or more independent dimensions) are merged into a final group that contains all the descriptor statements. This step can help highlight additional descriptor items in need of some refinement. Perhaps more important, it forces the modeling team to consider the similarity and distinctiveness of the dimensions in the second-generation model and may suggest ways to group the items that are more parsimonious and meaningful. Additionally, if there are a large number of dimensions to deal with, it may make sense to configure the dimensions into higher order groupings or factors. The sequential merge process brings to the forefront the relationships between the dimensions in the content domain and is a good way to guide the creation of a rational-based set of organizing factors.

A potential fourth step is a differential weighting analysis. This may be accomplished by dividing the descriptor items into three groups of equal size: those considered most important for successful performance in the target job or job group, those considered to be of intermediate importance, and those considered least important. Actually, it is easier to just sort items into the high and low importance categories and let the leftover final third of the items represent the middle. This sorting of work activities and competencies highlights the most critical subset of content and is one way to help establish the job-relatedness of the critical core set of items.

There are other questions about the descriptor content, other than importance, that can be useful to investigate. For example, one might want to look at variation in the strategic importance of the item content or the extent to which people have a chance to develop a competency on the job versus needing to be in full possession of a particular skill to hit the ground running from Day 1. The next chapter presents a number of potentially useful questions that may be applied to the modeling content in the form of a questionnaire. However, the same questions may be applied to the content in the form of a sorting task along the lines just described. The result of this process (i.e., Steps 1–2 and Steps 1–4 if desired) is a content model that provides an economical structure for building various job information displays and characterizing the similarities and differences among jobs.[43]

Approach 2: Fixed Structure Content Analysis

A second approach is simply to retranslate the pool of descriptor items into an existing classification structure. For example, perhaps a decision has been made to use a rigorously developed structure that has been used elsewhere in the organization or one reported in the literature for a similar job group. In some circumstances, one might also choose to use a generic classification scheme for a job category like the one for *management* in Appendix A. In these cases, proceeding through Steps 1 and 2 will still accomplish the intended purpose of identifying duplicate items, identifying items that may be combined or need to be rewritten, and so forth. The difference in the procedure is that the number of categories into which items are sorted is fixed and the categories are already clearly labeled and defined. The sequential merge process may still be used to investigate relationships among the categories and perhaps suggest a higher order or classification. Similarly, the differential weighting analysis may be used to reclassify descriptor content into categories reflecting different weighting in terms of degree or level of some characteristic.

Approach 3: Delphi-Based Content Analysis

A third approach involves using a modification of the Delphi technique. Named after the Greek oracle known for predicting events, this methodology for capturing expert judgments had its beginnings in the 1950s when a group of Rand Corporation scientists developed a system for combining individuals' judgments of how to bet at the horse races to the benefit of all.[44] Perhaps the defining feature of the technique is its iterative process, where the respondents are constantly interacting with the independently created solutions. A second important feature of the approach is the anonymity of the authors of the independently created solutions.

The way this technique works best in a modeling context is to start the process after Step 1 has been completed as described in the free-form content analysis approach (i.e., after the initial pool of descriptor items has been cleaned up and consolidated). Step 2 involves reproducing the consolidated set of descriptor statements on a new batch of 3 x 5 cards for each member of the subteam involved in producing the final solution. Armed with his or her own set of cards, each participant generates an independent classificatory solution and produces a written document illustrating and describing his or her solution and provides copies for the other participants.

In the third step, armed with all of the original solutions produced and after reviewing the products from the other participants, each member of the subteam works independently on a revised second-generation solution. Again, each participant produces a written document illustrating and describing his or her revised solutions for the other members. After two or three independent generations, a next step is likely to be a group meeting to discuss the second-generation solutions and work out a final model as a team.

The advantages of this approach are numerous. For example, the fact that there is anonymity during the process can lead to a freer expression of ideas, resulting in creative ways of modeling the descriptor content. The feature of anonymity also makes it more difficult for interpersonal factors of the group to impact the final solution. Further, the sharing and iterative process allows each participant to consider and build on the ideas of others. Additionally, given the design of the process, it can be managed without the participants ever having to be in the same room together, which helps when consulting and customer participants in the process happen to reside in different cities, countries, or continents. On the downside, this approach clearly has time and cost (based primarily on time) implications. For example, the modeling results using the Delphi procedure reported in Schippmann, Prien, and Hughes took more than a month to complete.[45]

Approach 4: Scaling-Based Content Analysis

Approach 4 is merely an extension of the first two steps described in the free-form content analysis. However, in terms of the second step, rather than having a subteam working as a group to conduct the second round of the content analysis, each individual independently sorts the descriptors into dimensions. When each person has completed the sorting task, the results may then be combined across people. In Approach 4, each person's sorting results are put in a matrix or table that has as many rows and columns as there are descriptor items sorted. The total number of people who put two items in the same category in their independently derived classification solutions is then entered into the cells of this matrix. Therefore, a high number in a cell indicates that many people put a particular pair of items in the same category, suggesting that the two items are conceptually similar. It is then possible to analyze this table to identify groupings of related items and develop the classification structure.

Of course, beyond a couple of dozen items, this procedure becomes cumbersome without relying on a computer and some standard statistical software packages to facilitate the management and analysis of these data. Then, too, rather than relying on the potentially fallible interocular test (i.e., eyeballing the data and drawing conclusions based on a straight visual inspection of the results), it makes sense to use factor or cluster analysis statistics to analyze the data matrix. However, at this point, we are moving pretty quickly away from a pure rational analysis of content toward an empirically based approach and the empirical methods get plenty of coverage starting in chapter 7.

It should be noted that one set of statistical procedures not discussed in chapter 7 includes the variety of techniques referred to as *multidimensional scaling (MDS) methods*. It is this class of methods on which this fourth approach is based. For those who are interested in using this approach for larger data sets or in a more sophisticated way, start by looking at an eminently readable discussion of MDS by Rosenberg and Sedlack.[46]

PROJECT MANAGEMENT TIPS

There are a number of tips associated with Step 3 of the SJM process. To begin, develop a clear picture of the target jobs, job families, organizational roles, relevant job levels, and included business units and locations before gathering reference and source materials. You will save time with a more refined and targeted search.

Next, try to keep the interview or focus group leader team small; it is easier to organize and integrate information if fewer people are involved. Also, if possible, take the time to pick the right people to participate as interviewers and focus group leaders and not just the right number. You want people who will have credibility with the interviewees or focus group participants. Be sure to prepare the interviewers or focus group leaders with plenty of background information, such as information on the customer organization, purpose and anticipated outcomes of the project, the organization structure, names and titles of the executive sponsor(s) of the project, as well as those of key members of the customer's project team and descriptive information on the target jobs, job families, organizational roles, and business units.

Carefully determine how much time you will need to conduct the interviews or focus groups and then stick to it. Depending on the extent of existing information, the experience of the interviewers/focus group leaders, and the intended use of the job information and resulting detail of information required, you can probably expect interviews with:

- job incumbents to require at least 1 hour.
- supervisors/managers of the target jobs to require between 1 and 2 hours.
- organizational visionaries to require between 1 and 2 hours.
- focus group meetings with four to eight people to require 2 to 4 hours.

Although interviews and focus groups are great ways of collecting information, it is also important to study work lives where they are really lived and not simply where the job modeler finds it convenient to look at them. This recognition may seem as bland and obvious as a cliché, but it is easy to succumb to what is expedient in the crush for speed. *Do not do it* ... the quality will suffer.

In terms of creating model content, it is often a good idea to have each interviewer and focus group leader independently create descriptor content that gets channeled into the overall pool (vs. coming together as a group and creating content as a team). Although more labor-intensive, it is often the best way to ensure comprehensive coverage of the content domain. Each modeling team member will certainly create a lot of similar items and overlapping content, but you will be in a better position to leverage the possibly important distinctions when you consolidate information later in the process. Of course, if the modeling team is larger than four or five people, you quickly reach the point of diminishing returns in capturing value added distinctions considering the accompanying increases in time and labor demands. When you have a large modeling team, consider breaking the total group into subteams and have the subteams generate independent content.

Also keep in mind that a whole slew of one-on-one interviews are more difficult to interpret than several focus groups due to the sequential versus simultaneous receipt of information. If your project includes a lot of interviews, give yourself some extra time at the end to consolidate information and create the rationally derived model.

Finally, Table 5.2 presents some of the more important advantages and disadvantages of different information-gathering methods. This kind of summary comparison of methods can be useful when consulting with your customer around the different options. You will note that I have jumped the gun a little bit by including information about questionnaire methods.

TABLE 5.2

Job Modeling Information-Gathering Methods

Review Existing Source Materials

Potential Advantages	Potential Disadvantages/Challenges
+ Potential to get a significant head start in understanding a particular work domain. + Nonreactive and nonintrusive way to gather lots of information.	− Not always easy to tell what is "good" information or to determine applicability to the current modeling situation.

Semistructured Interview (Face-to-Face)

Potential Advantages	Potential Disadvantages/Challenges
+ Terrific relationship-building potential. This level of personal attention and convenience often required when dealing with high-level managers and executives. + Allows consultant opportunity to immerse self in customer organization and gather information using all six senses. + Unforeseen deposits of useful information may be identified and mined "on the fly."	− Difficult to consolidate the results, particularly if there are many interviews and many interviewers. − Time-consuming to coordinate and conduct multiple interviews; as a result, is expensive. − Not everyone is a good interviewer. It takes a special blend of competencies to develop a rapport with people while staying focused and intent on getting meaningful answers to questions.

(continues)

TABLE 5.2 (continued)

Focus Group

Potential Advantages	Potential Disadvantages/Challenges
+ Cost-effective way to garner most of the benefits of the interview at a fraction of the time and cost.	– This kind of group interview puts special demands on the focus group leader, and skilled facilitators are not always easy to find.
+ Good relationship-building potential.	– Unless natural clusters of people exist in close geographic proximity, can be difficult to get large numbers of people to travel to a common location.
+ Allows consultant opportunity to immerse self in customer organization and gather information using all six senses.	
+ Interaction between participants often has a synergistic effect that can enhance the creativity and quality of the created content.	

Observation

Potential Advantages	Potential Disadvantages/Challenges
+ Puts the modeler smack dab in the middle of the work place with all the contextual richness that entails.	– As with the interview, it is time-consuming to coordinate and conduct multiple observations.
+ A trained observer is likely to generate information that is less biased than that offered up by a job incumbent, supervisor, and so on.	– Because of the above, it is expensive.
+ Enhanced perception by job holders that their job has been taken seriously.	– The act of observing people often changes their behavior.
+ In many cases, makes minimal demand on the job incumbent (i.e., causes little disruption for the person being observed).	– For many jobs, it can be difficult to infer the most important aspects of the job (e.g., problem solving).

(continues)

TABLE 5.2 (continued)

Questionnaire

Potential Advantages	Potential Disadvantages/Challenges
+ Terrific way to get lots of people involved and have them provide input to the modeling process.	– Can be viewed as cold and impersonal and, if not positioned correctly, may be viewed as something of a test.
+ In many respects, the most cost-effective way to gather and summarize large amounts of information.	– Questions and associated rating scales require a great deal of thought because the range of response options is predetermined.
+ Objective format circumvents having to find skilled interviewers and focus group leaders and having to rely on the interpretive and processing power of those facilitators.	– Related to the above, it can be difficult to write good item content for inclusion in a questionnaire.
+ Easily handles situations when the experts are numerous and/or in multiple and far-flung geographic locations.	– True meaning of the resulting numbers is not always as clear-cut as the black-on-white numbers on the printout might lead one to believe. Response bias introduces some unknown amount of error into the results.
+ At its best when there is a need to prioritize job content in some way or determine the degree to which some quality characterizes aspects of the job content (e.g., *Current Importance, Future Importance*).	– People are not always ready to stop what they are doing to complete a questionnaire; one needs to be prepared to handle low response rates.
+ Similarly, this method is well suited to describing and differentiating sets of related jobs or handling situations where people with the same job title do different things.	

REFERENCES

[1]Ashkenas, R., Ulrich, D., Jick, T., & Kerr, S. (1995). *The boundaryless organization.* San Francisco: Jossey-Bass.

[2]Voss, H. (1996, July–August). Virtual organizations: The furture is now. *Strategy and Leadership,* p. 14.

[3]Bridges, W. (1994). *Jobshift.* Reading, MA: Addison-Wesley.

[4]Aronowitz, S., & DiFazio, W. (1994). *The jobless future.* Minneapolis, MN: University of Minnesota Press.

[5]Rifkin, J. (1995). *The end of work: The decline of the global labor force and the dawn of the post-market era.* New York: Putnam.

[6]Prien, E. P. (1997). *Sales inventory.* Memphis, TN: Author.

[7]Borman, W. C., & Brush, D. H. (1993). More progress toward a taxonomy of managerial performance requirements. *Human Performance, 6,* 1–21.

[8]See Appendix A of this book.

[9]Prien, E. P. (1997). *Clerical inventory.* Memphis, TN: Author.

[10]Bernardin, J. H. (1988). Police officer. In S. Gael (Ed.), *The job analysis handbook for business, industry, and government* (Vol. 2, pp. 1242–1254). New York: Wiley.

[11]Kane, J. A. (1983). *A job analysis for the police officer job in the city of Washington, DC.* Unpublished manuscript.

[12]Dunnette, M. D., & Motowildo, S. J. (1975). *Police selection and career assessment.* Washington, DC: U.S. Government Printing Office.

[13]Baehr, M. E., & Orban, J. A. (1988). Municipal transit bus operator. In S. Gael (Ed.), *The job analysis handbook for business, industry, and government* (Vol. 2, pp. 1229–1241). New York: Wiley.

[14]Page, R. C., & Caskey, D. T. (1988). Computer programmer. In S. Gael (Ed.), *The job analysis handbook for business, industry, and government* (Vol. 2, pp. 1192–1205). New York: Wiley.

[15]Gael, S. (1988). *The job analysis handbook for business, industry, and government* (Vol. 2). New York: Wiley.

[16]Ash, R. A., & Edgell, S. L. (1975). A note on the readability of the position analysis questionnaire. *Journal of Applied Psychology, 60,* 765–766.

[17]Cornelius, E. T., & Lyness, K. S. (1980). A comparison of holistic and decomposed judgment strategies in job analysis by job incumbents. *Journal of Applied Psychology, 65,* 155–163.

[18]Cordery, J. L., & Sevastos, P. P. (1993). Responses to the original and revised job diagnostic survey: Is education a factor in responses to negatively worded items? *Journal of Applied Psychology, 78,* 141–143.

[19]Ackerman, P. L., & Humphreys, L. G. (1990). Individual differences theory in industrial and organizational psychology. In M. D. Dunnette & L. M. Hough (Eds.), *Handbook of industrial and organizational psychology* (Vol. 1, pp. 223–282). Palo Alto, CA: Consulting Psychologists Press.

[20]Hunter, J. E. (1986). Cognitive ability, cognitive aptitudes, job knowledge, and job performance. *Journal of Vocational Behavior, 29,* 340–362.

[21]Landy, F. J., & Vasey, J. (1991). Job analysis: The composition of SME samples. *Personnel Psychology, 44,* 27–50.

[22]Borman, W. C., Dorsey, D., & Ackerman, L. (1992). Time-spent responses as time allocation strategies: Relations with sales performance in a stockbroker sample. *Personnel Psychology, 45,* 763–777.

[23]Landy, F. J., & Vasey, J. (1991). Job analysis: The composition of SME samples. *Personnel Psychology, 44,* 27–50.

[24]Mullins, W. C., & Kimbrough, W. W. (1988). Group composition as a determinant of job analysis outcomes. *Journal of Applied Psychology, 73,* 657–664.

[25]Schmitt, N., & Cohen, S. A. (1989). Internal analyses of task ratings by job incumbents. *Journal of Applied Psychology, 74,* 96–104.

[26]Silverman, S. B., Wexley K. N., & Johnson, J. C. (1984). The effects of age and job experience on employee responses to a structured job analysis questionnaire. *Public Personnel Management, 13,* 355–359.

[27]Borman, W. C., Dorsey, D., & Ackerman, L. (1992). Time-spent responses as time allocation strategies: Relations with sales performance in a stockbroker sample. *Personnel Psychology, 45,* 763–777.

[28]Mullins, W. C., & Kimbrough, W. W. (1988). Group composition as a determinant of job analysis outcomes. *Journal of Applied Psychology, 73,* 657–664.

[29]Wexley, K. N., & Silverman, S. B. (1978). An examination of differences between managerial effectiveness and response patterns on a structured job analysis questionnaire. *Journal of Applied Psychology, 63,* 646–649.

[30]Conley, P. R., & Sackett, P. R. (1987). Effects of using high- versus low-performing job incumbents as sources of job analysis information. *Journal of Applied Psychology, 72,* 434–437.

[31]Morgeson, F. P., & Campion, M. A. (1997). Social and cognitive sources of potential inaccuracy in job analysis. *Journal of Applied Psychology, 82,* 627–655.

[32]Schippmann, J. S. (1996). *Key decision points in job modeling.* Minneapolis, MN: Author.

[33]Many of these ground rules are similar to those suggested for running successful brainstorming sessions. See Osborne, A. F. (1953). *Applied imagination.* New York: Charles Scribner's Sons.

[34]Ammerman, H. L. (1977). *Performance content for job training: Vol. II. Stating the tasks of the job* (R&D Series No. 122). Columbus, OH: The Ohio State University, The Center for Vocational Education.

[35]Gael, S. (1990). *Job analysis: A guide to assessing work activities.* San Francisco, CA: Jossey-Bass.

[36]Lawshe, C. H. (1989). *Describing work behavior: How to prepare job activity or task statements.* West Lafayette, IN: Author.

[37]McIntire, S., Bucklan, M. A., & Scott, D. (1995). *Job analysis kit.* Lutz, FL: Psychological Assessment Resources.

[38]Prien, E. P. (1991). *Action verb starter list.* Memphis, TN: Author.

[39]Murphy, W. F. (1966). *The application of readability principles to the writing of task statements.* Unpublished doctoral dissertation.

[40]Flesch, R. (1948). A new readability yardstick. *Journal of Applied Psychology, 32,* 221–233.

[41]Gunning, R. (1964). *How to take the FOG out of writing.* Chicago: Dartnell Corporation.

[42]McLaughlin, G. H. (1969). SMOG grading: A new readability formula. *Journal of Reading, 12,* 639–646.

[43]Schippmann, J. S., Hughes, G. L., & Prien, E. P. (1987). The use of structured multi-domain job analysis for the construction of assessment center methods and procedures. *Journal of Business and Psychology, 1,* 353–366.

[44]Rath, G., & Stoyanoff, K. (1983). The Delphi technique. In F.L. Ulschak (Ed.), *Human resource development: The theory and practice of needs assessment* (pp. 111–131). Reston, VA: Reston Publishing Company.

[45]Schippmann, J. S., Prien, E. P., & Hughes, G. L. (1991). The content of management work: Formation of task and job skill composite classifications. *Journal of Business and Psychology, 5,* 325–354.

[46]Rosenberg, S., & Sedlack, Z. (1972). Structural representations of perceived trait relationships. In A. K. Romney, R. N. Shepard, & S. B. Nerlave (Eds.), *Multidimensional scaling* (Vol. 2, pp. 133–162). New York: Seminar.

Chapter 6
Which Questions are Asked?

> ... I think that I may arrive at my facts most directly by questioning you. ...
> —Sir Arthur Conan Doyle's *Sherlock Holmes*—

In August 1854, the most terrible cholera epidemic in England's history broke out along Broad Street in London. At the time, the terrified people in the kingdom knew nothing about bacteria or the mode of the disease's transmission. All they knew was that, in the space of 10 days, there were more than 500 fatalities within a 250-yard radius of the intersection of Cambridge Street and Broad Street (and there would have been a lot more if people had not virtually deserted that part of the city within the first several days of the outbreak).

A chapter in Tufte's recent book describes the shrewd detective work of Dr. John Snow, who is widely credited with discovering the cause of the epidemic and bringing it to an end. In addition to sound medical analysis, Dr. Snow would have impressed even Sherlock Holmes with his investigative approach, which involved asking the right questions of the right people and employing quantitative procedures to help put the answers together in a way that was logical and reasonable.[1]

For example, despite that a bustling brewery had been operating smack dab in the middle of the decimated area, none of the 70 workmen suffered from the cholera. By surveying the proprietor and the workers, he found that a perk of the business was that each employee was allowed a daily quantity of malt liquor. Moreover, as a result of this benefit, they never had reason to visit the public Broad Street water pump to get anything to drink. It was this particular pump that was eventually implicated as the source of the contaminated water that fueled the epidemic. Saved by the beer!

However, this is not the moral of the story. The real lesson here was Dr. Snow's logical set of questions, which, when applied to a lot of people, allowed him to develop a basis of evidence that pointed him in the right direction. That is what the rest of this chapter is all about: asking clear, lucid questions from people who are in a position to tell you what you need to know and putting their answers together in a way that points you in the right direction.

POTENTIAL QUESTIONS

For any specific content unit, such as an item-level work activity or competency statement, a number of different questions can be asked of a job content expert, supervisor, organizational visionary, trained observer, or customer. The set of questions or rating scales discussed in this section certainly is not meant to be an exhaustive list. Rather, it is simply a subset of the questions I have found most useful, used singly or in combination, in the widest range of settings.

Current Importance

Rarely are the work activity and competency components of a job or job group (i.e., items, dimensions, or factors) of equal value or importance in contributing to effective performance. The *Current Importance* question (see Fig. 6.1, Part A, for a sample scale focusing on work activities) is one way to capture these differences for use in constructing a wide range of HR applications. In fact, this question is probably the most versatile of all the potential questions discussed in this section. Thus, although it is not possible to discuss all the ways this question might be used, I offer one applied example.

In the area of selection, there is a variety of methods that may be used to make preemployment predictions, including interviews, biodata, paper-and-pencil testing, simulations, and work sample tests, to name only a few. Regardless of the specific method, a vital first step is to identify and prioritize the most important aspects of the job(s). Clearly, it is not possible to set up a system for predicting an applicant's performance in a target job without a clear understanding of the target job's requirements.

Given this background, consider the effort to build a set of simulations and work samples for screening new hires into production jobs within a work-team environment for a large automobile parts manufacturer. Displeased with the results of an existing paper-and-pencil testing procedure, the operations leadership group wanted to employ more interactive procedures to assess the interpersonal characteristics and work habits of potential new team members. In this project, questions about the *Current Importance* of both work activities and competencies were built into the modeling questionnaire for the purpose of establishing the job relatedness of the resulting simulations.

For employment decisions to be job related, federal and professional guidelines require decisions to be based on important aspects of the job content domain that are necessary on entry. In this regard, the *Uniform Guidelines* state that measures are relevant to the extent that they "represent critical or impor-

CURRENT IMPORTANCE (PART A)

Use the *Importance* scale to indicate your answer concerning the importance of each work activity for full performance in the job in question. For each work activity statement, proceed in two steps. First, consider whether a work activity *is* or *is not* part of the job. If a work activity is not part of the job or does not apply, then you should rate this activity a "0."

If a work activity is part of the job, you must decide how important it is relative to other activities performed as part of the job. When deciding how important a work activity item is, think about how critical or important each activity is compared to all the other work activities that make up your job. Record your answer in the *Importance* column next to each work activity item. Remember, you are rating the importance of each work activity compared to all the other activities that make up your job. Thus, some activities will be relatively more, or less, important than others.

0 – The work activity is never done and is unimportant to the job.

1 – The work activity is of very little importance to the whole job, but is useful for some minor part of the job.

2 – The work activity is somewhat important for successful performance in either the whole job or some part of the job.

3 – The work activity is important for successful performance in either the whole job or a major part of the job.

4 – The work activity is very important for successful performance in the whole job or a significant part of the job.

5 – The work activity is critically important for successful job performance in the whole job.

❏ FUTURE IMPORTANCE (PART B)

Use the *Future Importance* scale to indicate your answer concerning the anticipated future importance of each competency for full performance in the job as it will look two years from now. First consider whether a competency *is* or *is not* expected to be a part of the job. If a competency is not expected to be a part of the job or does not apply, you should rate this competency a "0."

If the competency is part of the job, then you must decide how important it will be for the job that will exist two years from now, relative to other competencies expected to be required as part of the job. When making your ratings, try to anticipate changes in the way the work is performed, the introduction of new processes, technology, or other change factors that are likely to occur over the next two years.

0 – The competency will not be required.

1 – The competency will be of very little importance.

2 – The competency will be somewhat important for successful performance.

3 – The competency will be important for performing part of the job.

4 – The competency will be very important for performing a significant part of the job.

5 – The competency will be critically important for performing nearly all aspects of the job.

FIG. 6.1. Job modeling questions.

(continues)

❑ FREQUENCY (PART C)

Use the *Frequency* scale to indicate the frequency with which specific work activities are performed as part of the job. For each work activity, proceed in two steps. First, consider whether a work activity *is* or *is not* part of the job. If a work activity is not part of the job or does not apply, rate this work activity a "0."

Second, if the work activity is something that is performed as part of the job, then determine how frequently the activity is performed relative to other job activities using the following scale.

0 – The work activity is never done.

1 – The work activity is performed infrequently.

2 – The work activity is performed occasionally.

3 – The work activity is performed fairly often.

4 – The work activity is performed very frequently.

5 – The work activity is performed constantly.

❑ LEVEL OF MASTERY (PART D)

Use the *Level of Mastery* scale to indicate the degree of expertise required to perform specific competencies. First, consider whether a competency *is* or *is not* part of the job. If a competency is not required to perform the job or does not apply, rate the competency a "1."

Second, if the competency is required to perform the job, determine the level of mastery or expertise required to perform the competency relative to other required competencies using the following scale.

1 – The competency is not required.

2 – Minimal competence required. Job incumbents can be expected to handle only the simplest or least complex situations calling for this competency, and they will need significant support or assistance to handle anything but the easiest situations.

3 – Intermediate competence required. Job incumbents should be capable of handling many day-to-day situations calling for this competency, but they will need to seek assistance in difficult situations.

4 – Advanced competence required. Job incumbent should be capable of handling most day-to-day situations calling for this competency, though they might need to seek expert assistance in dealing will particularly difficult situations.

5 – Expert competence required. Job incumbents should be capable of handling all situations calling for this competency, and they could be expected to serve as role models and coach others on this competency.

❑ WHERE ACQUIRED (PART E)

Use the *Where Acquired* scale to indicate your answer concerning where an individual in the job would acquire each competency. In other words, you are to judge whether an individual should be competent in a particular area before entering the job, or if a person could gain proficiency on the job. Mark your answer in the space provided in the *Where Acquired* column next to each item.

0 – Does not apply.

1 – Proficiency in this competency must be acquired on the job. A new person is not be expected to perform this competency.

2 – For the most part, proficiency in this competency must be acquired on the job.

3 – Proficiency in this competency can be acquired while on the job or before entering the job.

4 – For the most part, proficiency in this competency must be acquired before entering the job.

5 – Competency cannot be gained on the job; proficiency in this competency must be acquired before entering the job.

FIG. 6.1 (continued). Job modeling questions.

❏ DIFFICULTY TO ACQUIRE (PART F)

Consider the difficulty an average employee would have in learning to perform a particular competency. Of interest here is not whether an individual has an opportunity to learn the competency, but rather the difficulty the individual would have in developing proficiency relative to other competencies. Mark your answer in the *Difficulty to Acquire* column next to each item.

0 – Does not apply.

1 – This competency is very easy to learn. Proficiency can be acquired in a very short time.

2 – This competency is easier than most others to learn. Proficiency can be acquired in a relatively short span of time without any great degree of difficulty.

3 – This competency is about average in terms of difficulty to learn compared with other competencies.

4 – This competency is harder to learn than most others. It can take a fairly long time to develop   proficiency in this competency.

5 – This is one of the most difficult of all competencies to learn. It requires a great deal of time and   practice to develop proficiency.

FIG. 6.1 (continued). Job modeling questions.

tant job duties, work behaviors, or work outcomes as developed from the review of job information" (p. 38300).[2]

Rating data from job incumbents and supervisors were collected using this scale to determine which work activities and competencies were most important and directly related to effective performance. This was accomplished, in part, by creating job information displays that rank ordered the important work activity and competency items. Chapter 7 discusses in detail techniques for prioritizing and displaying modeling results, so this chapter does not go too far down this path. For now, let me just say that only the most important content was included in the construction phase of the selection project (i.e., roughly 60% of the original pool of 200 work activity items and 50% of the original pool of 120 competency items).

The construction phase included creating a Test Budget Matrix by listing the retained competency items on one axis and work activities on the other, thus creating a mechanism for linking important competencies to important work activities. Two individuals from the customers' project team and two individuals from the consultant project team then, as a group, made a judgment as to whether a particular competency was important for performing a particular work activity. If the answer was "yes," a check was placed in the corresponding cell of the matrix. The completed Test Budget Matrix identified related groups of work activities requiring a particular competency.[3] Although not employed here, it should be noted that a more empirical means for making these competency-to-work activity linkages is available.[4,5]

Next, the project teams needed to make decisions concerning the most appropriate types of simulations and work samples that would allow candidates to demonstrate their degree of possession of the requisite competencies. This decision was aided by the creation of an Assessment Method Matrix, which consisted of competencies on one axis and several potential simulation and work sample methods on the other. As a group, the project teams discussed the advantages and disadvantages of using a particular type of simulation or work sample to get at the individual difference variability for each competency and placed a check in the appropriate cell of a logical competency-by-simulation-method combination.

Hence, sets of competencies that were judged best assessed using a particular type of simulation (e.g., leaderless group discussion, group problem solving, operations in-basket) were identified using the Assessment Method Matrix. The set of competencies judged best suited for measurement using a particular simulation (e.g., a group problem solving situation) were then reviewed in the Test Budget Matrix to identify the corresponding set of linked work activities. This done, the associated work activities were used to create scenario content and operations to be performed by assessors while the linked competencies were used to represent important (for full job performance) individual difference variability to be measured by assessors.

For example, 20 work activities were used to guide construction of the group problem-solving simulation to maximize the fidelity of exercise content to actual job demands and create opportunities to observe and assess the critical competencies. In other words, the problem solving simulation created a situation where participants were required to "collaborate with team members to generate solutions for machinery or system problems" and "investigate potentially conflicting information from multiple sources concerning the operation of instruments or machines." Based on observations of job candidates' performance in the simulation, which replicated critical work activities, assessors were provided the opportunity to observe and assess the degree of possession of the most important competencies linked to these activities.

Of course, the prior project example represents only one specific description for how *Current Importance* data might be used. Most of the references tagged with the list of HR applications presented in chapter 4 offer some description of how *Current Importance* data are used to guide the development of specific HR applications (e.g., workload analysis, job redesign, creation of job descriptions, selecting tests for an individual assessment program, conducting training needs analysis, conducting job evaluation, or investigating the comparable worth of jobs).

Future Importance

The *Future Importance* scale (Fig. 6.1, Part B) is a future-oriented derivative of the *Current Importance* scale. A critical, although often overlooked, element in job modeling involves identifying and estimating the importance of new work activities or new competency requirements as the job changes over time. Information about the importance of specific competencies for the envisioned future job can be used to guide thinking about anticipated changes in the competency requirements that might result from changes to the direction or emphasis of the business, changes to the configuration of the job resulting from work redesign, changes in knowledge requirements stemming from the introduction of new technology, or other changes.

In terms of a project example, consider some recent work with a diversified oil company. This organization operates in three primary areas: exploration and production of oil and gas, refining and distribution, and chemical products related to oil. Within the International Exploration division of the first area, the company was interested in developing a detailed model for the job of Manager of International Contracts and Negotiations. The results of the modeling process were to be used to guide the creation of tools for identifying high-potential candidates, evaluating company bench strength, and guiding individual development efforts of *high-po* employees.

The challenge was that the job was rapidly changing. In the past, those who succeeded were basically globe-trotting cowboys who worked independently to secure exploration and production agreements from government representatives all over the world. However, given the increased complexity of the negotiations and agreements, the need to work as a member of a team of specialists was becoming more important. Furthermore, because of increased emphasis on merging commercial contract law theories and precedents into the overall negotiation strategy (which impacted organizational concerns such as exploration time frames, revenue sharing, and options on the production period), it appeared as if some of the basic requirements of the job were changing.

Given the extent of anticipated change in job requirements, and given the internal politics surrounding this particular modeling effort, members from both the customer and consultant project teams quickly determined that it would be necessary to show, with some precision, the migration of job requirements. Hence, both *Current Importance* and *Future Importance* questions were used with both the work activity and competency sections of a questionnaire that was administered to a wide range of incumbents, supervisors, and potential negotiation team partners. Item-level ratings of current and future importance were rolled up and reported back at the dimension level using information displays like those found in chapter 7 (replacing the different job designations with the current and future requirement assessments for the same job of Manager of International Contracts and Negotiations).

The most critical competency dimensions and subsumed items for the emerging *future* job were then identified (again, more on how to do this in the next chapter) and used to build, among other things, an integrated assessment or forward-looking performance appraisal tool. [6,7] The idea behind integrated assessment is to use information that is already available in most organizations and provide a mechanism for systematically evaluating behavior as it occurs on the job to assess internal candidates for a promotional opportunity. The assumption is that, although it may not be possible to observe a promotional candidate in all the activities of a target job, it is possible to observe a candidate in a sample of situations that are approximations of activities that compose the target job. From these observations, it is possible to infer the degree to which a candidate possesses requisite competencies. In this context, ratings of *Future Importance* not only identified the most important dimensions to build into this procedure and offered a logical rationale for differentially weighting them, but the item-level descriptors were built right into the assessment tools. In summary, the *Future Importance* information now serves as the coordinates on a talent map, from which several applications have been constructed for the purposes of identifying and developing individuals in potential feeder positions throughout the company.

Frequency

The *Frequency* scale (Fig. 6.1, Part C) is based on the older *Time Spent* measure used in early job analysis work. *Frequency* ratings are usually related to ratings of *Current Importance*.[8,9,10] Clearly, if individuals spend most of their time performing a particular work activity, that activity is usually important for full job performance. For this reason, measures of importance are favored over questions about frequency. However, some jobs do include work activities that are performed infrequently yet are required and critical for job success. Thus, while these two scales are related, they are not identical.

An excellent illustration of the difference between measures of importance and frequency comes from the work of a colleague. Erich Prien has been involved in a number of projects involving law enforcement officers over the years. One of the consistent findings is the rating gap between *Current Importance* and *Frequency* ratings for crime-related activities. Specifically, activities like "firing one's weapon in the line of duty" or "using batons, mace, or tasers to subdue and control suspects" are always rated as important, despite that the frequency of occurrence is low.

Level of Mastery

The *Level of Mastery* scale (Fig. 6.1, Part D) captures the level or degree of possession of a competency needed to perform the associated work activities in a job. The *Level of Mastery* and the *Importance* scales differ in that a competency dimension such as Analyzing Issues can be equally important for two different jobs (e.g., sales representative and anesthesiologist), but the depth of skill/knowledge/competence is different. This has been referred to as the within-job-relative versus cross-job-relative frame of reference challenge.[11] In short, this scale is often a nice complement to the *Current Importance* scale, particularly when the modeling work covers a broad range of job levels and functions.

Such was the case with a modeling effort involving one of the most prominent hospital systems in the world. The modeling work covered *all* exempt and nonexempt medical and nonmedical jobs in the system. In these kinds of cases, the metamodel or superordinate map covers a lot of ground (see chap. 7 for one way to present a high-level description of the competency composition for an entire organization). Thus, a competency dimension like Numeral Acumen might need to apply to top-tier executive jobs such as hospital administrator or director of general service, as well as entry-level jobs like lab aide or supply clerk. Although the same basic competency may be involved in each, the level of mastery needed to perform effectively is certainly different.

Employing the *Level of Mastery* scale in the questionnaire in this setting allowed the project team to identify item-level content that operationally defined the competencies somewhat differently at three broad levels. For example, Numerical Acumen at the midlevel management through executive ranks required mastery in specific item-level competencies like "skill in grasping the full meaning of key financial indicators on overall business performance" and "using algebraic or complex formulas to solve problems." However, for many entry-level jobs, *Numerical Acumen* was defined as mastery in item-level content like "skill in performing routine calculations quickly and accurately" and "knowledge of basic arithmetic (e.g., addition, subtraction, multiplication, and division)."

Where Acquired

The *Where Acquired* scale (Fig. 6.1, Part E) is useful for distinguishing between competencies that should be used for selection and those used for training specifications. In this regard, the *Uniform Guidelines* state that test users should "take into account the extent to which the specific knowledges or skills which are the primary focus of the test are those which employees learn on the job" (p. 38301).[12] Further, the *Principles* state that "job content domains should be defined in terms of what an employee needs to do or know without training or experience on the job" (p. 22).[13] Because the *Where Acquired* scale is frequently used in combination with the *Difficulty to Acquire* scale, I will refrain from presenting a project example until both questions have been covered.

Difficulty to Acquire

Each of the questions described earlier involve judgments about a job. In other words, the responses to the *Current Importance, Future Importance, Frequency, Level of Mastery,* and *Where Acquired* scales are based on a particular frame of reference—the target job or jobs. For example, a particular work activity can be important for job performance in a particular job, or a related competency must be possessed prior to starting a particular job.

There are other questions that involve characteristics specific to the work activity or competency yet do not refer to a particular job. For example, take a look at the *Difficulty to Acquire* question in Fig. 6.1, Part F. This question is more complex than the previous questions because it requires a broad base of information about people and is aimed at getting information about how difficult it is for the average person to develop an adequate degree of possession of a particular competency. So, while a complex judgment to ask someone to make, it can be argued that it does tap a fairly stable underlying phenomenon. However, keep in mind that the rater's prior experience and individual abilities are likely to impact judgments even more so than for other questions we might ask about descriptor content.

Now for a case example. It may not surprise you to learn that more than 90% of private companies in the United States have some form of systematic training.[14] Given that training is not an inexpensive enterprise, it may surprise you to learn that few companies do much by way of formally identifying the competencies to be trained, matching appropriate training methods to relevant objectives, or evaluating the success of training initiatives.

A recent client in the consumer products business was an exception. A conscious decision had been made by the senior managers of the company to simplify and reduce the cost of the selection process for entry-level plant employees and pour more dollars into training new hires who have the basic building block competencies. Those HR managers in charge of orchestrating this shift from a *buy* to *develop* mode of operation were acutely aware of the need to go beyond informal discussions among training task force members to identify areas for emphasis in training and the in-house training curriculum.

In addition to collecting *Current Importance* data from job incumbents, a small group of supervisors and training managers were also selected to provide *Where Acquired* and *Difficulty to Acquire* ratings for the same item-level competencies. The *Where Acquired* data produced information that clearly distinguished content covered in the limited screening process versus content that should appear in some form in the training specifications.

For the competency content that ended up in the training camp, the *Difficulty to Acquire* data proved to be a valuable additional perspective. For example, competencies that were judged to be fairly easily acquired were to be developed through some minimal on-the-job coaching by a supervisor or experienced employee. Conversely, competencies judged to be difficult to learn were treated in a more formal way in classroom or apprenticeship training.

In addition, to help guide the level of emphasis of certain concepts and bodies of knowledge in the in-house training curriculum, we developed *Competency Training Composites*. That is, we calculated a composite index for each competency item by multiplying the averaged *Current Importance* judgments, the averaged *Where Acquired* judgments (where high numbers denote content that must be learned on the job), and the averaged *Difficulty to Acquire* judgments (where high numbers denote the most difficult content). Such a composite reflects the logic that competencies most deserving of emphasis in training curriculum content are those judged most important for job performance, those that must be developed on the job, and those for which it is most difficult to acquire proficiency.

Simply rank ordering the competency items according to this training composite index can be informative for curriculum evaluation and instructional design purposes. However, in this setting, it made sense to take the additional step of making formal comparisons of current training coverage to actual competency demands in the target job groups. This was accomplished by calculating the amount of training time devoted to each content area and then relating the results to the actual competency demands using a two-dimensional job requirement and training emphasis matrix.[15] In this way, training deficiencies and excesses were identified with reference to actual work demands, and the training program was modified where appropriate.

There Ain't No Rules Around Here

Henry Ford was fond of saying, "There ain't no rules around here; we're trying to accomplish something!" I feel the need to infuse a little of this "there ain't no rules around here" spirit into the chapter at this point. With this thought in mind, let me tee up another project example to illustrate some of the more nonconventional ways one may use modeling questions.

Let me first provide a little background on the 360-degree or multiperspective feedback methodology used for employee development. This approach has gained a great deal of popularity in recent years. The idea is to provide individuals with boss, peer, direct report, and perhaps even customer feedback (i.e., 360 degrees or from all points around the job compass) that can be used to highlight job-related strengths and development needs. Although the vast majority of multiperspective feedback interventions target management populations, the approach is increasingly being used for various technical or professional segments of the workforce (e.g., physicians, attorneys) as well as high-level individual contributors. Furthermore, although the majority of interventions use standardized tools, which tap fairly conventional competency dimensions associated with management work, there appears to be some increased interest in creating customized content that is built into a *shell* of a 360-degree delivery and processing vehicle.

The creation of custom content for a 360-degree tool for managers was the presenting need of an international organization referred to here as the Intercontinental Organization (ICO). The ICO has major operations in dozens of countries, and the investment strategies and operations in each country are guided by a *country manager*. In recent years, the ICO has found itself in the throes of change in terms of how the organization conducts business and fulfills its mission. Furthermore, in many ways, the country managers were at point for much of what was changing. Without going into too much detail, the implementation of the ICO's business strategy was becoming more complex, the criteria for success at the country level were becoming more abstract and multifaceted, the rules of engagement were much less clear, the job increasingly required working with and satisfying multiple constituencies, and the need to respond quickly to opportunities was becoming a critical success factor.

Within this context, the presenting concern was that the model for future job success was poorly understood by this critical group of ICO managers who were central to carrying out the business plan. Hence, identifying the model for success for country managers and building the content into a 360-degree feedback tool as part of an individual development effort was the scope of the original project.

Once we started the interviews with the incumbent country managers, however, some initial suspicions began to be confirmed. Although by any measure the ICO had succeeded for many years, this success had fostered a bureaucratic rigidity and strong resistance to change. In fact, the unwritten philosophy of the country managers was to "do things by the book and not create waves." Individual efforts to deviate from the established work protocol or attempts to suggest new and innovative ways of conducting business or revising the success metrics met with a boot being applied to the throat of the offending manager—or worse! More than one of the interviewed managers explicitly stated, and nearly all of them implied, that they knew what it took to really succeed in the new role. However, if they demonstrated some of these behaviors, they would get their heads handed to them by their bosses.

In summary, the firm's CEO and senior management team indicated an awareness that change was required in the management models of performance at the country level. Furthermore, the country managers articulated similar views about the need for change. The challenge seemed to be that several intervening layers of management, and years of established operating protocol, stood in the way of necessary change.

Sensitive about not wanting to dilute the focus of the project from the original goal—creating a model of success that could be built into a 360-degree feedback tool—we approached our counterparts on the client project team about modifying the game plan just a bit. Specifically, we recommended going forward with the modeling effort, but we also suggested expanding the information gathered from the questionnaire process. Instead of just building the rationally derived model into a questionnaire and asking supervisors and incumbents to provide ratings of *Current Importance* and *Future Importance*, we wanted to add an *Organizational Support* scale.

Adding this scale to the modeling questionnaire would provide us with data to identify organizational hot spots, which the client could then use to guide what appeared to be a much needed organizational change effort. The lead from the client's project management team presented the idea to the executive sponsors, all of whom bought into the plan (after ensuring that we were not going to be "raising more dust than we could settle"). As a result, we wound up upgrading our straightforward modeling effort into a staging area for a full-blown organizational effectiveness or change effort.

To begin, the client and consultant project teams huddled to identify the alterations and additions that needed to be made to the original game plan. First, the organizational support scale was developed (see Fig. 6.2). In the questionnaire, respondents first answered questions about a competency's importance and then about the level of organizational support. If you replace the *Where Acquire Proficiency* scale in Fig. 6.6 with the *Organizational Support* scale you have an idea of what the questionnaire looked like.

Next, we expanded the charter of the original project to include a mechanism for conducting the diagnosis that would result in action on identified problems. The author's FAST framework for organizational change (see Table 6.1) was used to structure thinking about additional activities and responsibilities that needed to be built into the project. Answers to the questions in Table 6.1 were quickly determined and the project moved forward.

More than 50 SMEs, roughly 90% of the target population, responded to the expanded questionnaire. Table 6.2 illustrates how we chose to present the results—juxtaposing the *Current Importance* and the *Organizational Support* data. In this case, an item was identified as critical to include in the model if the mean *Importance* rating was greater than 3.50 and the standard deviation was less

---

❑ ORGANIZATIONAL SUPPORT

Use the *Organization Support* scale to indicate your answer concerning the extent to which the ICO values and promotes the use of each competency. In other words, to what extent does the ICO culture encourage and reward the use of each competency versus creating barriers to demonstrating the competency?

1 – Clearly not supportive. Practically nobody at the ICO values this competency or supports its use.

2 – Not very supportive. Very few people at the ICO value this competency or support its use.

3 – Somewhat supportive. Some people at the ICO, at various organizational levels, value this competency or support its use.

4 – Very supportive. Many people at the ICO, at various organizational levels, value this competency or support its use.

5 – Extremely supportive. Almost everyone at the ICO, at all organizational levels, values this competency and supports its use.

FIG. 6.2. Organizational support rating scale.

TABLE 6.1

FAST Change for Organizations

Focus	Feedback	Action Planning	Scorecard	Tracking
• What is the impetus for change? • What do the prevailing issues seem to be? • How will the current state of the issues be measured? How will the diagnosis proceed?	• Who sees initial results and decides how to "frame" for broader review? • What process will be used to feed back results more broadly?	• Is there a need to follow-up on the results to clarify issues? If so, how will this be accomplished? • Given that specific issues are highlighted as a result of the measurement, what interventions will be taken to effect change? Specifically, what will be the: - objectives, - resources, - steps, - timeframes?	• How will the success of the interventions be evaluated? What kind of down-stream information will be collected, by whom, to gauge the impact?	• Is there a need to build a system for regularly tracking or monitoring the issue or evaluating the success of the intervention on a long-term basis? If so, how will this be accomplished? • Who owns the evaluation process and what are the implications of deviations from the expected path?

TABLE 6.2

ICO "Lead Courageously" Competency Dimension and Items

Dimension: 09   Lead Courageously   (N = 51)

Item	Scale	Mean	SD	Included in Model	Under Supported
34. Willingness to take a stand and face problems or resolve important issues.	Importance	4.52	0.79	Yes	Yes
	Support	2.81	1.36		
36. Willingness to challenge status quo practices or conventional thinking.	Importance	4.48	0.67	Yes	Yes
	Support	2.52	1.12		
35. Willingness to act decisively and drive hard to solve problems, capitalize on opportunities, etc.	Importance	4.45	0.80	Yes	Yes
	Support	2.92	1.04		
38. Willingness to show consistency of principles, values, and behaviors.	Importance	4.43	0.73	Yes	Yes
	Support	2.85	1.28		
39. Skill in projecting confidence and self-assurance in own abilities.	Importance	4.39	0.78	Yes	No
	Support	3.67	1.02		
37. Skill in championing new ideas, initiatives, or plans.	Importance	4.26	0.69	Yes	Yes
	Support	2.76	0.83		

High

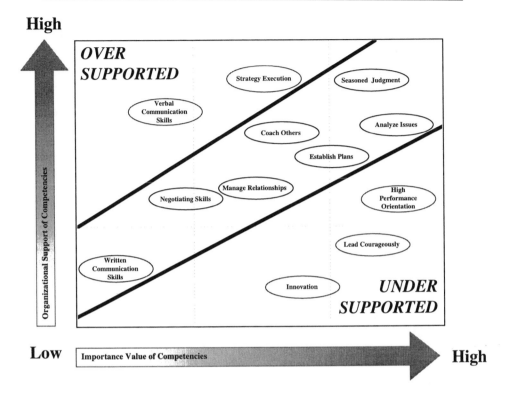

FIG. 6.3. Organization constraint analysis.

than 1.25 (a detailed discussion of the rationale behind these kinds of cutoffs is presented in the next chapter). Items were labeled *undersupported* if the mean *Importance* value was above 4.25 and the *Organizational Support* value was less than 3.00. In other words, we only wanted to highlight areas of constraint that were linked to critical aspects of expected performance. Only 7% of the number of competency items were highlighted in this way, but they were all grouped in 3 of the originally envisioned 12 dimensions: Lead Courageously, Innovation, and High-Performance Orientation.

Figure 6.3 illustrates how we chose to summarize the results for presentation to the executive sponsors. The magnitude of the challenge was readily obvious; at the time of this writing, we are in the middle of the Action Planning phase of the FAST change framework. At least one task force is being formed to scope out objectives, resource requirements, concrete action steps, and timeframes for managing the change effort.

Building Your Own Scales

By now it should be obvious that a variety of questions can be asked about activities, competencies, performance behaviors, or organizational features.[16,17,18] The types of questions used and how they are worded should be determined by the purpose of the job modeling effort. Table 6.3 presents some suggestions for linking specific questions to different HR applications. As this table illustrates, questions about the current and future importance of descriptor statements are particularly useful across a broad band of applications.

However, keep in mind that the potential questions discussed earlier do not represent a complete list. New situations and scale needs pop up all the time. Be willing to improvise and adapt. However, whether modifying an existing question or developing your own, also keep in mind the importance of a well-developed rating scale. For example, there is evidence that the most efficient number of response categories for a rating scale is between five and nine.[19,20,21,22] Fewer than five categories might result in a failure to capture meaningful variability in judgments, and ratings scales with more than nine categories require respondents to make finer discriminations than can be made. In fact, having too many response categories can have a negative effect on the quality of the data obtained.

In addition to numbers, words and phrases are typically used to tell the respondent the significance or meaning of making a rating at a given point. Here, too, there is some evidence indicating that different expressions of frequency (e.g., always, sometimes, or never) or amount (e.g., all, some, or none) have different meanings and interpretability relative to other expressions of frequency or amount.[23,24,25,26,27,28] For example, the words *never, infrequently, occasionally, fairly often, very frequently,* and *consistently* were carefully chosen to anchor different points of the 5-point *Frequency* scale in Fig. 6.1 because of the research describing the meaning (i.e., level of magnitude) of these words relative to one another.

INFORMATION SOURCES

As with questions concerning the target population and the kinds of questions asked, questions about where the information inputs come from in an empirical modeling approach are determined by the purpose of the job modeling study. For example, in some instances, it is important to collect information from job incumbents. In other situations or for other kinds of data, a panel of SMEs or visionaries might be used. In still other cases, observers or modeling experts can monitor the work of individuals and provide input data.

Regardless of the source, keep in mind that the usefulness of the results of the job modeling effort depend directly on the representativeness and adequacy of the respondent sample. Responses from a poorly designed information-gathering process can be viewed as the research equivalent of a four-leaf clover, from which one concludes that all clovers are green and possess four leaves.

TABLE 6.3

Appropriate Questions to Ask to Generate Relevant Information for Different Applications

Application		Current Imp.	Future Imp.	Freq.	Level of Mastery	Where Acquired	Difficulty to Acquire
Human Capital Planning							
1. Job design/redesign	Activity	★★★	★★★	★★★			
	Competency	★★★	★★★		★★	★	
2. Workload analysis	Activity	★★★	★★★	★★			
	Competency	★★★	★★★		★★	★	★
Recruitment							
3. Job desc. & minimum	Activity	★★★	★★★	★★★			
qualifications	Competency	★★★	★★★		★★		
4. Realistic job preview	Activity	★★★	★★	★★			
content	Competency	★★★	★★		★★	★	★
Selection							
5. Interview system	Activity	★★★	★★	★			
	Competency	★★★	★★		★★	★★	★★
6. Scored application	Activity	★★★	★★	★			
blank/biodata	Competency	★★★	★★		★★	★★	★★
7. P-&-P testing	Activity	★★★	★★	★			
(follow-up validation)	Competency	★★★	★★		★★	★★	★★
8. P-&-P testing	Activity	★★★	★★	★			
(validity generalization)	Competency	★★★	★★		★★	★★	★★
9. P-&-P testing	Activity	★★★	★★	★★			
(custom built)	Competency	★★★	★★		★★	★★★	★★
10. Sim'lns/content-oriented	Activity	★★★	★★	★★			
test construction	Competency	★★★	★★		★★★	★★★	★★
11. Individual assessment	Activity	★★★	★★	★			
for selection	Competency	★★★	★★		★★	★★★	★★
Classification Placement							
12. Job classification	Activity	★★★	★★	★★			
	Competency	★★★	★★		★★	★	★
13. Employee skills	Activity	★★★	★★	★			
bank & matching	Competency	★★★	★★		★★★	★★	★

(continues)

TABLE 6.3 (continued)

Training						
14. Training needs analysis	Activity	★★★	★★	★★			
	Competency	★★★	★★		★★★	★★	★
15. Training program design	Activity	★★★	★★	★★			
	Competency	★★★	★★		★★★	★★	★★★
Performance Appraisal						
16. BARS appraisal-oriented	Activity	★★★	★	★			
test construction	Competency	★★★	★		★★	★	
Compensation						
17. Job evaluation	Activity	★★★	★★	★★			
	Competency	★★★	★★		★★★	★★★	★★
Career Management						
18. 360 instruments	Activity	★★★	★★	★★			
for development	Competency	★★★	★★		★★★	★	★★
19. Individual assessment	Activity	★★★	★★★	★			
for development	Competency	★★★	★★★		★★	★★	★★
20. Career ladders/succession	Activity	★★★	★★★	★			
planning	Competency	★★★	★★★		★★★	★★	★★
21. Career planning	Activity	★★★	★★	★			
	Competency	★★★	★★		★★	★★	★
22. Coaching	Activity	★★★	★★	★			
	Competency	★★★	★★		★★★	★★	★★
Organization Structure						
23. Organizational analysis	Activity	★★	★★				
& change	Competency	★★	★★				

★★★ = Always an appropriate source for information of this type.

★★ = Often an appropriate source for information of this type.

★ = Seldom an appropriate source for information of this type.

Blank = Never an appropriate source for information of this type.

There are also types of information that are better suited for collection from different sources. For example, job incumbents or supervisors are usually the best source of information regarding the current composition or requirements for a particular job. In terms of the work activity and competency requirements for jobs that are undergoing change, being redesigned, or that do not currently exist, a small group of visionaries is likely the best source of information.

Furthermore, because the *Difficulty to Acquire* judgment is particularly difficult to make, a small panel of supervisors or subject matter experts often provides more reliable ratings. Similarly, a small group of SMEs will provide better data on whether a competency must be acquired before coming to the job or is acquired as a result of experience on the job (i.e., the *Where Acquired* judgment). Supervisors or individuals responsible for training in the organization are often used to make these judgments because of their opportunity to see a number of people enter the target job and observe their job performance in numerous situations over extended periods of time. Thus, this small group of experts is likely to have a more broad and informed base from which to make these difficult judgments than other groups. On the other hand, job incumbents are usually used to provide information about the importance of work activities or competencies for full job performance and about the frequency with which work activities are performed.

Yet another way to collect job modeling information is to use observers or modeling experts to monitor and record the incumbent's behavior. The advantage of using observers is that the data collected are a direct and independently observable account of the work being performed. Also, when observers are used, questions about the respondents' understanding of the rating task and motivation level are largely avoided. However, the presence of observers can be a distraction to the job incumbent and can possibly encourage or discourage certain activities. Furthermore, the usefulness of observers as the information filter can be limited in situations in which the work being performed is more complex and cognitive in nature. Finally, compared with other sources of information, the costs associated with using teams of observers is a consideration. Table 6.4 provides a summary chart that suggests the most appropriate information source for different types of questions.

TABLE 6.4

Appropriate Information Source for Different Questions

	Incumbents	Supervisors	Visionaries	Customers	Observers
Current Importance	★★★	★★★	★★	★★	★★
Future Importance	★	★★	★★★	★	★
Frequency	★★★	★★★	★	★	★★
Level of Mastery	★★	★★★	★★	★	★★
Where Acquired	★★	★★★	★		★
Difficulty to Acquire	★★	★★★	★		★

★★★ = Always an appropriate source for information of this type.

★★ = Often an appropriate source for information of this type.

★ = Seldom an appropriate source for information of this type.

Blank = Never an appropriate source for information of this type.

THE QUESTIONNAIRE

What is the questionnaire going to look like? This depends in large part on the type of content, mix of modeling questions, intended respondent group, and so forth. However, a fairly straightforward questionnaire, which focuses only on competencies and work context, might have the following four sections.

Section 1 should provide a brief overview to the questionnaire. As Fig. 6.4 illustrates, this is likely to include the purpose of the instrument, some mention of how the data are managed and used, a statement on how to complete the questionnaire (e.g., on company time) and by when, and clear directions for returning the responses along with a contact name if there are questions. Also, do what you can to drive home the point that the focus of this data-gathering device is the job and not the individual.

SECTION 1: OVERVIEW

The purpose of the [NAME OF ORGANIZATION] Job Modeling Questionnaire is to learn more about:

A.   The competencies or individual skills and knowledge required to perform the work activities comprising your job. The focus is **YOUR JOB** and not you.

B.   The work characteristics that define the environment where you work.

Your responses will be combined with those of about [ESTIMATED NUMBER OF RESPONDENTS] employees to help us define the role requirements and related competencies people need in order to perform successfully in a broad range of retail banking jobs. Your individual responses to this questionnaire will be kept *strictly confidential*. Only aggregated data for large job groups will be reported.

•   It should take you close to [ESTIMATED TIME REQUIREMENT] to complete the questionnaire.

•   Everyone's data is important. Complete the questionnaire on company time by [DEADLINE DATE]. Please [RETURN QUESTIONNAIRES, COMPLETED DISKS, ETC.] directly to [CONSULTANT ORGANIZATION] using [ENCLOSED ENVELOPE, DISK MAILER, ETC.].

•   Should you have any questions, please contact [CONTACT PERSON AND TELEPHONE NUMBER AND/OR E-MAIL ADDRESS].

•   Thank you for your time.

FIG. 6.4. Sample overview: Questionnaire with four sections.

SECTION 2: COMPETENCIES

The following section asks two questions about each of [NUMBER OF ITEMS IN QUESTIONNAIRE] competencies (i.e., personal skills and characteristics) that **might** contribute to successful performance in **YOUR JOB**. Please respond to both questions and make your ratings carefully.

Step 1. Importance of Competency to Your Job
Use the *Importance* scale described below to rate the importance of each competency to successful performance in your job. You may also find that a number of these competencies are *not* important in order to perform your job. Note: **Try to use the full range of the 6-point scale (i.e., use all six numbers) as you make your ratings.**

5 -   This competency is **Critically Important** for successful performance in my job.

4 -   This competency is **Very Important** for successful performance in my job.

3 -   This competency is **Important** for successful performance in my job.

2 -   This competency is **Somewhat Important** for successful performance in my job.

1 -   This competency is of **Minor Importance** for successful performance in my job.

0 -   This competency is **Not Important** for my job.

Step 2. Where Is Proficiency in the Competency Acquired (i.e., Before or After Job Entry)
Use the *Where Acquired* scale to indicate your answer concerning where an individual in your job would acquire each competency. In other words, you are to judge whether an individual should be competent in a particular area before entering the job, or if a person could gain proficiency on the job. Mark your answer in the space provided in the *Where Acquired* column next to each item.

5 -   **Must Be Acquired Before Entering the Job**; proficiency in this competency must be acquired before one starts the job, because there is no opportunity to "learn as you go."

4 -   **Primarily Acquired Before Entering the Job.**

3 -   **Acquired Before or After Entering the Job.**

2 -   **Primarily Acquired on the Job.**

1 -   **Must Be Acquired on the Job**; proficiency can only be acquired after one starts the job, a new person is not expected to possess this competency.

FIG. 6.5. Sample introduction to descriptor content section:
Two rating scales applied to competencies.

Section 2 should be the beginning of the guts of the questionnaire. As illustrated in Fig. 6.5, this means presenting clear and concise definitions of the modeling rating scales to be applied to the first domain of descriptor content and then, as illustrated in Fig. 6.6, listing the item-level descriptors with a place for individual responses. Regardless of whether questionnaires are presented in paper or electronic form, it is a good idea to reproduce at least an abbreviated version of the questions or rating scales on each respondent page (e.g., see Fig. 6.6).

Importance	Where Acquired		
_____	_____	1.	Skill in breaking down issues or problems into component parts to identify underlying issues.
_____	_____	2.	Willingness to face challenges or problems with an open mind and sense of curiosity.
_____	_____	3.	Skill in analyzing the flow to ensure existing processes facilitate, rather than hinder, the accomplishment of work.
_____	_____	4.	Skill in identifying the most probable long-term consequences of an action or decision given a large number of possible future outcomes.
_____	_____	5.	Knowledge of competitors' products, strategies, and business philosophies.
_____	_____	6.	Skill in organizing thoughts or facts in verbal communications in such a way that they facilitate understanding.
_____	_____	7.	Skill in preparing written communications that express information clearly and concisely.
_____	_____	8.	Skill in interpreting the nonverbal messages (e.g., crossed arms, facial expressions) that accompany a speaker's verbal communication.
_____	_____	9.	Skill in anticipating the interests and expectations of an audience when preparing a presentation.
_____	_____	10.	Willingness to be proactive and work at connecting with and building cooperative relationships with others.
_____	_____	11.	Skill in assertively presenting one's own point of view without offending or alienating others.
_____	_____	12.	Skill in adjusting one's work pace to keep up with rapidly changing events.
_____	_____	13.	Willingness to follow through on commitments and promises.
_____	_____	14.	Skill in conveying a sense of urgency to others to help team members focus on a limited set of priorities.
_____	_____	15.	Knowledge of basic principles of motivation and theories of work behavior.
_____	_____	16.	Willingness to take a stand on important matters when faced with difficult dilemmas or decisions.
_____	_____	17.	Willingness to persist in the face of difficulties (e.g., when work becomes complex, intellectually challenging, politically complicated).

FIG. 6.6. Sample rating page: Two rating scales applied to competencies.

Section 3 contains the instructions and content for the next domain addressed by the questionnaire. In Fig. 6.7, this is a brief set of items targeting work context. The same suggestions noted earlier apply here as well. Use a clear, concise rating scale and reproduce the scale on each page requiring a response.

Section 4 should be the background information page(s). Far from trivial, this is a critical section of the questionnaire because it determines how one can cut the data on the back end. Thus, it is really important to think ahead about all the relevant comparisons that need to be made. For example, it is often useful to make comparisons between:

- work locations,
- business units or areas of work,
- size of divisions or work groups (e.g., 0–50, 51–100, 101–200, 201–300, more than 300),
- gender and ethnic groups,
- levels in the organization (e.g., manager, supervisor, team leader),
- how people are paid (e.g., hourly wage, salary, commission, base plus commission),
- the hours people work (e.g., straight shift, swing shift, split shift), and
- number of people supervised (e.g., 0–5, 6–10, 11–15, 16–20, 21 or more).

Unless codes are developed and used in this section, it is difficult, if not impossible, to go back and figure it out later.

Consider adding a couple of questions to this section that may be used to establish the respondent as a job content expert. For example:

- tenure with the company,
- number of years in current job or spent supervising individuals in the target job, and
- ask the respondent, "How well do you understand the work activities and competency requirements of the job you are rating?" (e.g., *extremely well, very well, somewhat, not very well, not at all*).

In addition, I often conclude a modeling questionnaire with some question designed to evaluate the comprehensiveness of the content. For example: "To what extent do the work activities (or competencies) presented in this questionnaire describe or fully explain the work performed in the target job?" (e.g., 96% or better, 81%–95%, 71%–80%, 51%–70%, less than 50%). A slightly reconfigured background information page from a recent project with BANK ONE serves as the illustration in Fig. 6.8.

If this section is so important, why is it last? Good question. I suppose it is largely a matter of personal preference, but the reasoning behind it is that it usually makes sense to get your respondents into the meat of the questionnaire

SECTION 3: WORK CONTEXT

The following section describes 18 different job characteristics or features that are typically associated with different jobs. Use the 5-point scale described below to rate the extent to which each characteristic or feature is present in your job.

5 - **Strongly Agree**
4 - **Agree**
3 - **Neutral**
2 - **Disagree**
1 - **Strongly Disagree**

| Agreement |

WORK ITSELF

_____ 1. *Work Variety:* My job allows me to perform a variety of work activities throughout the day and provides opportunities to participate in different initiatives or projects throughout the year.

_____ 2. *Creativity:* My job provides some opportunity to try out new ideas, do things differently, or be creative in terms of how work activities are performed.

_____ 3. *Mentoring:* My job includes the opportunity to teach, mentor, or develop the skills of others.

_____ 4. *Autonomy:* My job provides me some latitude and discretion in setting daily goals and work direction.

_____ 5. *Authority:* My job provides me with the authority or responsibility needed to get the work done quickly and correctly.

WORK CONDITIONS

_____ 6. *Mobility:* My job requires me to physically move about the work location throughout the day to accomplish work.

_____ 7. *Structure:* My job provides me with most of the policies and guidelines I need to solve problems, interact with customers, and so on.

_____ 8. *Work Stress:* My job allows me some measure of control over the amount of work activities required during the day, and it is possible to adjust schedules to ease time pressure when necessary.

_____ 9. *Customer Contact:* My job requires proactive interaction with customers, such that I must initiate much of the contact versus passively waiting for them to come to me.

_____ 10. *Accountability:* People in my job have clear goals to strive for and are held accountable for results.

_____ 11. *Support:* People in my job receive the amount of training and level of supervisory support they need to succeed.

_____ 12. *Performance Tracking:* People in my job have their performance monitored closely and supervisors provide a lot of performance feedback.

WORK BENEFITS (INTRINSIC AND EXTRINSIC)

_____ 13. *Teamwork:* People in my job feel as though they are an important part of a team.

_____ 14. *Development:* My job offers opportunities to learn new work activities and develop new skills.

_____ 15. *Career Planning:* My job is part of a series of jobs that form a clear career path for advancement and clear criteria exist for what it takes to advance.

_____ 16. *Recognition:* People in my job are recognized for their work efforts.

_____ 17. *Strategic Business:* My job is part of an exciting business with a clear vision for the future.

_____ 18. *Compensation:* People in my job are paid appropriately for the work performed.

FIG. 6.7. Sample work context section: Used with white-collar employees.

BANK≡ONE.

Please answer the following background questions about yourself and your role at the bank.
Note: This information is used by the consultants to calculate questionnaire return rate data, and so that we may follow up with questions, if necessary. No one from BANK ONE will ever see individual-level data.

1. Indicate your job or primary work role by circling the appropriate number below.

Western	Midwestern	Southern	Eastern
1. CSA I	11. CSR I	22. CSR I	28. CSR I
2. CSA II	12. CSR II	23. CSR II	29. CSR II
3. CSA III	13. CSR III	24. CSR III	30. CSR III
4. Express Banker	14. Personal Banker I	25. Personal Banker	31. Relationship Banker
5. Relationship Banker	15. Personal Banker II	26. Banking Center Manager	32. Personal Banker
6. Banking Center Asst. Mgr.	16. Personal Banker III	27. Other:_____	33. Banking Center Manager
7. Express Assistant Manager	17. Banking Specialist I		34. Other:_____
8. Banking Center Manager	18. Banking Specialist II		
9. Express Manager	19. Banking Specialist III		
10. Other:_____	20. Banking Center Manager		
	21. Other:_____		

2. In what type of banking location do you work?

    1. Banking Center
    2. In-store
    3. Express

3. In which banking group do you work?

    1. Community
    2. Consumer
    3. Does not apply

4. Which of the following best describes the location of your branch?

    1. Metropolitan/Urban
    2. Outlying/Rural
    3. Suburban

5. How long have you worked for BANK ONE?

    _____ years   _____ months

6. How long have you worked in your current position?

    _____ years   _____ months

7. What is your name? **(OPTIONAL)**

    _____

FIG. 6.8. Background information section: A few general work roles
and many different work locations.

quickly and save the ostensibly ancillary stuff for later. Kraut made the additional point that if these background questions are placed at the beginning of the questionnaire and a respondent does not want to answer them, he or she may decide to stop right there and not answer any of the remaining questions either.[29] Once respondents have completed the bulk of the questionnaire, the thinking is that they will be more likely to complete the background section, perhaps omitting the one or two items of concern, and send it back.

Why might there be any concern? If the questionnaire offers the respondents anonymity, then adding demographic questions can cause respondents to feel that they could, with a little detective work, be identified. In these situations, take the time to think through how these questions will be perceived by respondents and be willing to scale back the number of questions; consider whether you can get by with making the needed comparisons at a more general level so you do not scare off the people you need to hear from.

SAMPLING PLAN

How many people do we need to send the modeling questionnaire to? The information needed for just about any intervention can be met by sampling the available expert pool rather than requiring every individual to participate in your information-gathering process or complete your data-gathering tool. Appropriate information can be collected and used to describe work on the basis of information obtained from a sample, and inferences can then be made about the work performed by the entire population based on the information gained from the responses of the sample. Furthermore, as I hope the discussion from the Information Sources section of this chapter made clear, there are multiple potential expert pools in an organization that are more or less relevant given the particular question(s) one is interested in asking. For a question about *Future Importance*, the entire expert pool for an organization might be judged to be five people. Similarly, the number of true SMEs for questions related to the level of mastery required for full job performance or the difficulty with which proficiency in certain competencies are acquired may be judged to be fairly small (e.g., 20–50 people even in large organizations). Although the concept of sampling applies in these situations, the real payoff of sampling occurs when there are hundreds or thousands of potential experts. In these cases, it makes a great deal of sense to identify that subset of people who will essentially provide you with the same information you would obtain if you had chosen to survey all individuals in the population.

Those situations where the potential expert pool is large typically include job incumbents and supervisors and typically involve surveys that ask questions related to *Current Importance* or *Frequency*. Of course, this information is usually the most basic and universally useful set of data captured in job modeling research (e.g., *Current Importance* data has three stars or is judged to be essential information for virtually every application listed in Table 6.3). Thus, although a discussion of techniques for determining the appropriate sample size for a particular questionnaire in a modeling project is pertinent for all of the potential questions listed in Table 6.4, it is most valuable with reference to the part of the project that uses questionnaires to collect information about the *Current Importance* of work activities and competencies (and perhaps the *Frequency* with which work activities are performed or competencies are utilized).

Unfortunately, fixed rules guiding the number of individuals needed to complete job modeling questionnaires targeting job incumbents and supervisors do not exist. As the sample size approaches the total size of the population in the target job, the sample data become more stable and accurate in reflecting the data that would have been obtained if all target job holders were included in the research. For many years, the only rule of thumb on which most experts would agree is this: The more job incumbents there were, the smaller the percentage of the population that needs to be sampled to obtain a sufficiently large sample. For example, Gael suggested that, when there are up to 300 job incumbents, the sample size might be 100%; if there are from 300 to 500 incumbents in a particular job, the sample size might drop to 60%; and if there are 1,000 to 4,000 incumbents in a particular job to be analyzed, the sample size might drop down to between 30% and 10%.[30] Drauden and Peterson,[31] McCormick,[32] and Roleau and Krain[33] offered similar rules of thumb, although the percentages vary. Somewhat more recently, several research efforts suggest that stable results may be obtained with smaller sample sizes (between 10 and 20 for every conceivable cut or breakout of data to be reported[34,35,36]).

Although broad guidelines based on population size—or those focusing entirely on the minimum samples required to establish numerical reliability—are useful, it is possible to take this line of thinking a couple of steps further. In other words, when evaluating the adequacy of a sample, there are a number of important factors beyond simply considering the relationship between sample and total population size. For example, a job modeling effort that focuses on a highly complex job group (i.e., one in which there are many job duties, the work is dynamic, the results of work are not observable and are difficult to define) requires a larger sample of respondents than an effort examining a job in which the work is low in complexity (i.e., one in which there are few job duties, the work is very routine, the results of work are observable and easy to define). Similarly, a greater number of individuals are required for the sample if the job modeling research is being conducted in a setting where there is expected to be high variability in job duties across work settings and locations rather than a setting where there is expected to be low variability in job duties across settings and locations.

To illustrate this second point, consider a modeling effort that was undertaken for the purpose of developing an assessment center for the individual banking department of First Tennessee Bank. First Tennessee has a large central headquarters and a number of smaller branch offices. In terms of personnel, the size of each branch office varied depending on the location and size of the community it served. Therefore, it was considered quite likely that job content would vary within job titles across the branches. Specifically, it was expected that the duties performed by a customer service representative in a 30-person metropolitan branch can be fairly specific in nature, whereas the same job in a rural, eight-person branch requires the performance of a number of different work activities and familiarity with a broader range of services. Thus, the possibility of variation in job content across branches had implications for how the content of the jobs was sampled; hence, care was taken to design the sampling plan accordingly.

Obviously, the simplest solution would have been to complete the project by collecting all of the information at the central headquarters and then making inferences from this information about what people did in jobs in the branch offices. Instead, we categorized branch offices in terms of size and location and made sure each of the titles included in the job modeling effort were adequately sampled so we could test for differences. Eventually we rolled the information up and used it for our subsequent purpose of developing Test Budget and Assessment Method Matrices to guide the creation of simulations.

Another factor that would increase the need for a larger versus smaller sample is the litigious nature of the environment in which the research is being conducted. If the work is being conducted as a precursor to developing a selection system and is the result of a court order, if there has been a great deal of union activity and interest in the research, if the organization has a history of Title VII challenges or if other similar factors exist, it is a good idea to increase the sample size to increase the surface acceptance of the research. This is not to say that in a nonlitigious environment, for purposes other than developing selection systems (e.g., developing specifications for training, developing a structure for a performance appraisal system, etc.), you can get away with a less than adequate sample. The suggestion here is that it might be worth the effort to go beyond the point of diminishing returns to include more people than would otherwise be deemed necessary, even though increases in the sample size are likely to result in only slight improvements in the quality of the data obtained. These factors illustrate the logical questions that need to be asked to determine whether the sample size is adequate.

Although each situation is different and has its own requirements and variables to be considered, Table 6.5 provides some guideposts that go beyond a one-dimensional rule of thumb. The Questionnaire Sample Determination Table works in the same way as the Interview/Focus Group Sample Determination Table did in chapter 5.[37] Simply determine the number of incumbents in the target job group and identify the base number of questionnaires required (i.e., the number in parentheses and bold print). Then multiply the base number by the multiplier associated with the appropriate response category for each of the remaining 12 impact variables.

TABLE 6.5

Questionnaire Sample Determination Table

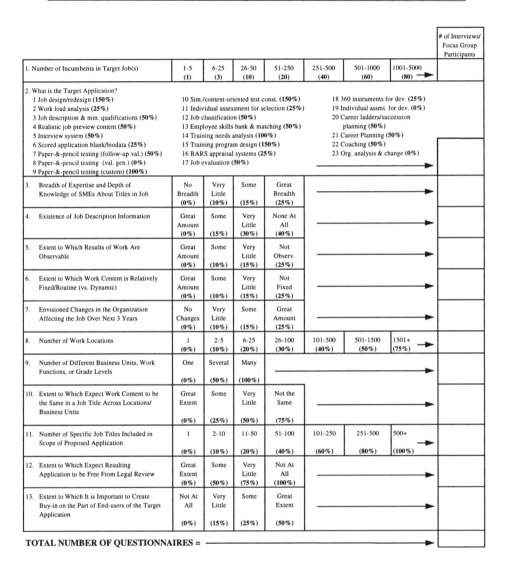

								# of Interviews/ Focus Group Participants
1. Number of Incumbents in Target Job(s)	1-5 (1)	6-25 (3)	26-50 (10)	51-250 (20)	251-500 (40)	501-1000 (60)	1001-5000 (80) →	

2. What is the Target Application?

1 Job design/redesign (150%)	10 Sim./content-oriented test const. (150%)	18 360 instruments for dev. (25%)
2 Work load analysis (25%)	11 Individual assessment for selection (25%)	19 Individual assmt. for dev. (0%)
3 Job description & min. qualifications (50%)	12 Job classification (50%)	20 Career ladders/succession
4 Realistic job preview content (50%)	13 Employee skills bank & matching (50%)	planning (50%)
5 Interview system (50%)	14 Training needs analysis (100%)	21 Career Planning (50%)
6 Scored application blank/biodata (25%)	15 Training program design (150%)	22 Coaching (50%)
7 Paper-&-pencil testing (follow-up val.) (50%)	16 BARS appraisal systems (25%)	23 Org. analysis & change (0%)
8 Paper-&-pencil testing (val. gen.) (0%)	17 Job evaluation (50%)	
9 Paper-&-pencil testing (custom) (100%)		

3. Breadth of Expertise and Depth of Knowledge of SMEs About Titles in Job	No Breadth (0%)	Very Little (10%)	Some (15%)	Great Breadth (25%)			→	
4. Existence of Job Description Information	Great Amount (0%)	Some (15%)	Very Little (30%)	None At All (40%)			→	
5. Extent to Which Results of Work Are Observable	Great Amount (0%)	Some (10%)	Very Little (15%)	Not Observ. (25%)			→	
6. Extent to Which Work Content is Relatively Fixed/Routine (vs. Dynamic)	Great Amount (0%)	Some (10%)	Very Little (15%)	Not Fixed (25%)			→	
7. Envisioned Changes in the Organization Affecting the Job Over Next 3 Years	No Changes (0%)	Very Little (10%)	Some (15%)	Great Amount (25%)			→	
8. Number of Work Locations	1 (0%)	2-5 (10%)	6-25 (20%)	26-100 (30%)	101-500 (40%)	501-1500 (50%)	1501+ (75%) →	
9. Number of Different Business Units, Work Functions, or Grade Levels	One (0%)	Several (50%)	Many (100%)				→	
10. Extent to Which Expect Work Content to be the Same in a Job Title Across Locations/ Business Units	Great Extent (0%)	Some (25%)	Very Little (50%)	Not the Same (75%)			→	
11. Number of Specific Job Titles Included in Scope of Proposed Application	1 (0%)	2-10 (10%)	11-50 (20%)	51-100 (40%)	101-250 (60%)	251-500 (80%)	500+ (100%) →	
12. Extent to Which Expect Resulting Application to be Free From Legal Review	Great Extent (0%)	Some (50%)	Very Little (75%)	Not At All (100%)			→	
13. Extent to Which It is Important to Create Buy-in on the Part of End-users of the Target Application	Not At All (0%)	Very Little (15%)	Some (25%)	Great Extent (50%)			→	

TOTAL NUMBER OF QUESTIONNAIRES = ————————————————→

Returning to the Bank Partners, Inc. case study presented in chapter 4, my assessment of the situation resulted in the following numbers of people being added to the questionnaire sample at each step:

Q1	80 people
Q2	40 people
Q3	8 people
Q4	32 people
Q5	8 people
Q6	12 people
Q7	20 people
Q8	60 people
Q9	0 people
Q10	60 people
Q11	8 people
Q12	60 people
Q13	20 people

The number of suggested questionnaire respondents in this case is 408. Again, this number should not be considered a fixed value. However, it should provide a pretty good starting point number to consider given the complexities and demands associated with the particular job modeling situation.

PROJECT MANAGEMENT TIPS

There are only several tips associated with this step of the Cheshire Strategic Job Modeling Process, but they are important. First of all, be forewarned that your customer, despite all your hard work to develop a wonderful tool, will likely react first to the length of the questionnaire and not the content. Although the questionnaire needs to be as long as it needs to be to serve the intended purpose, look for creative ways to format the questionnaire efficiently to minimize wasted space. More important, there may be ways to divide up the questionnaire content among clearly delineated job level, work function, process, and lines in the target sample. For example, unless it is necessary to make specific comparisons in work content between purely administrative and customer service staff, it may make sense to create two questionnaires by *a priori* culling out clearly unrelated content. Although there is the added burden of creating and managing data from two questionnaires, your customer respondents will have a smaller pill to swallow.

Even though it takes some self-discipline—because at this stage of the project you are probably frazzled from trying to keep up with the scheduled timelines—be sure to stop and pretest the questionnaire. At a minimum, ask several people who are representative of the target population to read the instructions and inventory of descriptor content for clarity and meaningfulness. Better yet, have several people actually respond to the questionnaire so you can verbally debrief them and examine their responses for anomalies.

At least 90% of your customers will want to talk about using various kinds of advanced computer or telecommunications technology to administer or collect questionnaire responses. The hope is that using some form of sophisticated technology will facilitate the process. Of this group, 90% will come to the realization pretty quickly that they are not quite ready, from a technological perspective, to capitalize on that hope. Nevertheless, there are increasing opportunities to take advantage of technology in this part of the endeavor. As you consult with your customer about the pros and cons of the different methods, Table 6.6 may help put some of the potential advantages and disadvantages in perspective.[38]

If you wind up creating paper versions of the questionnaire, it usually makes sense for the surveys to be distributed by the customer organization—for credibility reasons if nothing else. However, it usually makes sense to enclose a return envelope and have the questionnaires sent directly back to someone on the consultant's modeling team. If the questionnaires go out through the organization's own internal mail and distribution system, get an estimate of the time it will take from post to delivery and then double it. For example, if the customer says internal mail usually takes 3 days to get to the most remote locations on the system, assume it will take 6. The internal mail system never works as quickly as the customer thinks, hopes, or prays it will.

Finally, when deciding how many questionnaires to introduce into the system, be sure to build into your thinking the response rate you expect to see. Although I have not formally tracked this over the years, I suspect that a return rate of between 30% and 60% is pretty typical. It helps matters if you are able to clearly indicate on the questionnaire that the instrument is to be completed on company time. Arranging for questionnaires to be completed in a group administration format is a significant plus, but also frequently difficult to arrange. Do not forget that you will likely lose between 2% and 5% of your returned sample because of problems with individual responses identified by the data cleaning efforts described in the next chapter.

TABLE 6.6
Job Modeling Questionnaire Administration and Data Collection Methods

Paper & Pencil

Potential Advantages	Potential Disadvantages/Challenges
+ Low cost to produce and deploy (though mail costs can add up).	− Time to distribute and retrieve questionnaires. Setting up group administration is one way to speed up the process.
+ Recognizable methodology that is familiar and comfortable to most people. This advantage is diminished somewhat if scannable answer sheets are used, which can give the questionnaire the look and feel of a "test."	− Keeping track of the paper trail of responses from large projects can be an administrative challenge.
+ Can be completed anywhere and returned from virtually anywhere.	− Keypunching data for inclusion in electronic files is an extra step that (a) takes time and (b) introduces another way for errors to creep into data. Using a separate scannable answer sheet circumvents keypunching and speeds up the entry of responses, but expect a greater number of rating errors as respondents have to shift back and forth from questionnaire pages to answer sheet page.
+ Flexibility in handling different display formats and last minute changes to questionnaire content (i.e., at least until questionnaires are printed).	

Fax

Potential Advantages	Potential Disadvantages/Challenges
+ Low cost to produce and deploy (though phone costs can add up if there are long distance charges to consider).	− Keeping track of the paper trail of responses from large projects can be an administrative challenge. If multiple page answer sheets are used, this changes from challenge to nightmare.
+ Can be completed anywhere.	− Keypunching data for inclusion in electronic files is an extra step that (a) takes time and (b) introduces another way for errors to creep into the data.
+ Flexibility in handling different display formats and last minute changes to questionnaire content.	
+ Speed with which questionnaire can be put in the hands of respondents and returned for analysis.	− Can be hard to read responses, particularly if responses made on a faxed questionnaire, which is faxed back for analysis.
	− If data are to be completed in different locations, even your customer may be surprised to learn just how many sites do not have fax machines or PCs equipped with a fax board.
	− Potential confidentiality risks due to identification stamp which includes date sent and number of origin.

(continues)

TABLE 6.6 (continued)

Automated Telephone (Push Button, Not Interactive Voice Response)

Potential Advantages	Potential Disadvantages/Challenges
+ Can be completed anywhere there is a telephone.	− Phone costs for long distance charges.
+ Automated retrieval of responses and insertion into centralized data warehouse. Thus, retrieval time, keypunching costs, and potential for keypunching errors are all eliminated.	− Programming time and associated costs for building delivery system.
	− If using voice delivery of the questions, then long questionnaires can become tedious to listen to. If providing respondents with a hard copy of the questionnaire and only retrieving answers using phone number pad, user satisfaction still requires a shorter questionnaire.
+ Novelty and high-tech image, combined with user friendly technology, may lend itself to a higher response rate.	
	− Respondents need to deal with passwords.

PC Diskettes

Potential Advantages	Potential Disadvantages/Challenges
+ Automated retrieval of responses and insertion into a temporary data warehouse (i.e., diskette). Thus, keypunching costs and potential for keypunching errors are eliminated.	− Time to distribute and retrieve diskettes. Setting up group administration may be an option that can speed up the process.
	− Physical transfer of diskettes creates possibility of lost or damaged data files.
+ Novelty and high-tech image may lend itself to a somewhat higher response rate (though PC technology viewed as a hurdle by some people).	− Programming time and associated costs for building a delivery system (unless user needs can be met with off-the-shelf "shell" software).
+ Branching capabilities can be programmed into the software that create significant efficiencies in the administration of long and complex questionnaires.	− Disks fail 3% to 5% of the time.
	− Respondents need to deal with passwords.
	− If one disk designed to be passed around for capturing data from multiple respondents, one person can hold up the process.
	− As with fax-based methods, your customer may be surprised to learn just how many targeted respondents do not have access to PCs.

(continues)

TABLE 6.6 (continued)

E-Mail

Potential Advantages	Potential Disadvantages/Challenges
+ Low delivery costs (unless programming necessary to integrate multiple e-mail technologies across the organization).	− Large organizations may have different e-mail technologies across the system requiring integration and additional programming.
+ Speed with which questionnaire can be put in the hands of respondents and returned for analysis.	− Potential for questionnaires to get lost in individuals' e-mail clutter. This can be a real challenge in organizations where the technology has evolved to monster status, with many individuals receiving upward of 100 e-mails a day.
+ Easy to track actual receipt and opened/read dates.	− Potential confidentiality risks.
+ Reliable data return vehicle. Returned information can be easily harvested and built into files ready for analysis. Thus, retrieval time, keypunching costs, and potential for keypunching errors are all eliminated.	
+ No password required.	
+ High-tech image may lend itself to a higher response rate when dealing with respondent populations comfortable with the technology.	

Internet

Potential Advantages	Potential Disadvantages/Challenges
+ Can build "help" functionality to coach and coax respondents along.	− Requires technology sophisticated users, otherwise detailed supplemental instructions will be necessary.
+ Platform independent, so there should be no problems involving the integration of technology.	− Targeted respondents must have PC access. Moreover, phone line speed and browser capability not always uniformly available across the organization.
+ Reliable data return vehicle. Returned information can be easily harvested and built into files ready for analysis. Thus, retrieval time, keypunching costs, and potential for keypunching errors are all eliminated.	− If questionnaire to be completed anonymously, then there are potential confidentiality risks.
+ Branching capabilities can be programmed into the software that creates significant efficiencies in the administration of long and complex questionnaires.	− Respondents need to deal with passwords.
+ High-tech image may lend itself to a higher response rate when dealing with organizations and respondent populations comfortable with the technology.	

REFERENCES

[1]Tufte, E. R. (1997). *Visual explanations*. Cheshire, CT: Graphic Press.

[2]Equal Employment Opportunity Commission, Civil Service Commission, Department of Labor, & Department of Justice. (1978). Uniform guidelines on employee selection procedures. *Federal Register, 43*(166), 38295–38309.

[3]For a more detailed description of these procedures, see Schippmann, J. S., Hughes, G. L., & Prien, E. P. (1988). Raise assessment standards. *Personnel Journal, 67,* 68–79.

[4]Hughes, G. L., & Prien, E. P. (1989). Evaluation of task and job skill linkage judgments used to develop test specifications. *Personnel Psychology, 42,* 283–292.

[5]Vinchur, A. J., Prien, E. P., & Schippmann, J. S. (1993). An alternative procedure for analyzing job analysis results for content-oriented test development. *Journal of Business and Psychology, 8,* 215–226.

[6]Brush, D. H., & Schoenfeldt, L. F. (1980). Identifying managerial potential: An alternative approach to assessment centers. *Personnel, 57,* 68–76.

[7]Schippmann, J. S., & Prien, E. P. (1986). Psychometric evaluation of an integrated assessment procedure. *Psychological Reports, 59,* 111–122.

[8]Friedman, L. (1990). Degree of redundancy between time, importance, and frequency task ratings. *Journal of Applied Psychology, 75,* 748–752.

[9]Sanchez, J. I., & Levine, E. L. (1989). Determining important tasks within jobs: A policy-capturing approach. *Journal of Applied Psychology, 74,* 336–342.

[10]Sanchez, J. I., & Fraser, S. L. (1992). On the choice of scales for task analysis. *Journal of Applied Psychology, 77,* 545–553.

[11]Harvey, R. J. (1991). Job analysis. In M. D. Dunnette & L. M. Hough (Eds.), *Handbook of industrial and organizational psychology* (Vol. 2, pp. 71–163). Palo Alto, CA: Consulting Psychologists Press.

[12]Equal Employment Opportunity Commission, Civil Service Commission, Department of Labor, & Department of Justice. (1978). Uniform guidelines on employee selection procedures. *Federal Register, 43*(166), 38295–38309.

[13]Society for Industrial and Organizational Psychology. (1987). *Principles for the validation and use of personnel selection procedures* (3rd ed.). College Park, MD: Author.

[14]Goldstein, I. L., & Buxton, V. M. (1982). Training and human performance. In M. D. Dunnette & E. A. Fleishman (Eds.), *Human performance and productivity* (pp. 135–177). Hillsdale, NJ: Lawrence Erlbaum Associates.

[15]This procedure was conceptually similar to the technique described by Ford, K. J., & Wroten, S. P. (1984). Introducing new methods for conducting training evaluation and for linking training evaluation to program redesign. *Personnel Psychology, 37,* 651–665.

[16]Morsh, J. E., & Archer, W. B. (1967). *Procedural guide for conducting occupational surveys in the United States*. Lackland AFB, TX: Personnel Research Laboratory, Aerospace Medical Division, PRL-TR-67-11.

[17]Prien, E. P. (1988). *Job analysis manual*. Unpublished manuscript.

[18]Ammerman, N. L., & Pratzner, F. C. (1977). *Performance content for job training* (R & D Ser. 121–125, Vols. 1–5). Columbus, OH: Center for Vocational Education.

[19]Bendig, A. W. (1952). A statistical report on a revision of the Miami instructor rating sheet. *Journal of Educational Psychology, 43,* 423–429.

[20]Bendig, A. W. (1953). The reliability of self-ratings as a function of the amount of verbal anchoring and the number of categories on the scale. *Journal of Applied Psychology, 37,* 38–41.

[21]Bendig, A. W. (1954). Reliability and number of rating scale categories. *Journal of Applied Psychology, 38,* 38–40.

[22]Finn, R. H. (1972). Effects of some variations in rating scale characteristics on the means and reliabilities of ratings. *Educational and Psychological Measurement, 32,* 255–265.

[23]Reagan, R. T., Mosteller, F., & Youtz, C. (1989). Quantitative meanings of verbal probability expressions. *Journal of Applied Psychology, 74,* 433–442.

[24]Bass, B. M., Cascio, W. F., & O'Connor, E. J. (1974). Magnitude estimations of expressions of frequency and amount. *Journal of Applied Psychology, 59,* 313–320.

[25]Jones, L. V., & Thurstone, L. L. (1955). The psychophysics of semantics: An experimental investigation. *Journal of Applied Psychology, 39,* 31–36.

[26]Lodge, M., & Tursky, B. (1981). The social psychophysical scaling of political opinion. In B. Wegener (Ed.), *Social attitudes and psychophysical measurement.* Hillsdale, NJ: Lawrence Erlbaum Associates.

[27]Lodge, M., Cross, D., Tursky, B., & Tanenhaus, J. (1975). The psychophysical scaling and validation of a political support scale. *American Journal of Political Science, 19,* 611–649.

[28]Spector, P. E. (1976). Choosing response categories for summated rating scales. *Journal of Applied Psychology, 61,* 374–375.

[29]Kraut, A. I. (1996). Planning and conducting the survey: Keeping strategic purpose in mind. In A.I. Kraut (Ed.), *Organizational surveys: Tools for assessment and change* (pp. 149–176). San Francisco: Jossey-Bass.

[30]Gael, S. (1990). *Job analysis: A guide to assessing work activities.* San Francisco, CA: Jossey-Bass.

[31]Drauden, G. M., & Peterson, N. G. (1974). *A domain sampling approach to job analysis.* St. Paul, MN: State of Minnesota Personnel Department. (Available through the Journal Supplement Abstract Service, Catalogue of Selected Documents in Psychology, MS1447).

[32]McCormick, E. J. (1979). *Job analysis: Methods and applications.* New York: AMACOM.

[33]Rouleau, E., & Krain, B. (1975, September–October). Using job analysis to design selection procedures. *Public Personnel Management,* pp. 300–304.

[34]Pass, J. J., & Robertson, D. W. (1980). *Methods to evaluate scales and sample size for stable task inventory information* (Tech. Rep. No. NPRDC TR 80-28). San Diego, CA: Naval Personnel Research and Development Center.

[35]Fletcher, J., Friedman, L., McCarthy, P., McIntyre, C., O'Leary, B., & Rheinstein, J. (1993, April). *Sample sizes required to attain stable job analysis inventory profiles.* Poster presented at the eighth annual conference of the Society for Industrial and Organizational Psychology.

[36]Beatty, G. O. (1996, April). *Job analysis sample size: How small is large enough?* Poster presented at the 11th annual conference of the Society for Industrial and Organizational Psychology, San Diego, CA.

[37]As with the Interview/Focus Group Sample Determination table in chap. 5, these impact variables and associated weights are based primarily on a research effort designed to investigate the key decision points in job modeling projects. Schippmann, J. S. (1996). *Key decision points in job modeling.* Minneapolis, MN: Author.

[38]This exhibit extends some ideas presented by Macey, W. H. (1996). Dealing with the data: Collection, processing, and analysis. In A. I. Kraut (Ed.), *Organizational surveys: Tools for assessment and change* (pp. 204–232). San Francisco, CA: Jossey-Bass.

Chapter 7
How is the Information
Analyzed and Displayed?

> *... you should make everything as simple as possible,
> but not simpler. ...*
>
> —Albert Einstein

In his book *The Discoverers*, historian Daniel Boorstin discussed one of the great advances in learning that began in the Ch'in era of China (221-207 b.c.).[1] China had unified and the Chou emperor presided over a vast realm with many unique regions, many of which were uncharted. While the masters of geography in Europe were trundling along in their efforts to map out earthly space using a hodgepodge of fantasy and dogma, the cartographic talents in China were marching ahead toward a quantitative cartography. Phei Hsui, Minister of Works to the first emperor of the Ch'in Dynasty, wrote openly about his successful methods, which included providing error-free and comprehensive descriptions of the landscape using a quantitative means for making graduated divisions. Without these ingredients, he warned, "there is no means of distinguishing between what is near and what is far." The resulting maps, which provided meaningful receptacles in which the virtually endless territory could be discerned and described, "proved to be an indispensable apparatus for the empire" (i.e., they were a source of competitive advantage).

The leap from what the Chou emperor envisioned and the work that Phei Hsui completed is not as far removed from the work of a modern-day job modeler as the intervening millennia might suggest. The landscape of work and human capital remains poorly charted and understood in most organizations and, as a consequence, fantasy and dogma prevail. There are a number of ways a job modeler can proceed at this point to capture the contours of work performed by the people who populate an organization and configure and display the extensive regions of human talent. Although your own creativity and willingness to learn from mistakes will serve you best, my hope is that the approach and data-based information displays presented in this chapter are useful points of departure and landmarks.

The key is not to get lost as one navigates through the vast expanse of information that exists at this stage in the modeling research. Keeping your bearings is easier if you remember the four basic steps to analyzing modeling data generated from a questionnaire process: (a) establish data quality, (b) data reduction, (c) item-level data analysis, and (d) data display.

The conceptual gist of this chapter can be understood without a deep understanding of mathematics or statistics. I do not believe that everyone who drives to work in the morning needs to have an understanding of the internal combustion engine. Neither do I believe that everyone who has data to analyze needs to have an understanding of matrix algebra, statistical notation, and so forth. Feel safer now? Good. This does not mean that a rudimentary understanding of fundamental descriptive statistics (e.g., mean and standard deviation) and measures of association (e.g., correlation) would not help. It would. For this reason, a quick brush up on these concepts is provided as we move through the chapter. For those who are interested, in those places where the discussion leads down a more difficult path, some technical elaboration is provided in Appendix B.

Furthermore, perhaps the most convenient platforms for using the statistical techniques mentioned in this chapter are contained in popular software packages of statistical programs such as SPSS,[2] SAS,[3] and BMDP.[4] These packages provide relative computer neophytes (well, at least nonprogrammers) with fairly easy access to sophisticated statistical methods for researching a wide range of topics relevant for those who deal with people and business data. These packages also contain a full array of data screening and manipulation methods that can make potentially very complicated analyses fairly straightforward. To some extent, they also provide an introduction and description of the statistical methods they cover in associated manuals, pocket guides, and newsletters. In addition, a number of readable statistics texts are available that provide examples of how these software packages are used to analyze various data sets.[5,6]

ESTABLISH DATA QUALITY

The first consideration at this step of the strategic job modeling process is to evaluate the data obtained from the questionnaire sample, including job incumbents, supervisors, customers, or whomever, to determine if the data are clean and reliable. This is a quality control check—establishing the *goodness* of the data before they are used to guide subsequent decisions (i.e., decisions about what to include in a job description, identification of critical competencies to target in selection specifications, and so forth).

Data Cleaning

Errors in the data are like sugar in the gas tank of your project. If not caught early, they will gum everything up, bring you to a standstill at some point down the road, and cost you a lot of time as you look under the hood to try and find the problem. Actually, the worst-case scenario is that the errors will go undetected and result in incorrect conclusions that are translated into incorrect decisions or emphases in the subsequent HR applications. So, once questionnaire responses have been typed, scanned, or somehow recorded into electronic files, organize a hunting party to identify respondent and data coding errors.

Okay. Grit your teeth. It is time to introduce several basic statistical concepts before we move forward.

Frequency:	When data have been collected from a group of persons, it becomes possible to count the number of people who have the same response to a particular question. For example, for a question that uses a 5-point response scale, how many people selected a response value of 3? The answer is the frequency of that response.
Distribution:	A data display that shows the frequency or number of times a value occurs for each response option across the range of potential responses for a particular question.
Percentage:	Frequencies can easily be transformed into percentages in a couple of ways. First, each of the frequencies in a distribution could be multiplied by 100, then divided by the total number of cases or "N." Second, it is possible to find the quotient of 100/N to four decimal places and multiply each frequency by this ratio.
Mean:	The average response, which is an index of the center of the response values in a distribution. The mean is calculated by adding up the values of all the numbers in the distribution and dividing by the total number of values (i.e., the sum of the frequencies for each question or response category in the distribution).
Standard Deviation:	A measure of the amount of variation or spread of responses around the mean of a distribution. In other words, are all the responses tightly packed around the mean (i.e., small standard deviation)

or are responses spread out across the full range of response categories (i.e., large standard deviation)? This measure is computed by summing all the squared individual response deviations from the mean and dividing by N, yielding a statistic called the *variance*. The square root of the variance is the standard deviation.

Data cleaning can be best accomplished by examining frequency distributions to identify confirmed outliers or response values that fall outside the feasible response range for a question. For example, if we calculate the frequency with which each response option is endorsed for each question on a questionnaire that uses a 0–5 rating scale and we identify several 6s and 7s, we have flushed out some outliers. These outliers are confirmed because their values clearly fall out of bounds for what we know to be the real data range.

Potential outliers are a different kind of animal altogether and much more difficult to ferret out and deal with. Suppose we calculated response frequencies for a question that asks how frequently a work activity is performed. On review of the data, we see that 1 person selected a value of 1 (i.e., the activity is never performed), yet the other 15 respondents in the group, all with the same job title, endorsed this question at the 4 or 5 level. Have we uncovered someone who is using the rating scale incorrectly? Or is this person accurately portraying what he or she does do on the job and the fact of the matter is that he or she does something different?

As a first step, it makes sense to red flag these potential outliers and, on a case-by-case basis, investigate their other responses to see if there are other oddball answers that would lead us to consider excluding an individual's data from further analysis. Of course, if the questionnaire was not completed anonymously, it is always possible to go back to the individual and confirm the responses or check with supervisors to see if the responses could conceivably be correct. Despite that a few really out-of-whack values can distort the measures of group average (i.e., mean) and agreement (i.e., standard deviation) used to display the final results, it is best not to exclude any data unless you are sure you are dealing with random, or otherwise bogus, responses.

One tactic for identifying potential outliers is to use a random response scale, in which items are included that people would definitely endorse in a particular way if they were actually reading the items and taking the questionnaire seriously. For example, several items might be included in the work activity section of the questionnaire that we know all respondents do, in fact, perform, and several items we know all respondents do not, in fact, perform. A few items of this type in the questionnaire allows one to calculate a random response score and then exclude bad-apple respondents based on some agreed-on criterion with reference to this scale.[7,8,9,10]

Another early detection technique is to simultaneously compare two or more distributions of data. For example, if the questionnaire cuts across job levels in the organization, one might—based on the knowledge that females are underrepresented in higher level jobs in this organization—cross-tabulate gender and two or three breaks of job level. If the representation of females and males is not what you would expect to see as you move from lower to upper job levels, it might signal the presence of some congealed sweet stuff in your project's gas tank.

Finally, it sounds so trite that I hesitate to say it, but I will because it is so important: Understand your data! This implies an understanding of the organization and the people completing the modeling questionnaire. Having some idea of what you expect to find in the results and carefully checking these benchmark expectations will better serve you in efforts to identify potential problems than will any list of data cleaning techniques.

Data Reliability

Fundamentally, reliability concerns the consistency or repeatability of a measure. In a technical sense, this means that the data are free from random error variability resulting from people misunderstanding a question, having a lapse in motivation or focus regarding the rating task at hand, being distracted for any of a thousand reasons, and so forth. As Aldous Huxley so aptly put it, the only completely consistent people are the dead. Thus, to the extent that we limit ourselves to modeling research with live people, our data will have some built-in error. The question then becomes, how much? For a concept with such apparent simplicity, the measurement of reliability in job modeling research is a little convoluted and somehow often less than completely satisfying.

Let us start with the most straightforward situation first. Assume importance ratings are being collected from a panel of job content experts. Further, assume all of these experts have a clear mental picture of the job or role being modeled. In this case, it is possible to look at the degree of agreement in their ratings. Time to define another statistical concept:

Correlation Coefficient: An index of the degree of association between two entities, such as importance ratings by job incumbents for a work activity and ratings by supervisors for the same activity. The correlation or r coefficient has a potential maximum value of +1.0 and a potential minimum value of -1.0, indicating perfectly positive and perfectly negative relationships respectively. A positive value means high values on one entity tend to be related to high values on the second entity. When the correlation is perfectly positive (i.e., +1.0 ... but do not hold your breath, this is very rare) then the two entities covary in perfect unison. However, when there is no relationship between two entities, then $r = 0$. Finally, a negative relationship means as values on one entity go up, values on the second entity tend to go down (i.e., an inverse relationship).

In the situation described earlier, one could use a correlation coefficient to examine the level of agreement among all possible pairs of expert judges in their ratings across work activities, competencies, or whatever. However, using correlations as a measure of reliability with this kind of rating judgment works best when the people performing the rating task have a clear understanding of the work to be performed.

For example, if importance judgments are being collected from a broad range of job incumbents, the meaningfulness of looking at correlations among raters is greatly reduced. Different ratings from individuals with the same job title can reflect error in ratings. On the other hand, in this context, they can also reflect meaningful differences in work performed by people who just happen to have the same job title. To an extent, the value of between-rater correlations as an index of reliability is enhanced if they are calculated within consolidated job groups, as would be the case after using factor or cluster methods to identify relatively homogenous subgroupings of positions. Even then, however, one should proceed cautiously in interpreting the results.

It is also possible to readminister the modeling questionnaire to the entire respondent group, or a small subsample thereof, and use correlations to examine the stability of the ratings across two points in time. Because of the time and cost implications, this is seldom a realistic alternative.[11,12] Yet as with most things, the cost would probably be less of an issue if the gain were worth the pain. Unfortunately, this is rarely the case because of difficulties in interpreting these data as well. Brief time intervals between administrations may make the second installment of ratings as much of a test of memory or recall as an independent collection of rating information. Although it is certainly possible to underestimate the reliability of a modeling data set using this kind of Time 1, Time 2 design, it is likely that the more typical situation is an overestimation due to memory. Of course, if the interval between administrations is too great, low correlations could reflect low reliability or true changes to the job or role over time.

An intuitively appealing approach to tapping reliability is to repeat a small sample of items in the questionnaire and examine the consistency of the ratings in the same administration. However, whenever I have done this (either intentionally or unintentionally), it has been picked up on by the respondent group and they did not like it. The general feeling was along the lines that we were trying to sneak something past them ... and they slammed us for it.

The split-half method for assessing reliability can also be employed based on one administration of the modeling questionnaire. This method is useful with long, multidimensional questionnaires, where the group of items defining each dimension may be divided into halves and the scores on the halves correlated to obtain an estimate of reliability. The result would be a correlation for each subgrouping or dimension of items in the questionnaire. In actuality, these correlations would be the reliability of each half of the items in the dimension versus the entire dimension. Therefore, a statistical correction is necessary so that an estimate of the reliability for the complete dimensions may be found rather than for each half. This statistical correction is known as the Spearman–Brown prophecy formula; it was derived, as luck would have it, by a couple of fellows named Spearman[13] and Brown.[14] Used in this case, where each set of items in a dimension is twice as long as each half, the appropriate formula is:

$$r_{xx} = 2r/(1+r).$$

In this formula, r_{xx} is the reliability for an entire dimension of items and r is the split-half correlation.

Cronbach's alpha is a logical extension of the split-half method that does not require the splitting of items.[15] Instead, alpha depends on the average intercorrelation among all of the descriptor items comprising a particular dimension (i.e., versus calculating alpha for the entire inventory of items as a whole). In other words, alpha is proportionately equivalent to the mean of all possible combinations of split-half correlations for a particular dimension. From a somewhat different perspective, alpha can be thought of as an estimate of the expected correlation between one dimension of ratings with a hypothetical twin sister dimension with a distinct set of descriptor items.[16]

Unfortunately, receiving good data is not an inalienable right, so proceed carefully. Small oversights or flaws in your thinking early in the process can become huge problems later in the project. Protect yourself from building models with dubious data by taking the little bit of extra time needed to look at the reliability question from a couple of vantage points before moving forward and making decisions based on the data.

DATA REDUCTION

At this stage of the game, your data can be like a gushing, swollen river and, if you are not careful, you will drown. Consequently, the next step in this phase of the project is typically some form of data reduction to reduce the massive amounts of information into more discrete units. The focus of this data reduction can be either the job (assuming more than one job is being modeled) or the individual descriptor items. Each is discussed in turn.

Consolidating Jobs

As discussed in chapter 2, a position is easily defined because of its association with one employee. There are just as many positions in the organization as employees. Although it might not seem so at first glance, terms like *job, job group,* and *job family* are more difficult to clearly define. This is because, above the level of position, the titles we use to group clusters of jobs are mere labels that may change based on the composition of the group, which may change for any of a number of reasons. In fact, even the mix of work activities and competencies that comprise the material of a job or bundle of jobs is merely a contrivance designed to suit the needs of the organization, and these needs can change. As a result, the number and distinctiveness of jobs in most organizations is terribly unclear.[17]

For example, the work performed by assistant store managers of a recent client in the grocery retail business varied a great deal depending on the size of the retail outlet. Because store associate turnover was averaging about 180% in the larger metropolitan stores, which is another story altogether, assistant store managers in large stores were essentially working as staffing and training specialists. In the smaller stores, where both the base number of store associates and the level of turnover was lower, they were performing the same range of activities as store managers. The result was two pretty distinct job groups, although the job title was the same. To further complicate matters, an updated performance management system grouped the store managers, assistant store managers, and department managers into one job—entry level management—versus three distinct jobs. As this example illustrates, the definition and delineation of *jobs* can be a murky business.

Hence, the purpose of data-reduction techniques in this context is to discover the similarities and differences between the smallest number of meaningful groups of jobs. In this sense, the job consolidation effort is both a product and a process.[18] The product is a smaller and more meaningful set of bundled jobs, which is important for a wide range of organizationally relevant reasons. For example, instead of having to create unique selection tools for distinct job groups, the questionnaire data can be analyzed to discover broad groupings of jobs that require the same basic competencies and that may profit in terms of enhanced screening outcomes using the same selection procedures. Instead of having to develop and deliver different training offerings to jobs in different business units, job groupings may be established that cut across business unit boundaries, thereby increasing the efficiency of the training function. Further, instead of creating performance appraisal forms unique to every position in the organization, meaningful job groups may be identified that capture important similarities and, as a consequence, reduce the sheer number of unique forms used throughout the system. The absence of a meaningful way for organizing work and thinking about jobs is a major challenge to the efficient selection, development, and deployment of an organization's human capital.

A wide range of statistical procedures has been used to systematically arrange jobs into meaningful categories,[19] including repeated-measures analysis of variance (ANOVA),[20] canonical correlation,[21] and multidimensional scaling.[22] However, there are two predominant classes of grouping statistics: factor analysis and cluster analysis.

Based on the advice of every single person who read the original version of this chapter (10 in all), several of whom were downright threatening in the tone of their review, I decided to cull out the detailed discussion of these two grouping statistics. In so doing, I have smoothed out the level of complexity of the chapter immeasurably. However, this *is* supposed to be a how-to book. As Jean Valjean laments in *Les Miserables*, "How could I ever face myself again" if I didn't follow through on my promise? The answer is, I couldn't. So, what is a well-intentioned author to do? Well, I snuck it back in.

For those readers who can live without a detailed discussion of the technical ins and outs of this complex stage of the modeling process, the next several pages should suffice. For those who are interested in pursuing the topics further, scoot the dog out of your favorite reading chair, turn to the technical discussion in Appendix B, and settle down for an uninterrupted hour or so.

Q-Factor Analysis

Factor analysis refers to a family of statistical grouping techniques whose common goal is to take some large and confusing mass of potentially interrelated things and boil them down into a much smaller and understandable set of things. This becomes possible if we know the degree of association (e.g., correlation) or interrelationships between all possible pairs of things one wishes to analyze.

Specifically, one would use a variant of factor analysis that rotates the data matrix so that individual respondents are in the columns and are considered the *variables*, whereas the questions of the questionnaire from the rows assume the position of *subjects*. This technique is called *Q-factor analysis*. For example, suppose 300 people representing a broad mix of jobs in an organization each completed a 100-item questionnaire. The first step would be to use one of the statistical software packages noted at the beginning of this chapter to compute the correlation of each person's responses with every other (i.e., one position with another). One might then visually inspect the resulting table of 44,850 correlations. However, this mass of data is too big to try and work through visually to identify patterns or bundles of positions. Instead, you would be much better served turning to your favorite statistical software package and submitting the 300 x 300 matrix of correlations to a factor analysis. Actually, each of the statistical software packages listed earlier calculate the correlation matrix and run the factor analysis in one fell swoop.

The way factor analysis works is to analyze the matrix of interrelationships between all possible pairs of variables (i.e., positions in this case). The matrix is

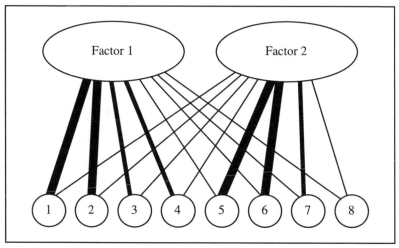

FIG. 7.1. General description of factor-analytic techniques (Note: the thicker the connecting line, the stronger the relationship.)

actually analyzed in a series of iterative passes through the data to identify factors or groups to which each variable could conceivably belong. In other words, this approach allows for overlap between groups, and variables can conceivably be grouped into more than one factor. This concept is illustrated in Fig. 7.1, where the circles across the bottom (1–8) represent individual positions. Want to learn more? Take a look at the more elaborate discussion and the BANK ONE case example presented in Appendix B.

Cluster Analysis

Cluster analysis refers to a second class of job grouping techniques, and the double entendre here is by design. Once referred to as the poor man's factor analysis because of its computational and conceptual simplicity,[23] cluster analysis is now one of the more widely used methods of job consolidation.[24] This despite that most cluster methods are merely loose collections of plausible algorithms for creating clustered groups of entities, which is in contrast to the extensive body of statistical reasoning supporting factor analysis.[25]

Cluster analysis procedures work in a manner that, in some ways, is quite different from factor analysis. Cluster analysis forms a symmetric matrix of interrelationships between all possible pairs of variables (which is what factor analysis does), but then it analyzes this matrix in a series of steps to create mutually exclusive clusters or groupings of variables (which is different from factor analysis). The idea behind this approach is characterized in Fig. 7.2. Again, the circles across the bottom represent individual positions. The number of circles at each

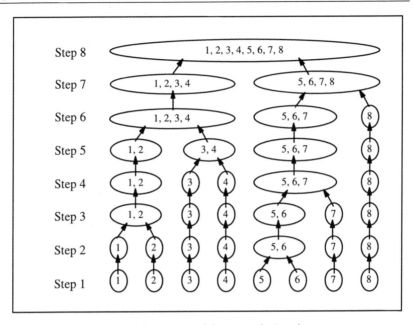

FIG. 7.2. General description of cluster analysis techniques.

stage represent the number of clusters at that stage of the analysis. Again, for those who desire a more elaborate discussion, take a look at the case study presented in Appendix B.

Consolidating Items

A second information-reduction effort focuses on the individual descriptor items. Frequently there are several hundred specific work activity, competency, and/or some other type of descriptor statements to be considered. The goal here is to reduce the total pool of activity items, competency items, and so on to a smaller set of basic categories to increase the meaning and usefulness of the results.

This classification work can proceed on qualitative or quantitative grounds. The rationally based content analysis procedures described in chapter 5 can be used here to group work activity and competency items for display purposes. Or, statistical procedures, such as factor analysis, can be used to group similar items together based on differences in degree with respect to some quality they have in common (e.g., using factor analysis to derive work activity dimensions based on *Current Importance* ratings of specific statements). Actually, this type of factor analysis (R-factor vs. Q-factor) is the more conventional way to use these statistics—where items serve as the variables to be grouped and not people or positions. Cluster analysis approaches may also be used to identify groups of items, but my view is that these procedures are better suited for job consolidation, rather than item consolidation efforts. For this reason, they are not considered in the discussion here nor are they covered in Appendix B.

ITEM-LEVEL DATA ANALYSIS

Once the job target (or targets) has been clearly grouped and defined, and once the configuration or grouping of descriptor content has been established, it is time to analyze the item-level responses to the questionnaire. Statistical analysis of the item-level ratings is used to identify and describe various aspects of jobs (e.g., the *Current Importance* or *Difficulty* of work dimensions and the specific statements subsumed in each). Typically this involves using means, standard deviations, and percentages created from the ratings and decision rules applied to these indexes to highlight and define these various aspects. Let us begin with the simple example in Table 7.1. Assume that a comprehensive work activity-based questionnaire has been given to a large sample of clerical workers at a consumer electronics company. Among other judgments, the respondents were asked to use a 5-point rating scale to evaluate the *Current Importance* of each activity statement. Three of the statements are reproduced below, along with the associated mean and standard deviation for the *Current Importance* ratings and the percent of respondents who reported performing the activities above a 2 on the 5-point rating scale.

To determine which activities should be used to describe the work performed by these clerical respondents, it becomes necessary to decide on some minimum statistical criteria that must be met to be considered important. To continue with the example, one might stipulate that a work activity item must have a mean rating of 3.00 or higher. The higher the mean, the more important the activity is to the job. The exact point you set the cutoff should be tied to the meaning of the interval definitions of the scale. In setting the cutoff at 3.00, we are stating that we are interested in selecting only those work activities that are

TABLE 7.1
Sample Item-Level Printout

	Activity	Mean	SD	% > 2
1.	Check forms or records against documents or master forms to ensure accuracy and completeness.	4.34	.56	91.7%
2.	Place forms, records, and correspondence in correct location in a systematic file.	3.12	1.41	71.5%
3.	Notify or remind certain individuals of meetings, rescheduled dates, or specific events.	2.15	1.11	44.1%

clearly *"important* for successful performance in either the *whole job* or a *major part of the job."* The language of this scale is linked to the language expressed in the *Uniform Guidelines*[26] and serves as an external standard. Depending on the intended purpose of the job analysis data and the specific setting in which data are collected, you might decide to adjust the cutoff downward (e.g., 2.5) or upward (e.g., 3.5). For this example, however, let us stick with 3.0. Thus, for those statements listed earlier, our criterion for inclusion indicates that we should use Items 1 and 2 to describe the work performed by these clerical workers.

A second cutoff point might require that a work activity have a standard deviation of 1.25 or lower. The lower the standard deviation, the greater the degree of agreement among respondents in the evaluations of importance. Use of this standard needs to be carefully monitored because variations in the number of respondents and the type of content being rated can affect the value of the standard deviation. Also, variability in ratings can represent either rating errors or real differences in job composition. Given these considerations, you may or may not wish to include the standard deviation as a fixed decision rule. In our example, when the standard deviation is used in combination with the mean *Current Importance* rating of 3.0 or higher, Statement 2 is dropped. As a result, only one of the three statements in the prior example is used to describe the work of the respondents (Item 1).

A third possible criterion might be that most respondents (e.g., 75% or more) must agree that the activity is at least somewhat important for successful job performance (i.e., ratings of 2.0 or higher using the *Current Importance* scale in chap. 6). Applying this criterion to our example, Statements 2 and 3 would be excluded from the description of work. At this point in the example, this does not change the final result, so only Statement 1 is retained.

Using these basic statistics and decision rules (singly or in combination), certain statements are retained and added to other statements to build or model various descriptions of work content. The descriptions can be in terms of important work content, as in the earlier example, the *Frequency* with which certain activities are performed, the *Difficulty* with which certain competencies are acquired, and so forth. In summary, the respondents' answers to these questions provide information for the definition of work content. The statistics and decision rules that are applied to the obtained data are then used to summarize information and create displays that may be used to guide future work (such as selecting, developing, or modifying various human capital management programs).

There is a substantial amount of human judgment involved in even the most technical aspects of a modeling endeavour. As Dunnette, Hough, and Rosse observed, "[we] know of no methodology, statistical technique, or objective measurement that can negate the importance of ... rational judgment as an important element in the process of deriving behavior and task information about jobs and of using that information to develop or justify human resource programs."[27] Thus, the quantitative procedures used to create empirically de-rived models do not remove or subjugate human judgment; they only permit a more systematic and enlightened form of judgment to occur.

DATA DISPLAY

First and foremost, it is useful to develop a high-level picture of the behavioral terrain being modeled. One way to do this is to create a map of the work activi-ties, competencies, and/or other descriptor content being modeled. If the mod-eling work was only conducted with a targeted job group, such as store manager jobs, this might mean a dimension-level description or map of the work land-scape. If you jump ahead a bit to Table 7.4, you will find an example displaying the competencies for a regional sales director.

However, if the modeling project was organization-wide and covered all func-tions and work levels, the map might be more involved. A map of the competen-cies for a semifictitous retail consumer electronics company appears in Table 7.2. There is no one best way to display topological information of this kind, so Table 7.2 should be considered only one possibility versus a prescription. In this exhibit, the complete list of competency dimensions identified in the modeling work is crossed by the four primary business units of the organization. Further, the organi-zation's competency dictionary (i.e., the comprehensive list of competency di-mensions) is segmented into those classes of competencies that are:

- core or organization-wide and that cut across all business units, job levels, and job functions;
- business unit specific and support the strategies of particular business groups;
- linked to job level and define the expectations of vertically arranged job groups; and
- functionally specific and define the technical knowledge and skills re-quired to perform successfully in different functional areas of the business.

Table 7.2 also makes the distinction between general transferable competen-cies (i.e., the first three classes of competencies defined in the exhibit) and tech-nical (or functional specific) competencies (i.e., the last category defined in the exhibit). The Xs in the table indicate that a particular set of competencies is im-portant for performing work for some job or class of jobs in a particular business unit. This conceptualization helps provide a basis for identifying what is com-mon across jobs versus simply looking at jobs and job groups individually. In ad-dition, this display structure permits an examination of the broader sets of worker attributes that may be important for organizational match above and be-yond job fit.

TABLE 7.2

Competency Map: Consumer Electronics Example

			Competency Dimension	BU#1 Corporate	BU#2 Domestic Markets	BU#3 Global Markets	BU#4 Product Develop'm't
General Transferable Competencies	**A.** Organization-Wide or Core Competencies		1. Analyze Issues	X	X	X	X
			2. Innovation	X	X	X	X
			3. Verbal Communication	X	X	X	X
	B. Business Unit-Specific Competencies		4. Build Org. Relationships	X			
			5. Entrepreneurial Risk Taking				X
			6. Customer Orientation	X	X	X	
			7. Negotiation Skills		X	X	
			8. Global Perspective			X	
	C. Job Level-Specific Competencies	Exec.	9. Visionary Thinking	X	X	X	X
			10. Champion Change	X	X	X	X
		Mgmt.	10. Champion Change	X	X	X	X
			11. Provide Direction	X	X	X	X
		Indiv. Contr.	11. Provide Direction	X	X	X	X
			12. Coach Others	X	X	X	X
			13. Listening Skills	X	X	X	X
		Non-Exempt	13. Listening Skills	X	X	X	X
			14. Work Efficiently	X	X	X	X
Technical/Functional-Specific Competencies	**D.** Job Function-Specific Competencies	Accounting	15. Financial Statements & Analysis	X	X	X	X
			16. Basic Bookkeeping and Accounting	X	X	X	X
			17. Management Accounting	X	X	X	X
			18. Auditing	X			
			19. Taxation	X			
		Computer Systems	20. Basic Computer Operation	X	X	X	X
			21. Hardware & Peripherals	X			X
			22. Computer Language/Programming				X
			23. Database Management	X	X	X	X
			24. Information Systems	X			X
			25. Computer Analysis Techniques				X
		Facilities Mgmt.	26. Tactical Planning				X
			27. Logistics Management				X
			28. Security	X	X	X	X
		Finance & Economics	29. Corporate Financial Management	X	X	X	X
			30. Global Economics			X	
			31. Investments	X			
			32. International Corporate Finance	X		X	

(continues)

TABLE 7.2 (continued)

Technical/Functional Specific Competencies	**D. Job Function-Specific Competencies**	**Marketing**	33.	Market Research & Analysis		X	X	
			34.	Product		X	X	X
			35.	Advertising	X	X	X	
			36.	International Marketing	X		X	
		Personnel & Management	37.	HR Planning/Forecasting	X			X
			38.	Staffing	X	X	X	X
			39.	Compensation	X			
			40.	Training	X	X	X	
			41.	Labor Relations	X			X
		Operations Mgmt.	42.	Process Planning				X
			43.	Process Design				X
			44.	Process Control				X
		Engineering	45.	Electromechanical Systems		X	X	X
			46.	Microelectronic Fabrication		X	X	X
			47.	Signals and Systems		X	X	X
			48.	Field and Wavelength Electromagnetics		X	X	X
			49.	Basic Math	X	X	X	X
			50.	Linear and Abstract Algebra				X
			51.	Differential Geometry				X
		Administrative	16.	Basic Bookkeeping and Accounting	X	X	X	X
			20.	Basic Computer Operation	X	X	X	X
			49.	Basic Math	X	X	X	X
			52.	Data Entry	X	X	X	X
			53.	Process Written Material	X	X	X	X
			54.	Scheduling and Coordinating	X	X	X	X
			55.	Research and Evaluation	X	X	X	X
		Sales	56.	Sales Prospecting		X	X	
			57.	Sales Presentation		X	X	
			58.	Overcoming Objectives		X	X	
			59.	Sales Management		X	X	

X = hardwired; this competency is a fixed part of the model for all jobs for this job family.

Keep in mind that this is just a kind of superordinate map, offering views from 20,000 feet. Observations closer to the ground are usually more useful and may be made using a variety of more detailed displays. This map and the subsequent sample displays in this chapter focus on competency information. The same ideas and displays may be used with work activities or other types of information. In fact, often two or three complementary maps of information are required to comprehensively describe the results of a modeling effort.

With reference to more precise displays, there are a variety of options. Broadly speaking, detailed data-based information displays can be developed for two primary purposes: (a) to create displays for making within-group com-

TABLE 7.3
Display Options

Within-Group Displays

1.	Within-Group Profile	Table 7.4	■	Makes within-group comparisons at the dimension-level and reports a graphic display and dimension mean averages (aggregating across items in a dimension).
2.	Item List	Table 7.6	■	Makes comparisons at the item level and reports a sorted listing of items and various descriptive statistics.
3.	Job Description	Figure 7.3	■	Creates a non-data-based display of sorted and ranked dimensions and items for activities, competencies, or both.
4.	Part-of-Job Wheel	Figure 7.4	■	Displays the relative weight, in terms of a percentage, of each dimension involved in the description of a group.

Across-Group Displays

5.	Group by Dimension Matrix	Table 7.10	■	Makes comparisons across target groups at the dimension-level by reporting mean averages.
6.	Group Comparison	Table 7.11	■	Makes graphic profile comparisons for multiple target groups at the dimension-level.
7.	Group Emphasis Distribution	Table 7.12	■	Makes a combined data and graphic display juxtaposing the relative emphasis weights (part-of-job or recruitment and selection focus or training and development focus) for multiple groups.

parisons (where *group* can mean a job, job family, class of jobs in a value chain, etc.), and (b) to create displays for making across-group comparisons. A snapshot description of some of the displays that can be useful in different settings appears in Table 7.3. A brief walkthrough description and example should highlight the potential value of each.

Within-Group Profile

This is probably the most basic and widely applicable display of the different samples presented in this chapter. Building on the consumer electronics company example, Table 7.4 illustrates a within-group profile for the regional sales director job from the Domestic Markets business unit. The display offers a box and whisker graph, which is a variation of the plot proposed by Tukey,[28] where the value in the box is the mean and the whisker represents one standard deviation on either side of the mean for the competency items that define each competency. In other words, all the items comprising a particular dimension are aggregated and the average rating and overall standard deviation across all respondents in the group are reported. The display allows for comparisons at the dimension level for a particular group of respondents applying some rating scale (such as Importance) to a common set of items.

Expanding out to give the big picture view, Table 7.5 presents the same information, but does so within the context of the entire competency map. A value of 0 in a box indicates a competency category that clearly was not part of the definition of the target job. As a result, it is part of a set of items that the respondent group, regional sales directors in this case, never even responded to in the ques-

TABLE 7.4

Within-Group Profile: Regional Sales Director, Domestic Markets

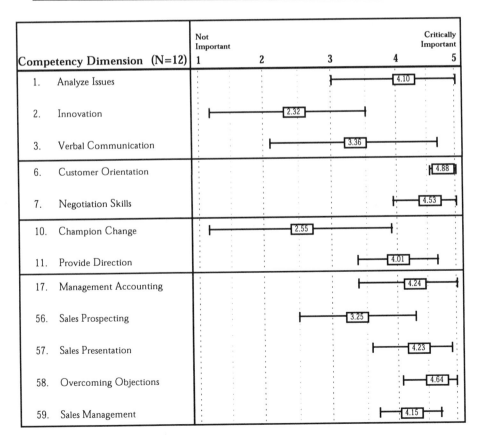

TABLE 7.5

Within-Group Profile: Regional Sales Director, Domestic Markets

		Competency Dimension	Not Part of Job 0	Not Important 1	2	3	4	Critically Important 5
General Transferable Competencies	**A.** Organization-Wide or Core Competencies	1. Analyze Issues					4.10	
		2. Innovation			2.32			
		3. Verbal Communication				3.36		
	B. Business Unit-Specific Competencies	4. Build Org. Relationships	0					
		5. Entrepreneurial Risk Taking	0					
		6. Customer Orientation						4.88
		7. Negotiation Skills						4.53
		8. Global Perspective	0					
	C. Job Level Specific Competencies — Exec.	9. Visionary Thinking	0					
		10. Champion Change	x					
	Mgmt.	10. Champion Change			2.55			
		11. Provide Direction					4.01	
	Indiv. Contr.	11. Provide Direction	x					
		12. Coach Others	0					
		13. Listening Skills	0					
	Non-Exempt	13. Listening Skills	0					
		14. Work Efficiently	0					
Technical/Functional-Specific Competencies	**D.** Job Function-Specific Competencies — Accounting	15. Financial Statements & Analysis	0					
		16. Basic Bookkeeping & Acctng.	0					
		17. Management Accounting					4.24	
		18. Auditing	0					
		19. Taxation	0					
	Computer Systems	20. Basic Computer Operation	0					
		21. Hardware & Peripherals	0					
		22. Computer Language/Program	0					
		23. Database Management	0					
		24. Information Systems	0					
		25. Computer Analysis Techniques	0					
	Facilities Mgmt.	26. Tactical Planning	0					
		27. Logistics Management	0					
		28. Security	0					
	Finance & Economics	29. Corporate Financial Mgmt.	0					
		30. Global Economics	0					
		31. Investments	0					
		32. International Corp. Finance	0					

(continues)

TABLE 7.5 (continued)

Technical/Functional Specific Competencies	D. Job Function- Specific Competencies			
		Marketing	33. Market Research & Analysis	☐ 0
			34. Product	☐ 0
			35. Advertising	☐ 0
			36. International Marketing	☐ 0
		Personnel & Management	37. HR Planning/Forecasting	☐ 0
			38. Staffing	☐ 0
			39. Compensation	☐ 0
			40. Training	☐ 0
			41. Labor Relations	☐ 0
		Operations Mgmt.	42. Process Planning	☐ 0
			43. Process Design	☐ 0
			44. Process Control	☐ 0
		Engineering	45. Electromechanical Systems	☐ 0
			46. Microelectronic Fabrication	☐ 0
			47. Signals and Systems	☐ 0
			48. Field and Wavelength Electromagnetics	☐ 0
			49. Basic Math	☐ 0
			50. Linear and Abstract Algebra	☐ 0
			51. Differential Geometry	☐ 0
		Administrative	16. Basic Bookkeeping and Accounting	☐ 0
			20. Basic Computer Operation	☐ 0
			49. Basic Math	☐ 0
			52. Data Entry	☐ 0
			53. Process Written Material	☐ 0
			54. Scheduling and Coordinating	☐ 0
			55. Research and Evaluation	☐ 0
		Sales	56. Sales Prospecting	⊢—[3.25]—⊣
			57. Sales Presentation	⊢—[4.23]⊣
			58. Overcoming Objections	⊢[4.64]⊣
			59. Sales Management	⊢—[4.15]—⊣

tionnaire. An X in this display indicates a dimension that is part of the target job, but the data are profiled elsewhere in the graph.

Item List

This display lists the specific items that are rated by questionnaire respondents and that get rolled up to form the dimension-level results used to create the within-group profile display. This display should also include all the relevant descriptive statistics associated with each item. In the case of the example in Table 7.6, this includes the mean, standard deviation, and percent greater than 2 for each of three questions used in the study (i.e., *Current Importance, Where Acquired,* and *Difficulty*). Often it makes sense to prioritize items based on some criteria. In Table 7.6, items are presented in descending order based on the *Current Importance* data.

TABLE 7.6
Item List: Single Competency Dimension

Dimension: 59 Sales Management (N = 12)						
Item	**Scale**	**Mean**	**SD**	**%>2**	**Selection Specifications**	**Training Specifications**
1. Knowledge of methods for analyzing client accounts to determine further potential for development.	Importance	5.00	0.00	100%	No	Yes
	Where Acq.	2.25	1.14	42%		
	Difficulty	3.75	1.06	92%		
2. Skill in evaluating competitor activity resulting from intelligence gathered from customers, observing offerings at trade shows, and so on.	Importance	5.00	0.00	100%	Yes	No
	Where Acq.	4.42	1.16	92%		
	Difficulty	3.17	1.19	75%		
3. Skill in identifying market trends and growth patterns in own geographic area of operation.	Importance	4.92	0.29	100%	Yes	Yes
	Where Acq.	3.42	1.24	75%		
	Difficulty	4.00	.74	100%		
4. Knowledge of procedures used to establish territory boundaries based on geographical area, customer base, accessibility, volume, and sales strategy.	Importance	4.83	0.39	100%	No	Yes
	Where Acq.	1.58	.65	8%		
	Difficulty	3.67	.78	100%		
5. Skill in communicating sales strategies and tactics to sales staff.	Importance	3.92	0.67	100%	Yes	Yes
	Where Acq.	3.33	.78	92%		
	Difficulty	3.17	.94	75%		
6. Skill in tailoring business unit sales strategy to specific objectives based on local market, economic, and competitive conditions.	Importance	3.67	1.07	83%	Yes	No
	Where Acq.	3.67	1.23	83%		
	Difficulty	4.33	.89	100%		
7. Skill in developing business-wide sales strategies that are aligned with corporate business plans and initiatives.	Importance	3.25	1.48	67%	No	No
	Where Acq.	4.00	1.13	92%		
	Difficulty	4.42	.79	100%		
8. Knowledge of formats for preparing status reports on pricing and the impact of special programs for review by management.	Importance	2.58	0.67	67%	No	No
	Where Acq.	1.50	.67	8%		
	Difficulty	1.58	.67	8%		

A complement to this display can be a simple interpretive table stating how the results are to be used (e.g., to create selection specifications, training specifications, etc.). In this example, items are included in the selection specifications if the mean *Current Importance* rating for an item is greater than 3.0, the standard deviation is less than 1.25 and percent greater than 2 is 75 or higher, and if the *Where Acquired* mean rating is 3.00 or higher (i.e., indicating an entry-level requirement for performance). Thus, Items 2, 3, 5, and 6 would be included in the selection specifications for the regional sales director job and a Y is entered in the appropriate box in the selection specifications column.

On the other hand, Training Specifications focuses on those competencies that are substantially acquired or developed on the job. Criteria for item inclusion are mean *Current Importance* ratings greater than 3.0, standard deviations less than 1.25, percent greater than 2 values of 75 or higher, and *Where Acquired* mean ratings of 3.5 or less. The band of inclusion around the *Where Acquired* mean ratings often overlaps with the selection band to cover competency content that may be part of the selection focus and yet may, in part, be further developed or honed while on the job. Also, note that two items from the Sales Management Dimension (7 and 8) are not included in either the selection or training specifications because they failed to meet at least one of the criteria for inclusion.

Job Description

This kind of display, which is based on the data yet narrative in nature, is often useful for general communication purposes. As Fig. 7.3 illustrates, this display may look a lot like a traditional job description minus the section on minimum qualifications. When used with competencies, the display can be segmented into core, business unit-specific, job level-specific, and functional-specific competencies. Within each dimension, it is often meaningful to sort the items into a prioritized order. In this case, items are sorted in terms of overall importance to the job, as can be seen by examining the items listed under Sales Management and referring back to the *Current Importance* means provided for this same dimension in Table 7.6.

Part-of-Job Wheel

This display is useful for illustrating the relative weight in terms of the importance of each dimension involved in the final composition of a modeled job or group of jobs. Continuing with the regional sales director example, take a look at the data in Table 7.7, which, for the most part, are an extension of the same *Current Importance* rating information found in Table 7.6.

The additional information is found in the last two columns of the exhibits. The Part-of-Job Value in the second to last column is calculated for each dimension by multiplying the dimension mean rating by the difference of the standard deviation from a control value of 3.0 (the purpose of this step is to create a number that gets bigger as the standard deviation gets smaller). The product of this step is then multiplied by the percent-greater-than-two value. The logic behind the calculations is that the most important dimensions (i.e., based on *Current Importance* mean), which everybody agrees are important (i.e., smaller standard

Job Summary

The regional sales director in domestic markets reports to the Vice President of Sales and Marketing. Responsibilities include establishing sales strategy; territory management; executing advertising/sales campaigns; gathering sales-related information; and evaluating financial information.

Requisite Competencies

Organization-Wide or Core Competencies	
1.	*Analyze Issues:* Ability to learn new information quickly; Ability to analyze problems from different points of view; Ability to look beyond symptoms to identify underlying causes of problems; Willingness to gather necessary information and data to fully understand issues or problems.
2.	*Innovation:* Willingness to approach problems with curiosity and an open mind; Ability to generate creative ideas and solutions to problems; Skill in stimulating creative ideas from others.
3.	*Verbal Communication:* Ability to speak clearly and concisely without loss of necessary detail; Ability to understand spoken input or instructions from others; Skill in using enthusiasm and expressiveness to underscore the important points of one's verbal communications.

BU-Specific Competencies	
6.	*Customer Orientation:* Willingness to encourage and listen to customer feedback; Ability to empathize with customers (either internal or external) when mistakes are made and they are upset; Willingness to "go the extra mile" to deliver on customer commitments.
7.	*Negotiation Skills:* Ability to understand the concerns and needs of other people; Willingness to assert one's ideas so they are considered by others and have a chance of being accepted; Willingness to work toward "win-win" solutions.

Job Level-Specific Competencies	
10.	*Champion Change:* Skill in creating buy-in and minimizing resistance to facilitate change; Willingness to go beyond every day assignments and identify areas in need of improvement.
11.	*Provide Direction:* Skill in providing clear direction and priorities for others to follow; Skill in orchestrating the pace of work activities to maintain operating effectiveness; Willingness to tackle problems head-on and work to resolve them without delay; Skill in delegating assignments to the lowest appropriate level.

FIG. 7.3. Job description (competency based) for regional sales director, domestic markets.

17. **Management Accounting:** Knowledge of capital budgeting processes; Knowledge of sales and profit analysis techniques; Knowledge of job order costing and process costing; Knowledge of variables involved in cost behavior analysis; Knowledge of regression analyses used for forecasting.

56. **Sales Prospecting:** Knowledge of industry sources for identifying and qualifying sales prospects; Skill in recognizing faces and recalling names; Knowledge of typical questions and problems in the target customer group; Skill in asking questions to qualify a customer or identify their needs; Skill in "connecting" quickly with account executives in face-to-face cold calls.

57. **Sales Presentation:** Skill in controlling the sequence and timing of events in a sales call; Knowledge of techniques for obtaining the active involvement of a target audience; Skill in maintaining composure and pace in sales presentations.

58. **Overcoming Objections:** Skill in identifying potential sales objections through evaluation of customer qualifying information; Ability to recognize the appropriate level of forcefulness with which to pursue a sale; Willingness to respond directly and succinctly to sales objections.

59. **Sales Management:** Knowledge of methods for analyzing client accounts to determine further potential for development; Skill in evaluating competitor activity resulting from intelligence gathered from customers, observing offerings at trade shows, etc.; Skill in identifying market trends and growth patterns in own geographic area of operation; Knowledge of procedures used to establish territory boundaries based on geographical area, customer base, accessibility, volume, and sales strategy; Skill in communicating sales strategies and tactics to sales staff; Skill in tailoring business unit sales strategy to specific objectives based on local market, economic, and competitive conditions.

FIG. 7.3 (continued). Job description (competency based) for regional sales director, domestic markets.

TABLE 7.7
Dimension-Level Data Used to Determine Part-of-Job for Regional Sales Director, Domestic Markets

	Competency	Importance Rating Mean	SD	%>2	Part of Job Value	Part of Job (%)
A.	1. Analyze Issues	4.10	1.01	82%	6.69	7.8
	2. Innovation	2.32	1.18	44%	1.86	2.2
	3. Verbal Communication	3.36	1.29	65%	3.73	4.3
B.	6. Customer Orientation	4.88	0.20	100%	13.66	15.8
	7. Negotiation Skills	4.53	0.58	98%	10.74	12.5
C.	10. Champion Change	2.55	1.34	38%	1.61	1.9
	11. Provide Direction	4.01	0.62	84%	8.02	9.3
D.	17. Management Accounting	4.24	0.84	86%	7.88	9.2
	56. Sales Prospecting	3.25	1.10	66%	4.08	4.7
	57. Sales Presentation	4.23	0.74	88%	8.41	9.8
	58. Overcoming Objections	4.64	0.70	96%	10.25	11.9
	59. Sales Management	4.15	0.57	90%	9.08	10.6

deviation), should be emphasized in weighting the different aspects of the job. The final multiplier in the equation (i.e., percent-greater-than value) is a combined measure of importance and rater agreement. The actual Part-of-Job Percentage indicated in the last column in Table 7.7 is found by dividing each dimension's Part-of-Job Value by the sum of the Part-of-Job-Values (86.01 in this case). One way to display the results of this analysis is to use the doughnut wheel in a manner similar to that found in Fig. 7.4. From a practice standpoint, performance evaluation and compensation for the regional sales director might be weighted along the lines outlined in this display.

An extension of this display format may be used to highlight the degree of focus for content used with other HR interventions. For example, the same basic calculations could be used to create a recruitment and selection focus wheel, which is what we have in Table 7.8 using the data from Fig. 7.5. The one real difference is that the *Where Acquired* versus *Current Importance* ratings are used in the calculations. The logic here is that we want to identify those facets of the job that must be fully present to perform the target job from Day 1. This is accomplished by dividing the Recruitment/Selection Point Value for each dimension by the sum total of point values. All that is left to do is appropriately weight the

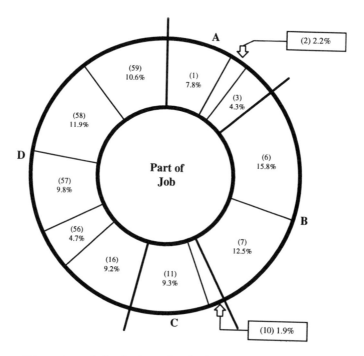

FIG. 7.4. Part-of-job wheel: Graphic display for regional sales director, domestic markets.

TABLE 7.8

Dimension-Level Data Used to Determine Recruitment and Selection Focus for Regional Sales Director, Domestic Markets

	Competency	Where Acquired Selection Rating Mean	SD	%>2	Recruitment/ Selection Emphasis Point Value	Recrtmt./ Selection Value (%)	Recruitment/ Selection Emphasis (%)
A.	1. Analyze Issues	3.89	1.42	74%	4.55	7.2	**7.5**
	2. Innovation	4.37	0.89	95%	8.76	13.8	**8.0**
	3. Verbal Communication	3.19	1.27	63%	3.48	5.5	**4.9**
B.	6. Customer Orientation	4.07	1.02	88%	7.09	11.2	**13.5**
	7. Negotiation Skills	3.62	1.10	79%	5.43	8.5	**10.5**
C.	10. Champion Change	3.57	1.33	84%	5.01	7.9	**4.9**
	11. Provide Direction	3.86	1.21	82%	5.67	8.9	**9.1**
D.	17. Management Accounting	4.15	0.70	92%	8.78	13.8	**11.5**
	56. Sales Prospecting	2.84	1.42	47%	2.11	3.3	**4.0**
	57. Sales Presentation	2.71	1.27	49%	2.30	3.6	**6.7**
	58. Overcoming Objections	3.99	0.98	87%	7.01	11.0	**11.5**
	59. Sales Management	3.08	1.34	65%	3.32	5.3	**7.9**

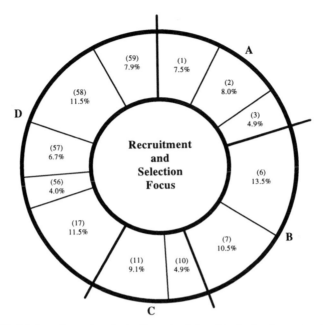

FIG. 7.5. Recruitment and selection wheel: Graphic display for regional sales director, domestic markets.

pure selection targets in terms of relative importance to the job, which is accomplished by simply averaging the Recruitment/Selection value percentages with the Part-of-Job percentages from Fig. 7.4. The result is an Emphasis percentage, which includes both *Current Importance* to the job and *Where Acquired* perspectives in the calculations. Again, the doughnut wheel can be used to graphically present the results of this analysis.

Similarly, the same base of information could be used to guide the creation or modification of training and development programs. The data in Table 7.9 and the visual display in Fig. 7.6 are both virtually identical to the Recruitment and Selection data and displays in the previous two sets of exhibits. The one exception is that the *Where Acquired* means used in the calculations have been transposed so that lower numbers become their higher number counterparts and vice versa (i.e., 5s become 1s, 1s become 5s, etc.). The rationale behind this transposition is to appropriately weight competencies that are often (or must be) acquired after job entry. The rest of the calculations used to complete Fig. 7.6 are exactly the same as those used to determine Recruitment and Selection Emphasis percentages. Although not built into this example, it can often be useful to incorporate the *Difficulty* level of the competencies into the creation of a Training and Development Focus Display.

TABLE 7.9

Dimension-Level Data Used to Determine Training and Development Focus for Regional Sales Director, Domestic Markets

	Competency	Where Acquired Training Rating Mean	SD	%>2	Training Emphasis Point Value	Training Value (%)	Training Emphasis (%)
A.	1. Analyze Issues	2.11	1.42	26%	0.87	6.5	**7.1**
	2. Innovation	1.36	0.89	7%	0.20	1.5	**1.8**
	3. Verbal Communication	2.81	1.27	27%	1.31	9.7	**7.0**
B.	6. Customer Orientation	1.93	1.02	14%	0.53	3.9	**9.8**
	7. Negotiation Skills	2.38	1.10	21%	0.95	7.1	**9.8**
C.	10. Champion Change	2.43	1.33	16%	0.65	4.8	**3.4**
	11. Provide Direction	2.14	1.21	18%	0.69	5.1	**7.2**
D.	17. Management Accounting	1.85	0.70	11%	0.47	3.5	**6.4**
	56. Sales Prospecting	3.16	1.42	53%	2.65	19.7	**12.2**
	57. Sales Presentation	3.29	1.27	51%	2.90	21.6	**15.7**
	58. Overcoming Objections	2.01	0.98	13%	0.53	3.9	**7.9**
	59. Sales Management	2.92	1.34	35%	1.70	12.7	**11.7**

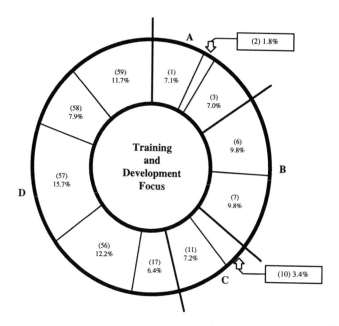

FIG. 7.6. Training and development wheel: Graphic display for regional sales director, domestic markets.

Group by Dimension Matrix

This display presents the mean average ratings for all dimensions comprising some mix of jobs or job groups. In other words, a job by dimension matrix is formed and each cell of the matrix contains the overall average (i.e., aggregating across items by dimension) for a particular job group and dimension pair. Table 7.10 shows how this display can provide a nice way to juxtapose and compare a set of jobs based on some value. This value can be any of your choosing, although the *Current Importance* data are often used for obvious reasons.

Group Comparison

As Table 7.11 illustrates, the group comparison display simply takes the data from the group by dimension matrix display and creates a graphic profile. In our example, the profiles for regional sales director (domestic markets) and regional sales director (global markets) are profiled. This kind of display can get visually busy very quickly. However, for two or three head-to-head comparisons, it does the job nicely. Having the capability to print the display in color lets one add another profile or two to the display without it becoming too messy to read. This kind of dis-

TABLE 7.10
Group by Dimension Matrix

		1	2	3	4	5
Data: Importance						
	Competency	VP Sales	Reg'l Sales Director	Store Mgr.	Dept. Lead	Sales Assoc.
A. Organization - Wide or Core Competencies	1. Analyze Issues	4.05	4.01	4.11	3.65	3.20
	2. Innovation	3.66	2.41	3.01	2.57	2.02
	3. Verbal Communication	3.55	3.49	3.44	3.50	3.33
B. Business Unit-Specific Competencies	6. Customer Orientation	4.02	4.70	4.55	4.86	4.80
	7. Negotiation Skills	4.44	4.35	4.11	4.05	3.71
	8. Global Perspective	4.75	4.31*	3.74	2.36	1.87
C. Job Level-Specific Competencies	9. Visionary Thinking	4.62	X	X	X	X
	10. Champion Change	4.22	3.00	2.04	X	X
	11. Provide Direction	X	3.41	4.66	X	X
	12. Coach Others	X	X	X	3.73	3.15
	13. Listening Skills	X	X	X	4.22	4.03
	14. Work Efficiently	X	X	X	4.15	3.96
D. Job Function-Specific Competencies	16. Basic Bookkeeping & Accounting	X	X	X	4.75	2.24
	17. Management Accounting	4.51	4.36	3.26	X	X
	56. Sales Prospecting	3.04	3.52	4.67	4.52	4.70
	57. Sales Presentation	3.53	4.16	4.70	4.37	4.28
	58. Overcoming Objections	4.08	4.35	4.44	4.61	4.59
	59. Sales Management	3.98	4.20	3.85	2.55	1.53

General Transferable Competencies

Tech/Funct Specific Comps

Note. Data from Global Markets only.

TABLE 7.11

Group Comparison: Regional Sales Director

——————— = Regional Sales Director, Domestic Markets (N=12)

— — — = Regional Sales Director, Global Markets (N=15)

		Competency Dimension	Not Important 0	1	2	3	4	Critically Important 5
General Transferable Competencies	**A.** Organization-Wide or Core Competencies	1. Analyze Issues						
		2. Innovation						
		3. Verbal Communication						
	B. Business Unit-Specific Competencies	4. Build Org. Relationships						
		5. Entrepreneurial Risk Taking						
		6. Customer Orientation						
		7. Negotiation Skills						
		8. Global Perspective						
	C. Job Level-Specific Competencies — Exec.	9. Visionary Thinking						
		10. Champion Change						
	Mgmt.	10. Champion Change						
		11. Provide Direction						
	Indiv. Contr.	11. Provide Direction						
		12. Coach Others						
		13. Listening Skills						
	Non-Exempt	13. Listening Skills						
		14. Work Efficiently						
Technical/Functional Specific Competencies	**D.** Job Function-Specific Competencies — Accounting	15. Financial Statements & Analysis						
		16. Basic Bookkeeping & Acctng.						
		17. Management Accounting						
		18. Auditing						
		19. Taxation						
	Computer Systems	20. Basic Computer Operation						
		21. Hardware & Peripherals						
		22. Computer Language/Program						
		23. Database Management						
		24. Information Systems						
		25. Computer Analysis Techniques						
	Facilities Mgmt.	26. Tactical Planning						
		27. Logistics Management						
		28. Security						
	Finance & Economics	29. Corporate Financial Mgmt.						
		30. Global Economics						
		31. Investments						
		32. International Corp. Finance						

(continues)

TABLE 7.11 (continued)

Technical/Functional-Specific Competencies	D. Job Function-Specific Competencies	Marketing	33. Market Research & Analysis
			34. Product
			35. Advertising
			36. International Marketing
		Personnel & Management	37. HR Planning/Forecasting
			38. Staffing
			39. Compensation
			40. Training
			41. Labor Relations
		Operations Mgmt.	42. Process Planning
			43. Process Design
			44. Process Control
		Engineering	45. Electromechanical Systems
			46. Micro Electronic Fabrication
			47. Signals and Systems
			48. Field and Wavelength Electromagnetics
			49. Basic Math
			50. Linear and Abstract Algebra
			51. Differential Geometry
		Administrative	20. Basic Computer Operation
			49. Basic Math
			52. Data Entry
			53. Process Written Material
			54. Scheduling and Coordinating
			55. Research and Evaluation
		Sales	56. Sales Prospecting
			57. Sales Presentation
			58. Overcoming Objections
			59. Sales Management

play is also a great way to compare differences in ratings for the same job (e.g., profiling *Current Importance* and *Future Importance* data).

Group Emphasis Distribution

Makes a combined data and graphic display by juxtaposing the relative emphasis weights (e.g., Part-of-Job or Recruitment and Selections Focus or Training and Development Focus) for multiple groups. Table 7.12, which is based on a display suggested by McCormick,[29] offers one such example and compares the regional sales director (domestic markets), regional sales director (global markets), and store manager jobs. It should be noted that the same type of emphasis distribution display may be used to highlight similarities and differences in emphasis across different HR interventions. Table 7.13 provides an illustration of how this might look.

TABLE 7.12

Group Emphasis Distributions

Regional Sales Director, Domestic Markets		Store Manager	
Organization-Wide Competencies			
1. Analyze Issues	6.9%	1. Analyze Issues	5.5%
2. Innovation	2.1%	2. Innovation	3.7%
3. Verbal Communication	3.2%	3. Verbal Communication	3.4%
Business Unit-Specific Competencies			
6. Customer Orientation	18.2%	6. Customer Orientation	14.1%
		7. Negotiation Skills	10.2%
7. Negotiation Skills	13.1%	10. Champion Change	1.0%
Job Level-Specific Competencies			
10. Champion Change	1.3%	11. Provide Direction	14.3%
11. Provide Direction	9.6%		
Technical/Functional-Specific Competencies			
17. Mng. Accounting	8.8%	17. Mng. Accounting	3.4%
56. Sales Prospecting	4.0%	56. Sales Prospecting	14.2%
57. Sales Presentation	9.7%	57. Sales Presentation	14.7%
58. Overcome Objections	12.0%	58. Overcome Objections	9.8%
59. Sales Management	11.1%	59. Sales Management	5.7%

TABLE 7. 13

Emphasis Distributions Across Different Human Resource Systems

	Part of Job		Recruitment and Selection Focus		Training and Development Focus	
Organization-Wide Competencies	1. Analyze Issues	6.9%	1. Analyze Issues	6.3%	1. Analyze Issues	6.1%
	2. Innovation	2.1%	2. Innovation	8.8%	2. Innovation	2.0%
	3. Verbal Communication	3.2%			3. Verbal Communication	6.1%
			3. Verbal Communication	4.1%		
Business Unit Specific Competencies	6. Customer Orientation	18.2%			6. Customer Orientation	11.2%
			6. Customer Orientation	15.0%		
					7. Negotiation Skills	10.2%
	7. Negotiation Skills	13.1%	7. Negotiation Skills	10.9%	10. Champion Change	2.8%
Job Level Specific Competencies	10. Champion Change	1.3%	10. Champion Change	4.0%	11. Provide Direction	7.3%
	11. Provide Direction	9.6%	11. Provide Direction	9.0%	17. Mng. Accounting	6.5%
	17. Mng. Accounting	8.8%	17. Mng. Accounting	12.7%	56. Sales Prospecting	14.0%
Technical/Functional Specific Competencies	56. Sales Prospecting	4.0%	56. Sales Prospecting	3.3%		
	57. Sales Presentation	9.7%	57. Sales Presentation	6.5%	57. Sales Presentation	14.9%
	58. Overcome Objections	12.0%	58. Overcome Objections	11.9%	58. Overcome Objections	8.2%
	59. Sales Management	11.1%	59. Sales Management	7.8%	59. Sales Management	11.0%

SUMMARY

The total meaning of a thing is simpler to understand and use than the multitude of smaller pieces that comprise it. However, the total package should give one clues as to the makeup of the constituent parts. This is the whole idea behind creating modeling maps from different vantage points, starting with the highest elevation first. However, it quickly becomes apparent that no single modeling map is ever complete. Each map should lead to and complement other maps that emphasize different parts of the conceptual information. This is part of the power of the approach, knowing that each part is related in a meaningful way to the whole. This in turn guides the connections and integration of the pieces of the HR system. Furthermore, the personally exciting aspect of the practice is knowing that no single map or set of maps will satisfy all situations or customer requirements. New situations and existing map configurations meet and breed more maps. The key ingredients to successful HR map musing are good information and creativity, with a healthy dose of practicality stirred into the mix. Do not be constrained by the ideas and illustrations that have been presented in this chapter.

PROJECT MANAGEMENT TIPS

Some of the most important suggestions I can offer at this stage of the ballgame revolve around the project feedback meeting. One trick of mine in preparing for a feedback meeting is this: Before I start pulling materials together, I look into a mirror and repeat the KISS mantra several times: "Keep It Simple, Stupid. Keep It Simple, Stupid. Keep It Simple, Stupid." Sometimes pounding on the mirror and yelling at the top of my voice helps drive the concept home, though this frequently has the accompanying effect of stopping work and drawing the attention of others in the office. Keep it simple! Easier said than done, however.

Why is this? Well, you have just spent a number of weeks talking to and working with some fascinating people from your customer's organization. Most recently, you have spent many hours pouring over the results of questionnaires and analyzing data. You are now in a position to recognize all kinds of interesting trends and discrepancies in the data. You are also in a position to make all kinds of elegant and insightful comparisons. Further, if you are like me, you will be tempted to do these things and try to share all this wonderful knowledge with the client. It is their data. They will be just as enamored with all the intricate richness as we are, right?

Well, most of the time, this probably is right. However, it is still the wrong thing to do. You are going to have some high-powered people in the room and you are going to have their attention only for a finite period of time. There are several key objectives to accomplish and one cannot afford to spend the entire meeting discussing the data. Moreover, the more involved and complex the presentation of the results, the wider you open the door for endless questions about the methodology and interpretation.

Rather than spending the entire meeting in a detailed discussion about the data, consider spending no more than the first 25% of the meeting reporting detailed results. Then move into your recommendations (e.g., how jobs should be redesigned, discussing how jobs should be grouped for job evaluation purposes, what to focus on in screening versus training, etc.). This should be the meat of the meeting. Discuss what the data mean and how they should be used. This is where you do want to get the people in the room reacting to what you are saying and engaged in some problem solving with you regarding the tough issues. Roughly 50% of the meeting should be spent working through your recommendations.

At the halfway mark of this discussion, stop and formally check in with those in attendance to ensure their needs are being met. For example, come right out and ask, "Are you getting the information you want?" or "How can we make best use of the remainder of our time?" At this point, you will be halfway through the discussion of recommendations *and* halfway through the allotted time for the meeting—enough time for them to get a clear indication of how things are going and enough time for you to shift gears and recover if necessary.

After the discussion of recommendations, the remaining 25% of the meeting should be used to address any concerns that have surfaced and to discuss next steps. If you do not specifically leave time for this activity at the end of the meeting, you may find the most important discussion winds up taking place, and subsequent decisions being made, while you are back at your desk, on the plane flying home, or whatever. Everyone's purposes are better served if the *real* discussion takes place with you in the room and in a position to add value to the decisions being made.

The project is not complete until the modeling process and results have been documented and presented in a way that the target audience finds useful. With respect to presentation, do not forget that, from a practical standpoint, how you state the results is as important as the results themselves. Keep the needs of the target audience clearly in mind.

Of course, the modeling work may not constitute a stand-alone report, but may be a section of a report describing the development of a particular HR application. However, for broad, multifaceted efforts, the modeling work warrants its own report. With this broader effort in mind, a proposed report format follows.

Title Page:	Should present a brief title that captures the focus of the modeling research. The title page should also clearly identify who the report is "submitted to," who it is "submitted by," and include a statement of confidentiality (if required).
Executive Summary:	A one-page summary of the modeling context and key results. This is the kind of description that captures the highlights for someone who needs an update but not intimate details. It is also a description that may be dropped into a company newsletter for broader communication purposes.
Modeling Context:	Should include a description of the organizational issues which prompted the need for modeling and outlines the project scope. It may be useful to reproduce

a figure like the one in Fig. 2.1 and use arrows or shading to point out the level of differentiation in the world of work hierarchy and the level of detail in the relevant job and situation description hierarchies that is intended.

Project Approach: Should detail the procedures followed in conducting the work. Depending on the type of project, this part of the report may include all, or some subset of, the following subsections.

- Preliminary Research: Description of the work that was conducted to understand the organization's business and culture, previous modeling work with the target job group, relevant modeling work that may be drawn on in the published literature, etc.
- Interview/Focus Group Methods: Specifies sample selection criteria (e.g., full time, at least 1 year in current job, two consecutive performance reviews at "Excellent" level), sampling plan, list of participants (including name, title, location and date of interview/focus group), and a description of the procedures followed in the interviews/focus groups and the results.
- Questionnaire Methods: Specifies sample selection criteria, sampling plan, relevant breakdowns of the obtained sample (often expressed in terms of a percent of total number of available respondents by break out [e.g., geographic location, business unit, gender, ethnic group]), and a description of the procedures used.

Analysis Procedures and Results:

Description of the analysis procedures used in the modeling effort, which may be the qualitative content analysis procedures used to sort descriptor content, or it may be the data analysis procedures used to empirically evaluate rater reliability, techniques for consolidating jobs or items, or both. As a standard to shoot for, one ought to be able to pick up this section of the report 5 years down the road and clearly reconstruct what was done and how the analysis led to the subsequent results. The major part of the report will likely consist of the description of your results and the displays for summarizing the key findings.

Implications of Results and Conclusions:
The information in the previous section of the report is a virtual roadmap leading to many valuable human capital initiatives, and this is the section where you outline how the information may be used to realize these objectives. In addition, if there are issues or questions raised by the results, this is where they should be outlined.

Bibliography:
Should include a complete list of the publications and documents consulted or referred to during the modeling project and noted in the report.

Appendices:
Should include copies of all tools and instruments (e.g., focus group leader's guide, modeling questionnaire) used during the project.

You are still not quite finished. Do yourself a favor in terms of your long-term development and take the time to do a project debrief and document the lessons learned. Take stock of what worked or went well and what did not. If you have read this book through to this point, I'll bet modeling work is more than a one-time event for you. A lessons-learned memo for your personal development file is a great way to make sure you take full advantage of your experience. Okay. Now you are finished. Take the time to pat yourself on the back for a job well done and celebrate your accomplishment!

REFERENCES

[1]Boorstin, D. J. (1983). *The discoverers.* New York: Random House.
[2]SPSS, Inc. (1986). *SPSS user's guide* (2nd ed.). New York: McGraw-Hill.
[3]SAS Institute, Inc. (1985). *SASSR user's guide: Statistics, version 5 edition.* Cary, NC: Author.
[4]Dixon, W. J. (1985). *BMDP statistical software: 1985 printing.* Berkeley, CA: University of California Press.
[5]Stevens, J. P. (1996). *Applied multivariate statistics for the social sciences.* Hillsdale, NJ: Lawrence Erlbaum Associates.
[6]Tabachnick, B. G., & Fidell, L. (1989). *Using multivariate statistics.* New York: Harper & Row.
[7]Green, S. B., & Stutzman, T. (1986). An evaluation of methods to select respondents to structured job analysis questionnaires. *Personnel Psychology, 39,* 543–564.
[8]Green, S. B., & Veres, J. (1990). Evaluation of an index to detect inaccurate respondents to a task analysis inventory. *Journal of Business and Psychology, 5,* 47–61.

[9]Pine, D. P. (1995). Assessing the validity of job ratings: An empirical study of false reporting in task inventories. *Public Personnel Management, 24,* 451–460.

[10]Locklear, T. S. (1992). The exploration and evaluation of an index to detect inaccurate respondents to structured job analysis questionnaires. *Dissertation Abstracts International, 53* (5-B), 2572.

[11]Cragun, J. R., & McCormick, E. J. (1967). *Job inventory information: Task and scale reliabilities and scale interrelationships.* (PRL No. TR-67-15). Lackland Airforce Base, TX: Personnel Research Laboratory.

[12]Wilson, M. A., Harvey, R. J., & Macy, B. A. (1990). Repeating items to estimate the test-re-test reliability of task inventory ratings. *Journal of Applied Psychology, 75,* 158–163.

[13]Spearman, C. (1910). Correlation calculated from faulty data. *British Journal of Psychology, 3,* 271–295.

[14]Brown, W. (1910). Some experimental results in the correlation of mental abilities. *British Journal of Psychology, 3,* 296–322.

[15]Cronbach, L. J. (1951). Coefficient alpha and the internal structure of tests. *Psychometrika, 16,* 297–334.

[16]Nunnally, J. C. (1978). *Psychometric theory* (2nd ed.). New York: McGraw-Hill.

[17]Katz, D., & Kahn, R.L. (1978). *The social psychology of organizations* (2nd ed.). New York: Wiley.

[18]Fleishman, E. A., & Quaintance, M. K. (1984). *Taxonomies of human performance.* Orlando, FL: Academic Press.

[19]For a great discussion of the issues involved in creating job families, see Pearlman, K. (1980). Job families: A review and discussion of their implications for personnel selection. *Psychological Bulletin, 87,* 1–28.

[20]Arvey, R. D., Maxwell, S. E., Gutenberg, R. L., & Camp, C. (1981). Detecting job differences: A Monte Carlo study. *Personnel Psychology, 34,* 709–730.

[21]Cornelius, E. T. (1983). *Canonical correlation as a job classification technique.* Paper presented at the annual meeting of the American Institute of Decision Science, San Antonio, TX.

[22]Sackett, P. R., Cornelius, E. T., & Carron, T. J. (1981). A comparison of global judgment vs. task oriented approaches to job classification. *Personnel Psychology, 34,* 791–804.

[23]Tryon, R. (1939). *Cluster analysis.* New York: McGraw-Hill.

[24]Harvey, R. J. (1986). Quantitative approaches to job classification: A review and critique. *Personnel Psychology, 39,* 267–289.

[25]Aldenderfer, M. S., & Blashfield, R. K. (1984). *Cluster analysis.* Newbury Park, CA: Sage.

[26]Equal Employment Opportunity Commission, Civil Service Commission, Department of Labor, & Department of Justice. (1978). *Uniform guidelines on employee selection procedures.* Federal Register, 43(166), 38295–38309.

[27]Dunnette, M. D., Hough, L. M., & Rosse, R. L. (1979). Task and job taxonomies as a basis for identifying labor supply sources and evaluating employment qualifications. In G. T. Milkovich & L. Dyer (Eds.), *Affirmative action planning.* New York: Human Resource Planning Society.

[28]Tukey, J. W. (1977). *Exploratory data analysis.* Reading, MA: Addison-Wesley.

[29]McCormick, E. J. (1979). *Job analysis: Methods and applications.* New York: AMACOM.

III

THE FUTURE
OF STRATEGIC JOB MODELING

Chapter 8
Final Comments
and Prognostications

> ... *you don't need a weatherman to know which way the wind blows....*
> —Bob Dylan

Boudreau and Ramstad have initiated a fascinating line of work that investigates the different information systems associated with different economic periods throughout human history.[1] Wrapped up in this discussion is an attempt to highlight the constrained resources and critical assets linked to success in each economic phase. Table 8.1, which is an adaptation of their original work, outlines some of these ideas. The idea is that the constrained resources for each of these periods are the primary avenues of opportunity that lead to success. Similarly, the associated critical assets are the key ingredients required to turn these opportunities into reality during each slice of human history.

A couple of things are intriguing about this conceptualization. First of all, after 200,000 generations of the Tribal Period, 400 generations of the Agricultural Period, and so on, today's Homo Sapiens find themselves in the early stages of the rapidly changing Information Age with only two generations behind them. This means the Tribal Age has had 20,000 times more influence on the evolving human DNA blueprint and genetic makeup than the Industrial Age and 100,000 times more influence than the Information Age.[2] In other words, you and I are living anachronisms because our biological machinery has been bred for a different age!

Second, and more to the point, this work nicely outlines the advance of the "brave new world" of business, where the constrained resource that must be managed is not something physical like grain, ships, or factories. In this new age, success in business and industry is the product of knowledge and know-how, and the critical asset is people.[3,4]

TABLE 8.1
Measurement Systems Associated With Different Economic Phases

Economic Phase	Constrained Resource	Critical Asset	Measurement/ Information Systems
Tribal Period (1,500,000 B.C. to 8,000 B.C.)	Food, shelter, safety	Weapons and tools	
Agricultural Period (8,000 B.C. to 2,000 B.C.)	Food	Crop land	Weather records, land surveys, agricultural universities
Trade Period (2,000 B.C. to 1700 A.D.)	Distribution	Transportation systems	Road maps, railroad timetables, time zones
Industrial Period (1700 to 1960)	Tangible goods	Capital	Security and Exchange Commission/Financial Accounting standard
Information/Services/ Intangible Period (1960 to Present)	Intellectual capital	People	The next generation of management information systems will meet this emerging need

Consider the variance between the market value and book value of many of today's companies. Although Microsoft produces revenues of $5.9 billion and General Motors $140 billion, Microsoft would likely be sold for more than General Motors. Why? Its higher market value reflects the ideas and know-how created by its living, breathing, thinking assets. The intellectual capital these people have created is the stuff that continues to shape an entire industry.[5]

In fact, it may be more appropriate to think of the Information Age as yesterday's news, having been eclipsed by the Intelligence Age. In the Intelligence Age, rather than just the ability to create new ideas, what differentiates organizational winners from losers will be the ability to extract meaning quickly and efficiently from the ocean of information that *does* exist. Why? Because without this ability, organizations will be unable to recognize and respond to the quickly changing market conditions that characterize today's business landscape. More than ever, people are likely to emerge as the hard assets of business.

Think this is an interesting, but somewhat tangential, topic? Well, think about this. Of all the measurement systems available to provide input to the information base of the Third Millennium Enterprise and of all the metrics used to track and manage the important assets of an organization (e.g., land, physical structures and machines, financial capital), the one area that is in its evolutionary infancy involves charting the human capital of the organization. As I have tried to establish throughout this discussion, this is widely becoming recognized as the most important one!

Enter the HR professional, stage right. Decisions about how to best leverage human capital to accomplish organizational objectives will become preeminent concerns, and HR managers will be on the spot. Relatively new partners to the management team, these individuals will need to make sense of complex streams of information and make recommendations and choices that have a broad and telling impact. They will rise to the challenge and succeed in this new role, but they will succeed through new approaches applied to a changing and more complex business landscape.

Further, I submit that one of these new approaches will be the next generation of job analysis methods. As much OD as job analysis, the job modeling methodology presented in this book provides an approach for charting and leveraging one aspect of the human capital information system that will be a cornerstone of the Third Millennium Enterprise. The information created and captured using this approach represents the plutonium power cells that feed the thermonuclear engine that drives and guides the human might of the organization.

From an applications perspective, whether the goal is to develop a selection system to bring high-caliber performers into the organization, an assessment tool for identifying training and development needs, a performance management system focusing on relevant organizational behaviors, and so forth, the first step is to start with a clear definition of effective performance and an understanding of the human capabilities needed to achieve it—now and in the future. Firms that bankroll expensive HR initiatives without these information models at their core have HR systems that are like huge, muscle-bound giants with little pea brains on top: clueless and uncoordinated. If you take one of these giants and give him the intellectual horsepower to wield his might effectively, then you have a champion—a competitive asset that can be worth more than natural resources, machines, factories, and financial capital.

Now I would like to call your attention to that tremendous roar you've heard building over your left shoulder for the past couple of years. Go ahead, take a look. Do you see it? That is the sound of the second generation of networked client/server computer technologies rumbling across the business terrain. Do not run away. Do not try to hide. There is nowhere to go where you will not be found. You might as well turn to face the stampeding herd.

This breed of computer systems uses desktop personal computers linked together into so-called *client/server networks* to process complex sets of information in far more efficient ways. At the hub of each network is the server—a computer dedicated to controlling user traffic on the network and storing information on sophisticated relational databases. The extensions around the periphery of the server are the client computers—desktop personal computers used by individuals to accomplish a wide range of information entry and analysis activities.

Newer and more powerful superservers, coupled with client computers using far simpler graphical user interfaces (i.e., icons vs. arcane computer code), are reducing to rubble the fortresslike walls that kept all but a small clan of information-system wizards from taking full advantage of the power of the organization's programs.[6,7] Intranet, internet, and wireless communications technologies will continue the assault until the walls are completely obliterated and even the smallest business enterprise, and even the tiniest departments within the largest organizations, are connected and integrated.

Another interesting side topic, you say? Maybe. However, when one considers the explosive developments in information technology, things like open, networked client/server systems, which are both workable and affordable, you get the feeling we are on the brink of something big. My inclination is to think it will be a big step up toward the realization of the integrated, information-driven, high-performance Third Millennium Enterprise versus a big drop into a spiraling abyss of valiant and expensive nonsense, although I suppose the latter is a possibility.

Why the optimism on my part? Keep in mind that HR is that piece of the organization that is truly enterprise-wide, spanning applications, functions, work process groups, business segments, geographic regions, and job levels. Probably more so than other emerging information system interventions focusing on areas like manufacturing, logistics, and finance, the emerging HR systems have been hamstrung by the numerous and varied computing platforms that exist in even small organizations. Intranet and fledgling Internet solutions are effectively leveling the playing field and will allow open access to even the most remote (either in terms of distance or platform compatibility) users in the Third Millennium Enterprise.[8] Thus, visions of human resources information systems (HRIS) that hold the promise of a human capital management architecture, which is a single, integrated, cross-application, cross-functional, cross-business-group, cross-regional, cross-work-group, cross-job-level information system, is now more a substantive reality than merely an ethereal hope.

Of course, many of the current HRIS pseudosystems focus primarily on the administrative aspects of HR—things like payroll and benefit information, employee and applicant tracking (e.g., name, address, phone number, work history, recruitment source), and the like. Nice, useful, but less than earth-shattering stuff. The second-generation HRIS systems will start making inroads to managing information that truly reflect the value of the organization's human capital. These version 2.0 HRIS systems will concern themselves with the management of the more valuable data related to the HR applications described in chapter 4 (HR planning, recruitment, selection classification and placement, training, performance management). This is where the tie-in with job modeling occurs. The next generation of job analysis methods will be required to provide the underlying data warehousing and information access architecture for the HRIS systems that will serve the high-performance Third Millennium Enterprise. The

HR professional who understands the ideas and techniques of strategic job modeling will find himself or herself at the vortex of a profound change event that will be responsible for recasting the very role of HR.

CONCLUSION

No book can cover *every* option. No single methodology can provide *all* the answers. Nothing in business *always* works. I believe these words to be true. That said, I also believe the basic ideas and methods presented between the covers of this book are central to the success of HR in the Third Millennium Enterprise. My hope is that it will quickly become one of the most thumbed-through, dog-eared, written-in reference books on your bookshelf as you adapt and expand on the contents to suit your job modeling needs in your organization or consulting work.

REFERENCES

[1]Boudreau, J. W., & Ramstad, P. M. (1997). Measuring intellectual capital: Learning from financial history. *Human Resource Management, 36,* 343–356.

[2]Ramstad, P. M., Janz, T., & Neumann, D. (1998). *Surviving the shift to a human asset economy.* Unpublished manuscript.

[3]Brooking, A. (1996). *Intellectual capital.* London: International Thompson Business Press.

[4]Stewart, T. A. (1997). *Intellectual capital: The new wealth of organizations.* New York: Doubleday/Currency.

[5]Hamel, G. (1995, October). *Tomorrowday 1995.* Paper presented at the Masters Forum, Minneapolis, MN.

[6]Greengard, S. (1994). The next generation. *Personnel Journal, 73,* 40–46.

[7]Greengard, S. (1995). Catch the wave as HR goes on-line. *Personnel Journal, 74,* 54–68.

[8]Cortese, A. (1996, February 26). Here comes the Intranet. *Business Week,* pp. 76–84.

Appendix A
Work Activity and Competency Taxonomies for Management

> *... I don't think I can tell you what a manager is. But I know one when I see 'em....*
>
> —Anonymous

A broad taxonomic description of management work activity and competency domains are presented in Parts 1 and 2 of this appendix, respectively. In the main, these two taxonomies are the result of Schippmann, Prien, and Hughes' research effort, which included a systematic review of 35 years of research on the content of management work and used the results of 32 independent studies as input for analysis.[1] Specifically, the taxonomic structures and descriptor statements in these two appendixes were guided by the results of these 32 studies and involved an initial pool of 358 work dimensions, over 5,500 descriptor statements, and input and ratings from more than 6,000 managers in a wide variety of different organizations. Enhancements to the original work activity and competency taxonomies have been made as a result of recent additions to the management literature.[2,3,4]

There are several reasons for reproducing these two taxonomies. The first is to provide a detailed frame of reference for illustrating a number of the ideas presented in the book. For example, these two solutions provide examples of (hopefully) well-written work activity and competency items. They also show how the concept of factors may serve as the organizing structure for dimensions and dimension the organizing structure for items.

Second, the hope is that these two solutions, which leverage the results of work by many researchers, may provide a meaningful starting point for job modelers who are doing work with management populations. Although the information presented here may be too general for some interventions and too detailed for others, it should provide a useful initial solution in many contexts.

PART 1:
MANAGEMENT WORK ACTIVITIES

FACTORS	DIMENSIONS	
People Management	I.	Staffing
	II.	Supervise People
	III.	People Development
	IV.	Personnel Administration
	V.	Labor Relations
	VI.	External Relations
General Operations Management	VII.	Supervise Work Operations
	VIII.	Materials Management
	IX.	Information Management
	X.	Facilities & Safety Management
	XI.	International Business Management
Functional Management	XII.	Research & Development Management
	XIII.	Accounting & Financial Management
	XIV.	Marketing & Sales Management
	XV.	Strategy Development
	XVI.	Internal Consulting

I. Staffing

1. Examine strategic business objectives to identify staffing issues related to achieving these objectives.
2. Review the organization structure (e.g., reporting relationships, responsibility flowcharts) of a work group or division to ensure it supports the business vision and strategy.
3. Identify employees in own department or other parts of the organization who are backups to replace key individuals who may be promoted, leave the organization, and so forth.
4. Identify the relevant work activities and associated skills, knowledge, and experiences needed to successfully perform a role or job.
5. Evaluate the cost and effectiveness of recruiting efforts to guide changes in recruiting focus, sources, strategies, and so forth.
6. Conduct screening or employment interviews to collect information relevant for a target role or job.
7. Monitor state, federal, and local legislation, bulletins, and guideline updates for changes that affect the staffing process.

II. Supervise People

8. Assign work assignments and priorities to employees to ensure the best distribution of individual talents.
9. Establish performance standards for employees to clarify goals and performance expectations.
10. Design individual and/or work group goals that are mutually supportive to encourage cooperation and discourage competition.
11. Meet with employees to discuss their perceptions of the work they do to clarify role requirements and work responsibilities.
12. Measure employees' progress toward goals or assignment completion to evaluate individual performance and provide performance-related feedback.
13. Identify opportunities for rewarding positive work behavior and outcomes to reinforce activities that are aligned with the goals of the work group and the organization.

III. People Development

14. Conduct informal or formal orientation of new hires to provide new employees with an overview of the organization's policies, work rules, role or job responsibilities, and so forth.

15. Review the current job assignments of employees and, with reference to their individual performance, identify assignments or work experiences that will be challenging and require growth and development.

16. Identify performance deficiencies or training needs of individual employees to guide coaching efforts, training interventions, and creation of individual development plans.

17. Select training courses or developmental interventions for individuals or groups of employees that address competency gaps resulting from the introduction of new technology, new work processes, redesigned jobs, and so forth.

18. Deliver training courses, seminars, or workshops designed to develop a job-related expertise, skill, or awareness.

19. Evaluate the effectiveness of training courses, workshops, or other developmental interventions that have been designed to address the training needs of individuals or groups of employees.

IV. Personnel Administration

20. Explain personnel policies, programs, procedures, rules, and so on, for employees to ensure understanding.

21. Conduct exit interviews to identify reasons for the separation.

22. Conduct personnel research (e.g., turnover or job classification analyses) designed to provide broader management with information for use in evaluating organization practices, interventions, policies, and so forth.

23. Develop and administer policies related to working hours and absences, work and vacation schedules, and so forth.

24. Conduct job evaluation research and compensation surveys to evaluate wage and salary equity and make recommendations to broader management.

25. Administer and monitor expenditures for various benefit programs such as workman's compensation, unemployment compensation, layoff income benefits, and so forth.

26. Maintain employee files to systematically document information related to employee performance, compensation, development, and so forth.

V. Labor Relations

27. Investigate employee grievances (e.g., collect facts, identify issues, research organization policies) to build a basis for discussions.

28. Develop negotiation strategies for dealing with union demands based on research of union expectations, grievance analyses, contract analyses, and so forth.

29. Develop relations with employee representatives from unions, professional groups, and so on, to lay the groundwork for future negotiations.
30. Review labor contract proposals to identify implications and bargaining points having to do with issues like job security, compensation, working conditions, grievances procedures, and union security.
31. Represent the organization's interests and strategy in negotiations with employee bargaining groups.
32. Monitor state or federal legislation, professional regulations, and so on, to stay abreast of changes that may affect employee relations activities, contracts, and negotiations.

VI.   External Relations

33. Provide board of directors or other external advisory or oversight groups with verbal or written updates to communicate trends or deviations from plans and highlight financial changes or operating results.
34. Develop a portfolio of regular contacts within the financial community (e.g., security analysts, financial press) to develop a financial public relations program.
35. Communicate planned organization actions (e.g., expansions, acquisitions, changes in operational focus, personnel changes) to local press, radio, and television outlets.
36. Represent the organization at community affairs and public functions to promote awareness and create goodwill.
37. Develop and/or administer corporate giving policies (i.e., relating to charities, fundraisers, donations to foundations) designed to promote goodwill and create a sense of positive corporate citizenship.
38. Respond to inquiries or requests for information from external sources such as the press or representatives from other organizations interested in benchmarking.
39. Consult with community and governmental representatives or other economic partners on ways to improve the business climate.

VII.   Supervise Work Operations

40. Coordinate work with other groups to ensure smooth progress and a seamless integration of effort.
41. Develop flowcharts that describe the relationship of one process to another via visual descriptions of the work cycle to guide the creation of new work systems or procedures.

42. Identify inefficiencies or roadblocks in work procedures to guide change in work flow, physical layout of the work area, work processes, and so forth.

43. Chart business measures of timeliness, quality, quantity (e.g., sales billed, orders received, products returned) for work groups or departments to help understand variations and their causes and to communicate information to others.

44. Set timetables and intermediate checkpoints for others to follow to keep track of progress toward objectives.

45. Prepare reports of business activities or projects in own area of responsibility to update management.

46. Conduct cost–benefit analyses to determine the productivity and efficiency payoff of purchasing new technology, updating existing equipment, purchasing additional equipment, and so forth.

VIII.   Materials Management

47. Evaluate potential vendor or supplier options to identify agreements that match needs of the organization in terms of price, delivery, service, technical assistance, and so forth.

48. Monitor the delivery of materials and supplies to counter-check amounts against requisitions, ensure quality of deliverables, oversee proper storage and placement, and so forth.

49. Develop inventory monitoring systems to track stock, material, or resource availability, allow for checks of perpetual inventories, and so forth.

50. Monitor the flow of materials or the delivery of services throughout the logistics system to audit the efficiency and cost-effectiveness of materials movement or service delivery.

51. Develop inventory control policies to hold inventory investments within bounds consistent with efficient operation.

52. Create master schedules for production, processing, or service delivery to guide workload distribution, efficient purchasing of materials or supplies, identify subcontracting needs, and so forth.

53. Conduct capacity utilization analyses to identify bottlenecks in production, processing, or service delivery centers.

IX.   Information Management

54. Conduct information needs analyses to determine the information and reporting requirements of an individual manager, department, business area, and so forth.

55. Utilize computer-aided software engineering (CASE) products to facilitate data modeling and the design of database management systems.

56. Interpret business data for the purpose of identifying patterns, trends, and variances in company operations.

57. Create data flow diagrams to illustrate business procedures or processes and flows among these procedures/processes.

58. Develop database strategic plans that map specific subject databases against their prospective uses for supporting management's monitoring, analyzing, and planning activities.

59. Monitor information-processing systems and specific processing outputs to ensure data quality.

X. Facilities & Safety Management

60. Monitor facility/store/plant operations to assess compliance with industry regulations, state or federal laws, or company policies.

61. Review quality control and reliability data to ensure procedural compliance and identify areas in need of improvement.

62. Develop and/or monitor the implementation of policies designed to promote safety or security, reduce accidents, and control work hazards.

63. Inspect buildings, facility layout and functioning, and so on, to determine their soundness, operational status conformity to security guidelines, and so forth.

64. Research potential facility/store/plant location sites to maximize sales and productivity, minimize labor and transportation costs, and so forth.

65. Design facility/store/plant physical layouts to accommodate optimum product/process flow, maximize space utilization, incorporate requisite handing and transportation equipment, and so forth.

XI. International Business Management

66. Identify communications technology that may be used to facilitate the transmission of data and ideas across international boundaries.

67. Negotiate license agreement terms to achieve international objectives for penetrating foreign markets.

68. Conduct import product analyses to develop cost of business computations that take into account finding fees, FOB and freight costs, U.S. duty, wharfage, cartage, warehouse expenses, and so forth.

69. Investigate culture, education, and business training variables to determine the feasibility of delegating management functions to foreign nationals.

70. Research issues related to financing facilities for short-term credit or equity-capital needs, trademarks, licenses, trade names, patents, copyrights and other intangible assets when conducting business abroad.

71. Evaluate the political, social, economic, and competitive conditions and long-range requirements of a potential host country to assess the attractiveness of investing in or relocating all or part of a business.

XII.   Research & Development Management

72. Evaluate the strategic fit of research and development projects with the organization's objectives to guide the allocation of human, financial, and technological resources.

73. Generate and inventory basic and applied research ideas to develop a portfolio of future business possibilities.

74. Identify new products, product uses, processes, process or system improvements, ways to utilize by-products and waste, and so on, that may contribute to an organization's existing stable of offerings.

75. Evaluate the technical feasibility of research and development ideas to guide recommendations concerning the allocation of human, financial, and technological resources.

76. Oversee research and development work conducted by outside facilities, such as independent laboratories, research institutes, academic institutions, consultants, trade associations, and so forth.

XIII.   Accounting & Financial Management

77. Use spreadsheet or specialized financial software programs to analyze cash flow, sales forecasts, budget forecasts, staffing projections, and so forth.

78. Develop budget or annual profit plan, including planned operations, time schedules, utilization of funds, anticipated financial position, and so forth, to be used in broader management planning and control.

79. Monitor expenditures to identify trends and evaluate variances in relation to an established budget.

80. Review subdepartmental budgets to reconcile differences and make sure that an overall budget includes comprehensive data for determining general costs for items such as supplies, staff personnel, facilities management, and so forth.

81. Review contracts, purchase agreements, and other financial arrangements to ensure compatibility with business goals and expectations about profitability.

82. Forecast the impact of business decisions and expected outcomes on overall financial results.
83. Monitor financial and economic information to identify trends and indicators that may impact business operations, planning, investments, and so forth.
84. Evaluate the profitability of new investments to guide decision making using standard measures of investment worth, such as payback period, book return on book investment, internal rate of return, and contribution to net present worth.

XIV.   Marketing & Sales Management

85. Research customer product or service needs to develop proposals, make recommendations for change in existing product or service lines, and so forth.
86. Monitor competitor pricing of equivalent products or services to help others make pricing decisions.
87. Evaluate packaging (i.e., both functional and merchandising) and branding recommendations for specific products or services.
88. Research markup and cost factors of a product or service to guide price setting.
89. Develop advertising or promotional strategies designed to attract customers, compete successfully with other comparable businesses, promote company image, build employee morale, and so forth.
90. Evaluate the sales performance of groups or regions to identify areas in need of additional coverage, training, realignment, special sales actions, and so forth.
91. Prepare status reports on sales, results of promotional programs, impact of pricing changes, and so on, to update management.

XV.   Strategy Development

92. Review statistical data and other economic, political, and market information to identify opportunities and risks associated with potential business decisions.
93. Establish profit objectives (e.g., profit growth, level, and stability) for a business or business unit to guide long-range planning.
94. Evaluate the growth of a business enterprise to identify a course of competitive action for moving into the future by considering variables like market size and scope, market maturity, competitor rivalry, changes in product demand, access to capital, and so forth.

95. Evaluate the human, technological, infrastructure, financial, and cultural strengths and weaknesses of an organization or business to see what there is to work with when responding to opportunities and threats in the external environment.

96. Review or propose business strategies designed to achieve targeted returns for shareholders, owners, employees, customers, and so forth.

97. Identify specific revenue-generating or cost-saving initiatives in one's own functional area to bring business operations in alignment with the broader organizational strategy.

XVI. Internal Consulting

98. Read manuals, books, technical journals, research publications, and so on, to stay abreast of new developments in own area of expertise.

99. Research the relevant literature (e.g., manuals, books, technical journals, research publications) to find information for answering specific questions or to build a base of information for supporting a specific action or decision.

100. Provide professional advice or specialized assistance and technical instruction to other employees with questions in one's own area of expertise.

101. Attend conferences, seminars, professional association meetings, and so on, to stay informed about industry and competitor practices.

102. Investigate problems (involving equipment, hardware, business processes or operations, etc.) requiring the application of technical or sophisticated procedures, tools, analysis techniques, and so forth.

103. Monitor the organization's practices or operations with reference to laws, regulations, guidelines, industry practices, and so on, to assess compliance, risk, and exposure.

PART 2:
MANAGEMENT COMPETENCIES

FACTORS	DIMENSIONS
Thinking	I. Analytical Agility II. Creativity III. Short-Term Planning IV. Strategy Development & Deployment V. Business-Specific Knowledge
Communications	VI. Verbal Communications VII. Written Communications VIII. Listening Skills IX. Public Speaking
Inter/Intrapersonal	X. Business Relationship/Teamwork XI. Influencing Skills XII. Adaptability XIII. Dependability & Trust
Leadership	XIV. Supervisory Skills XV. Motivation Skills XVI. Decisiveness XVII. Work Commitment
General Operations Management	XVIII. Materials Management XIX. Facilities & Security XX. Information Management & Computers XXI. International Operations & Alliances
Functional Business Knowledge	XXII. Economics XXIII. Accounting & Finance XXIV. Marketing & Sales XXV. Human Resources

I. Analytical Agility

1. Skill in breaking down issues or problems into component parts to identify underlying issues.
2. Skill in recognizing gaps in existing information that is important for fully understanding an issue or problem.
3. Skill in quickly gaining job-related knowledge and using newly acquired knowledge to help understand issues or solve problems.
4. Willingness to reflect on and analyze own mistakes to learn from experience.
5. Skill in grasping the complexities and understanding intricate relationships among issues or problems.

II. Creativity

6. Skill in analyzing issues or problems from different points of view to identify alternative courses of action.
7. Skill in generating ideas and solutions in response to business issues and problems.
8. Skill in making intuitive, inferential leaps in thinking that are logically grounded.
9. Willingness to develop solutions or consider proposals that challenge status quo assumptions or pro forma operations.
10. Willingness to face challenges or problems with an open mind and sense of curiosity.

III. Short-Term Planning

11. Skill in analyzing the work flow to ensure existing processes facilitate, rather than hinder, the accomplishment of work.
12. Skill in translating business or work group strategies into specific objectives and tactics.
13. Skill in balancing day-to-day activities with long-term objectives.
14. Skill in estimating the time and resources required to carry out a work objective.
15. Skill in coordinating the activities of multiple work groups to eliminate duplication of effort and inefficiencies in getting work accomplished.
16. Skill in identifying the most appropriate sequence in which activities should be conducted to efficiently complete a project.

IV. Strategy Development & Deployment

17. Skill in identifying the most probable long-term consequences of an action or decision given a large number of possible future outcomes.

18. Skill in recognizing the broad or long-term implications of business decisions and plans.
19. Skill in recognizing strategic business opportunities resulting from changes in the economic, technological, political/legal, or social environments.
20. Skill in seeing the relationship between one's own work group or business unit and other departments or functions in the organization.
21. Skill in recognizing alliances, either internal or external to the organization, that are complementary and benefit the competitive position of multiple parties.
22. Knowledge of the microenvironment variables that can impact the strategic management process (e.g., buyer switching costs, concentration of customers, competitor business strategies).
23. Knowledge of variables in the organization environment that can impact competitive positioning and long-term business planning (e.g., morale and commitment of key talent, technological assets available to the organization, organizational structure, and decision-making styles).

V.   Business-Specific Knowledge

24. Knowledge of competitors' products, strategies, and business philosophies.
25. Knowledge of the organization's mission, goals, product, service lines, associated competitive strengths and weaknesses, and so forth.
26. Knowledge of how other parts of the organization function (e.g., in other functional or geographic divisions, practice areas, business units).
27. Knowledge of the perspectives and agendas of key decision makers in the organization that may impact project planning, policy development, resource distribution, and so forth.
28. Knowledge of who in the organization needs to be involved if decisions are to be well received.

VI.   Verbal Communications

29. Skill in organizing thoughts or facts in verbal communications in such a way that they facilitate understanding.
30. Skill adapting speaking style (e.g., enthusiasm and expressiveness) to fit the situation and audience.
31. Skill in selecting words that convey the intent of a verbal message precisely and without ambiguity.
32. Skill in using nonverbal behavior (e.g., gestures and eye contact) to underscore important points in verbal communications.

33. Skill in using questions and verbal probes to elicit information or clarify issues with others.

VII. Written Communications

34. Skill in preparing written communications that express information clearly and concisely.
35. Knowledge of basic rules of grammar, punctuation, and sentence structure.
36. Skill in scanning reports, memos, or other documents to identify key points.
37. Skill in creating written material that has a logical flow of thoughts and ideas.
38. Skill in reviewing reports, memos, or other written material for flaws in logic or unsupported recommendations.
39. Skill in preparing reports, manuals, or other documents that contain complex information and are intended to be read by others without a technical background.

VIII. Listening Skills

40. Skill in interpreting the nonverbal messages (e.g., crossed arms, facial expressions) that accompany a speaker's verbal communications.
41. Skill in using open-ended verbal probes to get others to open up and elaborate on a topic.
42. Skill in using paraphrasing and summarizing techniques to clarify the content of a speaker's verbal communications.
43. Willingness to listen to and demonstrate empathy for the concerns of others.
44. Willingness to listen to others express disagreements in an effort to understand issues or explore another point of view.

IX. Public Speaking

45. Skill in anticipating the interests and expectations of an audience when preparing a presentation.
46. Skill in demonstrating confidence and poise during large-group discussions or formal presentations.
47. Skill in controlling the timing and sequence of events during a formal presentation.
48. Knowledge of various visual aids (e.g., slides, flipcharts, videos, computer presentation software) that may be used to augment a presentation and an understanding of the advantages and disadvantages of each.
49. Knowledge of social codes and standards governing behavior in business or social settings where one is identified with the organization.

50. Skill in "thinking quickly on one's feet" and "handling questions from the floor" during large-group discussions or formal presentations.

X.   Business Relationships/Teamwork

51. Willingness to be proactive and work at connecting with and building cooperative relationships with others.
52. Willingness to ignore personal likes and dislikes in work relationships and focus on the work at hand.
53. Willingness to consider the feelings or concerns of other team members when making decisions.
54. Skill at anticipating the reactions of other people in response to comments and feedback, decisions, and so forth.
55. Willingness to demonstrate an interest in the work-related and personal concerns of other team members.
56. Willingness to confront racist, sexist, ethnocentric, or other insensitive behavior in the workplace.
57. Willingness to promote work policies and structures that promote teamwork or enhance the functioning of work teams.

XI.   Influence Skills

58. Skill in assertively presenting one's own point of view without offending or alienating others.
59. Skill in building a strong logical argument and compelling rationale to support one's ideas and recommendations.
60. Knowledge of effective negotiating tactics and techniques (e.g., reframe vs. reject outright another party's position, specify how objectives will benefit the other party).
61. Skill in investigating and understanding another person's needs or negotiating position to guide the development or framing of one's own argument.
62. Skill in creating a strong personal presence that commands attention and respect in groups.

XII.   Adaptability

63. Skill in adjusting one's work pace to keep up with rapidly changing events.
64. Skill in shifting one's attention between multiple activities and competing demands.
65. Willingness to accept criticism without overreacting or becoming defensive.

66. Willingness to remain open to and assimilate new information or data that impact a previous decision, course of action, and so forth.
67. Skill in keeping a cool head and positive focus in stressful situations.

XIII. Dependability & Trust

68. Willingness to follow through on commitments and promises.
69. Skill in communicating information in an open and sincere manner that promotes credibility (e.g., honest answers to tough questions).
70. Willingness to act carefully and responsibly with sensitive or classified information (e.g., compensation figures or proprietary technical information).
71. Willingness to accept responsibility for own mistakes.
72. Knowledge of theories and techniques for enhancing an organization's ethical and moral consciousness.
73. Knowledge of social responsibility concepts in business and industry (e.g., concepts of relativism and stakeholder analysis).

XIV. Supervisory Skills

74. Skill in conveying a sense of urgency to others to help team members focus on a limited set of priorities.
75. Willingness to focus on employee development and training activities despite the daily rush to get work done.
76. Knowledge of existing development resources that can be used to support the skill development of team members (e.g., books, seminars, training programs).
77. Skill in identifying assignments designed to stretch and develop others' capabilities.
78. Willingness to monitor work assignments to stay on top of work progress.
79. Skill in communicating the goals of a work group or business unit to team members so that individual work behavior is aligned with broader strategies.
80. Skill in setting priorities and work directions for others so they have a clear idea of performance expectation.
81. Skill in assigning the appropriate level of authority to coincide with delegated work activities.

XV. Motivation Skills

82. Knowledge of basic principles of motivation and theories of work behavior.

83. Skill in creating an energetic and enthusiastic work environment where people have positive attitudes about their work.
84. Willingness to take the time to track and reinforce positive work behaviors in others.
85. Skill in conveying to others the feeling that their work is valued and that they are important members of the team.
86. Willingness to involve others in planning and decision making.

XVI.   Decisiveness

87. Willingness to take a stand on important matters when faced with difficult dilemmas or decisions.
88. Willingness to make decisions in the face of uncertainty or when tough choices are required.
89. Skill in setting priorities and developing a work direction in ambiguous situations.
90. Skill in delivering clear and action-oriented instructions in crisis situations requiring quick action.
91. Willingness to step forward and champion new initiatives and improvements in the organization that require broad commitment or change.

XVII.   Work Commitment

92. Willingness to persist in the face of difficulties (e.g., when work becomes complex, intellectually challenging, and politically complicated).
93. Skill in maintaining a high energy level to keep up with the pace of daily work activities.
94. Willingness to set high standards of personal performance.
95. Willingness to take the initiative in seeking out new work challenges and increase the variety and scope of one's job.
96. Willingness to bring issues to closure by pushing forward until a resolution is achieved.
97. Skill at staying focused on work priorities and working through or around frequent interruptions.
98. Willingness to pursue continuous learning to stay current with advances in own area of expertise.

XVIII.   Materials Management

99. Knowledge of purchasing fundamentals and techniques (e.g., forecasting techniques, purchasing control processes, procedures for establishing and maintaining vendor relations).

100. Knowledge of storage and inventory concepts (e.g., methods for determining storage layout, coding and marking, balancing and controlling inventory costs).

101. Knowledge of order processing (e.g., methods for entering orders, invoicing orders, measuring customer service).

102. Knowledge of logistics engineering (e.g., procedures for measuring reliability and maintainability, analyzing system functions, analyzing logistics support).

103. Knowledge of work process planning (e.g., job design concepts, work measurement procedures, variables impacting capacity planning and facilities layout).

104. Knowledge of process design and implementation (e.g., production and service designs, quality improvement concepts, project management and control).

105. Skill in setting clear priorities and work directions for others.

106. Skill in communicating the goals of a work group or business unit to individuals on one's team.

XIX.   Facilities & Security

107. Knowledge of facilities tactical planning (e.g., general site/location analysis, basic ergonomics, regulatory laws governing facilities).

108. Knowledge of preventive maintenance guidelines and procedures for equipment and facilities.

109. Knowledge of start-up procedures and facility implementation (e.g., procedures for monitoring equipment and furniture installation, obtaining municipality permits, contracting outside services).

110. Knowledge of procedures for establishing physical security (e.g., intrusion prevention techniques and devices, fire protection techniques and devices, disaster recovery plans).

111. Knowledge of procedures for establishing personnel security (e.g., background investigation procedures, monitoring techniques and tools, checks and balances, and separation of duties).

XX.   Information Management & Computers

112. Knowledge of information systems and information management (e.g., techniques for defining user requirements and data structures, statistical procedures for analyzing system functioning).

113. Knowledge of database manipulation and management (e.g., techniques for designing databases, storage and access methods in computer systems, CASE tools, data modeling).

114. Knowledge of project management tools and techniques.
115. Knowledge of decision support and expert systems in information management (e.g., neural networks, platform design features, compatibility issues).
116. Knowledge of computer hardware and peripheral devices (e.g., storage media such as tape drives, imaging devices, file server set-up and configuration).
117. Knowledge of computer operations and support tools (e.g., software utilities, job schedulers, data transfer tools).
118. Knowledge of computer network management tools (e.g., wireless technology, LANs and WANs, system network architecture).
119. Knowledge of computer information system development tools (e.g., program development standards, compilers and linkers, automated debugging and testing tools).

XXI.   International Operations & Alliances

120. Knowledge of international economics (e.g., variables impacting international trade and capital flows, production mobility factors, trade policy assessment).
121. Knowledge of international marketing (e.g., business customs and practices in global marketing, export trade mechanics and logistics, international distribution systems).
122. Knowledge of global human resources management (e.g., ethical issues in international management, impact of different value systems on decision making, cultural diversity influences, organizational behavior).
123. Knowledge of international corporate finance (e.g., currency trading and parity relationships, economic and political risk evaluation, international monetary arrangements).

XXII.   Economics

124. Knowledge of basic economic concepts and theories (e.g., marginal cost and benefit evaluations, production and consumption relationships and measurement).
125. Knowledge of microeconomics (e.g., variables involved in understanding consumer behavior, procedures for determining optimal input combinations and cost functions for an organization).
126. Knowledge of macroeconomics (e.g., commodity and credit markets, factors impacting capital accumulation and economic growth, variables impacting the demand for money).

127. Knowledge of labor economics (e.g., wage determination tables, stagflation concepts, trade union organization and functioning).

128. Knowledge of econometrics (e.g., descriptive statistics, linear regression models, disequilibrium models).

129. Knowledge of economic development (e.g., social aspects of development, trade policies of developing countries, agriculture policy and relationships to economic development).

130. Skill in using economic indicators to forecast trends and business cycles.

XXIII. Accounting & Finance

131. Knowledge of financial statements and analysis (e.g., balance sheets, cash flow statements, equity analysis).

132. Knowledge of management accounting procedures (e.g., cost–volume–profit analysis, return on investment calculations, capital budgeting).

133. Knowledge of auditing procedures (e.g., payroll and personnel cycles, sales and collection cycles, divisible profit calculations).

134. Knowledge of basic principles of finance (e.g., calculating net present value, risk assessment, asset pricing models).

135. Knowledge of corporate finance principles (e.g., debt financing, credit and cash management, methods for evaluating market efficiency).

136. Knowledge of corporate investment management (e.g., tax shelters, contrarian investment strategies and stock reversals, diversification concepts).

137. Knowledge of financial markets (e.g., primary and secondary markets, monetary and fiscal policy, security analysis).

138. Knowledge of financial risk measurement and management (e.g., volatility forecasting, risk capital calculations, credit risk management).

139. Skill in analyzing financial statements to evaluate an organization's fiscal health and locate causes of variance in business operations.

XXIV. Marketing & Sales

140. Knowledge of marketing research and analysis (e.g., sales forecasting, product and pricing research, marketing research designs).

141. Knowledge of product design and management (e.g., new product development strategies, product life-cycle concepts, market segmentation and positioning).

142. Knowledge of retail marketing and merchandising (e.g., techniques for modifying store image, planogram uses and misuses, pricing and promotion strategies).

143. Knowledge of consumer behavior (e.g., marketing communications that impact consumer behavior, economic and psychological theories about consumer behavior, sociocultural factors affecting consumer behavior).
144. Knowledge of sales management (e.g., methods for analyzing existing accounts, techniques for estimating sales based on trends).
145. Knowledge of territory management (e.g., procedures used to establish territory boundaries, methods for monitoring territory performance).
146. Skill in evaluating what constitutes desirable features or options in a product/service with reference to potential customer base or target market.
147. Skill in identifying customer needs and careabouts and matching or modifying products/services accordingly.

XXV. Human Resources

148. Knowledge of strategic human resource planning (e.g., techniques for inventorying internal labor supplies, modeling personnel flows, forecasting resource requirements).
149. Knowledge of labor laws and government regulations impacting human resource management (e.g., EEOC and OFCCP regulations, Civil Rights laws, labor laws such as the Wagner Act and Taft-Hartley Act).
150. Knowledge of job modeling techniques and outputs (e.g., interview and questionnaire approaches, creating models of work for jobs or groups of jobs).
151. Knowledge of employee selection and placement methods (e.g., interviewing best practices, ability and personality testing, validating decision-making processes).
152. Knowledge of employee compensation and reward systems (e.g., strategies for designing pay systems, conducting pay surveys, creating incentive programs).
153. Knowledge of performance appraisal approaches and methods for tracking individual performance (e.g., requirements of a relevant appraisal system, pros and cons of different methods, potential uses and misuses of appraisal data).
154. Knowledge of training programs and techniques (e.g., on-the-job methods, use of simulations, training evaluation methodology).
155. Knowledge of procedures and techniques for organization analysis and development.
156. Knowledge of employee and health and safety issues and regulations (e.g., health programs for employees, OSHA standards, reporting and enforcement, workers' compensation and disability programs).

REFERENCES

[1]Schippmann, J. S., Prien, E. P., & Hughes, G. L. (1991). The content of management work: Formation of task and job skill composite classifications. *Journal of Business and Psychology, 5,* 325–354.

[2]Borman, W. C., & Brush, D. H. (1993). More progress toward a taxonomy of managerial performance requirements. *Human Performance, 6,* 1–21.

[3]Johnson, J. W., Schneider, R. J., & Oswald, F. L. (1997). Toward a taxonomy of managerial performance profiles. *Human Performance, 10,* 227–250.

[4]Spreitzer, G. M., McCall, M. M., & Mahoney, J. D. (1997). Early identification of international executive potential. *Journal of Applied Psychology, 82,* 6–29.

Appendix B
Data-Reduction Techniques in Job Modeling

> *... each statistic by itself can be a little daunting, but mass them together and they are terrible indeed....*
>
> —Unknown

Welcome to the technical appendix, you adventurous soul! I am going to try my darndest to show that you have not misplaced your faith in me by venturing deep into the hinterland of this book.

There are three subsections to this appendix. The first two, Q-Factor Analysis and Cluster Analysis, concern data-based techniques for consolidating jobs. The third subsection, R-Factor Analysis, involves a brief discussion of a data-based technique for consolidating descriptor content or items. Ready to forge ahead into the foreboding mist? Screw your courage to the sticking place, keep your eyes on the path in front of you, and I'll bet you make it through unscathed!

Q-FACTOR ANALYSIS

As noted in chapter 7, factor analysis refers to a broad family of statistics. However, when using Q-factor techniques to guide the consolidation of jobs, one would use exploratory factor analytic statistics to see if meaningful subdivisions occur (as opposed to confirmatory factor approaches, which may be used to test specific expectations about the underlying job structure). Do not be thrown by the use of the term *exploratory*. This does not mean that we do not know something about what we are looking for or what we might find.

In general, regardless of the specific procedure, the first step in a factor analysis involves deciding whether to use principal component or common factor techniques. In the strictest sense, principal components analysis is somewhat distinct from factor analysis and yields groups of components versus factors. However, not much is lost in the translation if one simplifies matters and considers both to be factor analytic approaches that produce homogenous groupings of whatever is targeted by the analysis (i.e., positions in this case). This said, the purpose of principal components analysis is to create factors in such a way that the resulting groups are completely independent. In contrast, common factor approaches create factors that only approximate independence.

Furthermore, there are a number of ways to extract the initial grouping solution using the common factor approach—primarily maximum likelihood and least squares techniques. These basic ideas are represented in Table B.1, which is a statistical analysis cheat sheet that may be referred to when faced with questions about consolidating jobs. The top row of this table refers to factor analytic procedures and decision points. Actually, the top half of Table B.1 refers to Q-factor analysis, which, as noted in chapter 7, is a variant of the more traditional R-factor analysis. More on the R versus Q distinction later.

From a job consolidation perspective, both the principal component and common factor approaches have their supporters and detractors.[1,2] However, most of the debate is rooted in a theoretical brouhaha about the underpinnings of the analyses and impact of these foundational differences on the interpretability of the results. In fact, dozens of personal efforts examining the comparability of the results with various sets of real data, combined with similar findings from the reported research of others,[3,4,5] lead me to conclude there is little practical difference between the two (unless one is interested in investigating the theory underlying the resulting solution or generalizing the grouping outcomes to other settings or situations[6,7,8]). For these reasons, the remaining discussion is limited to principal components analysis, although the reader who is interested in learning more about common factor approaches can turn to a number of excellent sources, starting with Weiss,[9] moving on to Kim and Mueller,[10,11] and progressing to more involved discussions by Overall and Klett[12] and Gorsuch.[13] Using your favorite Web browser to search for keywords like *factor analysis* can also link you up to numerous homepages with useful information, working examples, and so on.

The second step in a factor analysis, as illustrated in Table B.1, is to determine how many groupings or components best organize the total number of things being analyzed (in this case, individual respondents representing specific positions). The determination of the number of groups that best organize the entities being grouped is typically based on a combination of statistical and judgmental decisions. From a purely statistical vantage point, one might use the Kaiser criterion,[14] which recommends retaining groups with eigenvalues greater than one, particularly when there is a large (e.g., 10 to 1) ratio between subjects and variables,[15] which translates to items and respondents or positions in a Q-factor situation. Eigenvalue, you say! Just what is an eigenvalue? In short, this is the total amount of variability in the matrix of correlations explained by

TABLE B.1
Statistical Cheat Sheet

Grouping Statistic	Use When	Specific Grouping Technique	Use When	Secondary Analysis	Specific Secondary Analysis Technique	Use When
Q-Factor Analysis	• Jobs being classified are fairly similar in terms of the description content being collected (i.e., work activities, competencies). OR • The classification effort is being based on descriptor content that is written at a general level of detail.	Principal Components	• Interested in a very pragmatic grouping of positions which maximize one's ability to explain the interrelationships among these positions (which is most of the time in most job consolidation efforts).	Rotation	Orthogonal (e.g., Varimax)	• Interested in moving quickly to a conceptually clean grouping of jobs, which emphasizes the independence or distinctiveness of the groupings.
		Common Factor Approaches (e.g., Maximum Likelihood, Least Squares)	• Interested in generalizing the results to other settings or situations or for testing specific hypotheses and building theory-based solutions.		Oblique (e.g., Promax, Quartimin, Oblimin, Orthoblique)	• Willing to take the time to produce and compare a variety of rotational techniques (no one type of method prevails and each yields slightly different solutions) and work with more complex (i.e., correlated) factors.
Cluster Analysis	• Jobs being classified are quite distinct in terms of the descriptor content being collected. OR • The classification is being based on descriptor content that is written at a fairly detailed level of specificity.	Average Linkage Correlation	• Grouping functionally different jobs (e.g., cutting across families like sales and clerical). OR • Grouping jobs traversing a wide range of levels (e.g., cutting across hourly, supervisory, and management). OR • Grouping jobs with vastly different numbers of people performing each job or reflected in your sample.			
		Wards Minimum Variance	• Grouping jobs where there is very little idea about what the underlying structure or job configuration ought to look like.			
		Average Linkage Distance	• Grouping jobs within a particular family and within a restricted content range (e.g., clerical and secretarial jobs), although probably better off using factor analysis.			

each factor; the first factor accounts for the largest amount of variance in the sample and successive factors contribute progressively smaller amounts to explaining what groupings exist in the data.

Consider the following subset of data from a project with BANK ONE, a full-service consumer and commercial bank with more than 1,500 banking offices. The project involved analyzing questionnaire responses from six jobs in the retail banking part of the business: Banking Center Manager (BCM), Banking Center Assistant Manager (BCAM), Relationship Banker (RB), and Customer Service Associate (CSA) I, II, III. The questionnaire asked job incumbents to rate the importance of 112 work activities using a 5-point rating scale. As an illustration, 30 cases have been selected from a much larger set of project data—five cases representing each job. This mini data set was submitted to a principal components analysis, yielding the initial set of extraction statistics in Table B.2. This exhibit lists the total number of extracted factors (which equals the number of variables being factored), associated eigenvalues (i.e., total variance explained by the factor), corresponding percent of variance (i.e., the percentage of total variance attributed to each factor), and the cumulative percent (i.e., the running total of explained variance as one moves down the list from larger to smaller factors).

TABLE B.2
Initial Factor Statistics

Factor	Eigenvalue	Percent of Variance	Cumulative Percent
1.	10.3807	34.6	34.6
2.	5.6396	18.8	53.4
3.	4.3960	14.7	68.1
4.	1.4362	4.8	72.9
5.	0.7069	2.4	75.3
6.	0.6656	2.2	77.5
7.	0.5575	1.9	79.4
8.	0.5551	1.9	81.3
⋮	⋮	⋮	⋮
30.	0.0827	0.3	100.0

In this example, the results of which mirror the results from the actual study, four eigenvalues are greater than one, suggesting a four-factor solution. Often this rule for identifying the best number of underlying groups has been criticized for producing too many factors. Although not true in this case, it frequently produces as many factors as one third of the number of original variables.

A more judgmental means of identifying the best number of groupings to retain is Cattell's scree test,[16] where scree is the geological term referring to the loose stones and debris that accumulates at the base of a rocky mountain slope. This rule suggests identifying that point where the eigenvalues begin to smooth out and form a gradual slope (i.e., the scree or debris that litters the base of the main mountain of factors). Using the BANK ONE data, Fig. B.1 illustrates a scree plot, which suggests a couple of breaks in the data—a clear one at three and a second smaller one at four. It is at these points that our rock climber, superimposed on the scree plot in Fig. B.1, would have to break out his tools and climb versus continuing to walk up an inclining slope.

There are other factor determination techniques out there, such as parallel analysis,[17] minimum average partial correlation procedures,[18] tests of the equality of the last eigenvalues,[19,20] and others.[21] However, no single end-all, beat-all

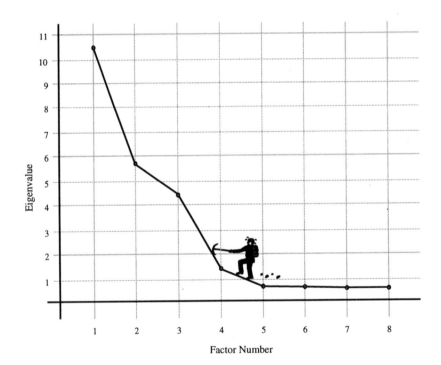

FIG. B.1. Scree plot.

method has emerged. In fact, my sense is that most practitioners end up using multiple combinations of rules to reach a satisfactory solution. Furthermore, because there is some evidence to suggest that it is better to err on the side of overestimating versus underestimating the best number of groups,[22,23,24] a number of writers suggest that a wise strategy is to start with the largest solution first and work down until the best categorization is found.[25,26] In fact, some practitioners identify the number of factors suggested by the technique of choice and then add 2. When the factor procedures are re-run, these plus-2 factors often act as the factor analytic equivalents of a couple of garbage cans and collect the statistical litter from variables that do not fit in the targeted factors. These two garbage factors are then left uninterpreted and the associated variables are excluded from further analysis. In summary, the best solution is rather abstractly defined as the categorization that is most reasonable given the data in hand and the practical realities that are interwoven with the modeling context.

The third step in the principal components analysis is to improve the meaningfulness of the initial factor solution by re-running the factor analysis to the specified number of extracted factors and then submitting the resulting factor matrix to a follow-up analysis called *rotation*. The rotation step has two primary options—orthogonal rotation or oblique rotation. In the simplest terms, *orthogonal rotation* produces factors that are substantively uncorrelated (i.e., emphasizes distinctness in the groupings), whereas *oblique rotation* allows the factors to be correlated. Here, too, it is possible to find proponents and detractors of the different methods. Champions of the orthogonal approach highlight the method's simplicity and conceptual clarity.[27] Fans of the oblique approach claim that the additional complexity is a small price to pay for some added precision in explanatory value. When used in job modeling work to consolidate jobs, I think arguing about the best rotational method is kind of like arguing about who makes the best barbecue. It depends on who you ask (although for my money it is a wonderful little place called Interstate BBQ in Memphis; if you find yourself in town and decide to stop by, be sure to try the barbecue spaghetti). There really is no overwhelming support for either side; there is only a choice between *this* way of doing things and *that* way of doing things.

At this point, a final factor solution exists and one is left to the business of interpreting the resulting groupings of positions. Interpretation typically involves looking at both the positive and negative factor loadings based on the idea that the resulting labels are more meaningful when they consider both what is and is not in the factor.[28] Time to define another term:

Factor Loadings: Describe the correlations between factors emerging from a factor analysis and the original entities used to create the factors. In a Q-factor analysis this means a correlation between individual respondents or positions and the smaller set of job factors.

Conventional practice is such that only entities with loadings greater than .30 or .40 should be considered practically significant. To create distinct classifications, one might go one step further and only select positions to represent a group if the factor loadings are .40 or higher on a given factor and all other loadings on the remaining factors are less than .30.

Take a look at the matrix of factor loadings in Table B.3. Each row contains the correlations (in the case of uncorrelated factors such as those resulting from a principal components analysis) between variables (i.e., persons/positions) and the resulting factors. When using Q-factor procedures to classify persons/positions, it is usually most meaningful to associate each respondent with one and only one factor. This is done by using each individual's highest factor loading as the criterion for belonging to an exclusive group.

Inspection of the matrix of factor loadings in Table B.3 with the simple exclusivity criterion in mind indicates a readily interpretable breakdown in terms of factor composition (i.e., group membership in this situation). Factor 1 is clearly a Relationship Banking job group. It may appear a little confusing to see the CSA II positions loading highly on this factor. The confusion clears up when one understands that BANK ONE, at the time, used this job as the training ground for moving into the more sales-oriented Relationship Banker job. Rather than performing a broad range of customer service activities, CSA IIs were really serving as a Relationship Banker understudy.

Factor 2 is composed of all the CSA I and IIIs. Although there were some differences in the performance expectations between these two job titles, the employees were substantively performing the same kinds of activities. Thus, subsequent work to create selection tools, training programs, and so on, might proceed most economically by considering these two classes of employees as a group. However, Banking Center Managers and Banking Center Assistant Managers broke out separately as Factors 3 and 4. Consequently, these two classes of employees might be considered as a collective job group in future efforts to build various HR applications, roll-up data for reporting various kinds of operational data, and so forth.

In summary, Q-Factor principal components analysis is a wonderful tool for making sense of the many and varied interconnections among jobs in most organizations. Although I am not aware of any data to support the point, I suspect it is the preferred method among practitioners, particularly when the positions of interest are expected to be highly correlated. This view has received some recent empirical support by Colihan and Burger,[29] who conducted a series of studies that indicate the technique is superior to its closest competitor—cluster analysis—in recovering known groupings. Nevertheless, cluster analysis is a popular technique, and our discussion would be incomplete if it were not also covered. To be fair, I'll bet that, although

TABLE B.3
Matrix of Factor Loadings

Person/Position	Factor 1	Factor 2	Factor 3	Factor 4
Person 21 / RB	*.88340*	.16237	-.03807	.00201
Person 19 / RB	*.84093*	.09126	.15115	-.11375
Person 27 / RB	*.83452*	.19953	.23421	-.04411
Person 20 / RB	*.82187*	.21716	.01560	.03987
Person 08 / CSA II	*.81660*	.24054	-.09311	.04797
Person 30 / RB	*.80972*	-.04328	.02767	-.11303
Person 24 / CSA II	*.80580*	.19102	.12161	.14996
Person 07 / CSA II	*.80363*	.21882	.21140	.06357
Person 05 / CSA II	*.77013*	.36467	.05682	-.04141
Person 06 / CSA II	*.72204*	.36094	-.17992	.15222
Person 23 / CSA I	.06798	*.84373*	-.05005	-.04862
Person 02 / CSA I	.20975	*.84114*	-.17734	.09290
Person 29 / CSA I	.21696	*.82799*	-.04806	.06213
Person 25 / CSA III	.27173	*.80942*	-.03767	-.01625
Person 04 / CSA I	.17249	*.80017*	-.20347	.08954
Person 03 / CSA III	.14540	*.78676*	-.16408	.15378
Person 22 / CSA III	.02621	*.75748*	.16971	.27362
Person 26 / CSA I	.25310	*.73782*	-.16290	.14085
Person 01 / CSA III	.42666	*.65392*	.03003	.17841
Person 28 / CSA III	.33906	*.63211*	-.18986	.10312
Person 16 / BCM	.05072	-.19551	*.86074*	.14124
Person 15 / BCM	.20494	-.10436	*.85856*	.09561
Person 14 / BCM	.05611	-.24343	*.84198*	.12860
Person 18 / BCM	.13285	-.10931	*.81131*	.36395
Person 17 / BCM	-.04269	-.01076	*.77785*	.37380
Person 09 / BCAM	.06498	-.04186	.15520	*.85825*
Person 11 / BCAM	-.05230	.14268	.07768	*.82007*
Person 12 / BCAM	-.06434	.35415	.15909	*.76295*
Person 13 / BCAM	.03661	.27250	.34889	*.71570*
Person 10 / BCAM	.05044	.07720	.39231	*.70934*

many, if not most, practitioners may start with a factor analysis, they end up doing a cluster analysis as well and compare the results. Harvey took this approach a step further and suggested employing a hybrid technique in which a matrix of factor loadings is submitted to a cluster analysis.[30]

CLUSTER ANALYSIS

As with factor analysis and perhaps even more so, a considerable variety of cluster methods are available.[31,32,33] These methods may be clustered themselves into five major families of techniques: hierarchical agglomerative, hierarchical diversive, iterative partitioning, density search, and factor analysis variants. Of the five, hierarchical agglomerative is the most frequently used overall[34] and most certainly the most popular for job consolidation purposes.

Within the hierarchical agglomerative family, there are a number of specific techniques, although all use a hierarchical procedure for grouping purposes. In each, the first step of the analysis starts by considering all variables (i.e., persons/positions) as separate clusters. That is, at ground zero, there are as many clusters as there are variables (i.e., persons or positions). At Step 2, two variables are combined to form a single cluster. At Step 3, either a third case is added to the existing two-variable cluster or two new variables are combined to form a new cluster. This continues on up the ladder, as illustrated by the dendrogram or tree diagram in chapter 7.

Unlike factor analysis, the initial solution created by the cluster procedure is the only solution. In other words, there is no secondary analysis, like rotation, used to sharpen up the results. Thus, selecting the best method right out of the chute is important.

In a terrific paper designed to make sense of the pros and cons of the various techniques in this family (e.g., average linkage correlation, average linkage distance, Ward's minimum variance), Garwood, Anderson, and Greengart compared the usefulness of the different techniques for grouping positions from different kinds of data sets.[35] Their results and recommendations serve as the primary information source for the bottom half of the statistical analysis cheat sheet in Table B.1.

The nested tree structure of a dendrogram is the preferred method for displaying the results of a cluster analysis. Figure B.2 presents the Average Linkage Correlation Dendrogram for the BANK ONE micro data set. Kind of interesting, right? Just how many meaningful clusters are represented in this pretty picture? Well, as with factor analysis, there are no fixed decision rules. Probably the most prevalent procedure is a subjective decision on where to prune the tree based on the length of the branches.[36] The longer the line, the bigger the difference between the two entities that get grouped together at a particular step.

In Fig. B.2, we might start at the top and work our way down. At Level 16 there are two large groups, one consisting of BCMs and BCAMs and one com-

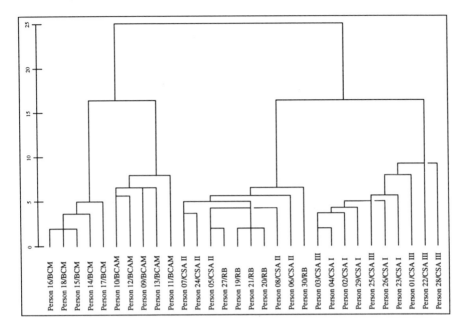

FIG. B.2. Average linkage correlation dendogram.

prised of RBs and CSA I, II, and IIIs. Below this point, there are long branches all the way down to Level 10 and beyond, suggesting some distinct clusters of position. If we examine these clusters, we see BCMs and BCAMs breaking out separately from the higher level cluster on the left and RBs/CSA IIs and CSA I/IIIs breaking out as subgroups from the higher level cluster on the right. At this point, we have the same solution as that provided by the factor analysis. Clearly this procedure is judgmental; the final judgment is likely to be better the more one understands the data and has a sense of what the correct grouping of positions is likely to look like.

A somewhat more data-based technique for deriving the best number of clusters is to examine and/or plot the amalgamation coefficients, which is the squared Euclidean distance between two variables, or variable clusters, which are combined at a particular step. Put simply, the amalgamation (i.e., linkage) coefficient is a numerical value that represents the point at which variables merge to form a cluster. More specifically, it is the value of the distance between the two most dissimilar points of the clusters that are being merged. By examining a list of these values, as seen in Table B.4 using the BANK ONE data, it is possible to identify jumps in the value of the coefficient. A jump means that two dissimilar clusters have been combined and suggests that the number of clusters

TABLE B.4

Amalgamation Coefficient List

Cluster Number/Step	Coefficient
1.	.771201
2.	.770867
3.	.752844
4.	.752651
5.	.748638
6.	.743124
7.	.733785
↓	↓
29.	.049612

prior to the combination is a possible solution (kind of like examining the length of a branch in a dendrogram). Jumps occur between two and three and between four and five.

As Thorndike originally suggested, it is also possible to plot the amalgamation coefficients in a manner that is similar to the scree test in factor analysis. A flattening in this type of plot suggests that no new information is contributed by the following cluster combinations.[37]

In summary, clustering approaches to job consolidation have their advocates.[38] A potentially nice feature of the cluster methods is that they clearly put each variable (i.e., person/position) into one, and only one, group. Thus, there is none of this business of examining factor loadings across multiple factors. On the downside, this also means that potentially useful information is unavailable. Furthermore, the fact that different clustering methods can, and do, yield different results can be disconcerting. Then, too, there is the limitation that cluster routines make one, sequential pass through the data to generate a result. As a consequence, poor decisions by the statistical algorithms to merge variables early in the pass through the data cannot be undone or reconsidered as additional information is channeled into the analysis. This means that simply reordering the variables in the data set can impact what the final solution looks like.

Finally, the presentation format of most cluster methods makes it difficult to really see what is going on in large data sets. Imagine a dendrogram like the one in Fig. B.2 with 150 variables versus 30. Nevertheless, it still often makes sense to generate a cluster solution after factoring a data set to confirm the results and, in some cases, even add a little precision in interpretation.

R-FACTOR ANALYSIS

We are not going to get into a full-blown discussion of R-factor analytic techniques. Much of what is important has already been covered in the section on consolidating job information using Q-factor methods.

A good example of a quantitatively based classification system using job analysis questionnaire data is Hemphill's work with management jobs.[39] Hemphill's questionnaire contained 575 activity items that were factor analyzed using principal components to produce 10 separate dimensions of management work. Research of this kind uses factor analysis on data sets in which the statements are treated as variables and the responses from raters completing the questionnaire are treated as observations. The basic data are cast in a work activity (or competency) by rater matrix, as opposed to the rater by activity (or competency) matrix used in Q-mode factor analysis.

Using factor analysis with item content from modeling questionnaires is a widespread activity. However, it should be noted that factoring importance ratings can be misleading when the ratings have been collected with reference to a single job.[40] The argument is that if a single job is targeted, and assuming there was perfect agreement among the raters about the value of the job characteristics being rated, their resulting patterns of disagreement would reflect response bias, idiosyncratic value systems, and unreliability, rather than any true differences in job content. As a result, factor analyses of ratings in this situation would capture spurious patterns of disagreement and not meaningful patterns of relationships among sets of questionnaire items. In this isolated context, when a single job is studied, this argument rings true. Far more typical in practical modeling situations, however, are occasions to model the work spanning multiple jobs.

Furthermore, for the results from a factor analysis to supplant the structure obtained from the content analysis, a large sample size is required. Some writers have suggested 5[41] or 10[42] times as many raters as items. Although recent work suggests that smaller sample sizes and rater-to-item ratios yield meaningful results,[43,44,45] as a general rule one should have at least two times as many raters as items. Unfortunately, such large sample sizes are not always available. Consequently, the results of the content analysis often have driving influence in determining the structure of work (i.e., classifying activities and competencies into subsets of items that are similar).

REFERENCES

[1]Ford, K. J., MacCallum, R. C., & Tait, M. (1986). The application of exploratory factor analysis in applied psychology: A critical review and analysis. *Personnel Psychology, 39*, 291–314.

[2]Velicer, W. F., & Jackson, D. N. (1990). Component analysis versus common factor analysis: Some issues in selecting an appropriate procedure. *Multivariate Behavioral Research, 25*, 1–28.

[3]Velicer, W. F. (1977). An empirical comparison of the similarity of principal component, image, and factor patterns. *Multivariate Behavioral Research, 12*, 3–22.

[4]Velicer, W. F., Peacock, A. C., & Jackson, D. N. (1982). A comparison of component and factor patterns: A Monte Carlo approach. *Multivariate Behavioral Research, 17*, 371–388.

[5]Arrindell, W. A., & van der Ende, J. (1985). An empirical test of the utility of the observations-to-variables ratio in factor and components analysis. *Applied Psychological Measurement, 9*, 165–178.

[6]Gorsuch, R. L. (1997). Exploratory factor analysis: Its role in item analysis. *Journal of Personality Assessment, 68*, 532–560.

[7]Tucker, L. R., Koopman, R. F., & Linn, R. L. (1969). Evaluation of factor analytic research procedures by means of simulated correlation matrices. *Psychometrika, 34*, 421–459.

[8]Kenny, D. A. (1979). *Correlation and causality.* New York: Wiley.

[9]Weiss, D. J. (1976). Multivariate procedures. In M.D. Dunnette (Ed.), *Handbook of industrial and organizational psychology* (pp. 327–362). Chicago: Rand McNally.

[10]Kim, J. O., & Mueller, C. W. (1978). *Introduction to factor analysis: What it is and how to do it* (Sage University Paper Series on Quantitative Applications in the Social Sciences). Beverly Hills, CA: Sage.

[11]Kim, J.O., & Mueller, C.W. (1978). *Factor analysis: Statistical methods and practical issues* (Sage University Paper Series on Quantitative Applications in the Social Sciences). Beverly Hills, CA: Sage.

[12]Overall, J. E., & Klett, C. J. (1972). *Applied multivariate analysis.* New York: McGraw-Hill.

[13]Gorsuch, R. L. (1974). *Factor analysis.* Philadelphia, PA: W. B. Saunders.

[14]Kaiser, H. F. (1974). Little Jiffy, Mark VII. *Educational and Psychological Measurement, 34*, 111–117.

[15]Robbins, S. (1980). On eigenvalues greater than unity and the true structure of tests. *Educational and Psychological Measurement, 40*, 875–877.

[16]Cattell, R. B. (1965). Factor analysis: An introduction to essentials. (1) the purpose and underlying models, (2) the role of factor analysis in research. *Biometrics, 21*, 190–215, 405–435.

[17]Horn, J. L. (1965). An empirical investigation of various methods for estimating common factor scores. *Educational and Psychological Measurement, 25*, 313–322.

[18]Velicer, W. F. (1976). Determining the number of components from the matrix of partial correlations. *Psychometrika, 41*, 321–327.

[19]Bartlett, M. S. (1950). Tests of significance in factor analysis. *British Journal of Psychology, 3*, 77–85.

[20]Bartlett, M. S. (1951). A further note on tests of significance in factor analysis. *British Journal of Psychology, 4,* 1–2.

[21]Jackson, D. N., & Morf, M. E. (1973). An empirical evaluation of factor reliability. *Multivariate Behavioral Research, 8,* 439–459.

[22]Guertin, A. A., Guertin, W. H., & Ware, W. B. (1981). Distortion as a function of the number of factors rotated under varying levels of common variance and error. *Educational and Psychological Measurement, 41,* 1–9.

[23]Levonian, E., & Comrey, A. L. (1966). Factorial stability as a function of the number of orthogonally-rotated factors. *Behavioral Science, 11,* 400–404.

[24]Rummel, R. J. (1970). *Applied factor analysis.* Evanston, IL: Northwestern University Press.

[25]Ford, K. J., MacCallum, R. C., & Tait, M. (1986). The application of exploratory factor analysis in applied psychology: A critical review and analysis. *Personnel Psychology, 39,* 291–314.

[26]Hakstian, A. R., Rogers, W. T., & Cattell, R. B. (1982). The behavior of number-of-factors rules with simulated data. *Multivariate Behavioral Research, 17,* 193–219.

[27]Nunnally, J. C. (1978). *Psychometric theory* (2nd ed.). New York: McGraw-Hill.

[28]Rummel, R. J. (1970). *Applied factor analysis.* Evanston, IL: Northwestern University Press. ·

[29]Colihan, J., & Burger, G. K. (1995). Constructing job families: An analysis of quantitative techniques used for grouping jobs. *Personnel Psychology, 48,* 563–586.

[30]Harvey, R. J. (1986). Quantitative approaches to job classification: A review and critique. *Personnel Psychology, 39,* 267–289.

[31]Anderberg, M. (1973). *Cluster analysis for applications.* New York: Academic Press.

[32]Blashfield, R. K. (1976). Mixture model tests of cluster analysis: Accuracy of four agglomerative hierarchical methods. *Psychological Bulletin, 83,* 377–388.

[33]Milligan, G. W. (1981). A Monte Carlo study of thirty internal criterion measures for cluster analysis. *Psychometrika, 46,* 187–199.

[34]Blashfield, R. K., & Aldenderfer, M. S. (1988). The methods and problems of cluster analysis. In J. R. Nesselroade & R. B. Catell (Eds.), *Handbook of multivariate experimental psychology* (pp. 447–473). New York: Plenum.

[35]Garwood, M. K., Anderson, L. E., & Greengart, B. J. (1991). Determining job groups: Applications of hierarchical agglomerative cluster analysis in different job analysis situations. *Personnel Psychology, 44,* 743–762.

[36]Aldenderfer, M. S., & Blashfield, R. K. (1984). *Cluster analysis.* Newbury Park, CA: Sage.

[37]Ibid.

[38]Mobley, W. H., & Ramsey, R. S. (1973). Hierarchical clustering on the basis of inter-job similarity as a tool in validity generalization. *Personnel Psychology, 26,* 213–225.

[39]Hemphill, J. K. (1960). *Dimensions of executive positions.* (Research Monography No. 98). Columbus, OH: Ohio State University, Bureau of Business Research.

[40]Cranny, C. J., & Doherty, M. E. (1988). Importance ratings in job analysis: Note on the misinterpretation of factor analysis. *Journal of Applied Psychology, 73,* 320–322.

[41]Gorsuch, R. L. (1974). *Factor analysis.* Philadelphia, PA: W.B. Saunders.

[42]Nunnally, J. C. (1978). *Psychometric theory* (2nd ed.). New York: McGraw-Hill.

[43]Gorsuch, R. L. (1997). Exploratory factor analysis: Its role in item analysis. *Journal of Personality Assessment, 68,* 532–560.

[44]Guadagnoli, E., & Velicer, W. F. (1989). Relation of sample size to the stability of component patterns. *Psychological Bulletin, 103,* 265–275.

[45]Reddon, J. R. (1990). The rejection of the hypothesis of complete independence prior to conducting a factor analysis. *Multivariate Experimental Clinical Research, 9,* 123–129.

References

Ackerman, P. L., & Humphreys, L. G. (1990). Individual differences theory in industrial and organizational psychology. In M. D. Dunnette & L. M. Hough (Eds.), *Handbook of industrial and organizational psychology* (Vol. 1, pp. 223–282). Palo Alto, CA: Consulting Psychologists Press.

Age Discrimination in Employment Act of 1967 (Pub.L. 90-202) (ADEA), as amended, 29 U.S.C. 621 *et. seq.*

Aldenderfer, M. S., & Blashfield, R. K. (1984). *Cluster analysis.* Newbury Park, CA: Sage.

American Psychological Association. (1985). *Standards for educational and psychological testing,* Washington, DC: Author.

Americans with Disabilities Act of 1990 (Pub.L. 101-336) (ADA), as amended, 42 U.S.C. 12101 *et. seq.*

Ammerman, H. L. (1977). *Performance content for job training; Vol. II. Stating the tasks of the job* (R&D Series No. 122). Columbus: The Ohio State University, The Center for Vocational Education.

Ammerman, N. L., & Pratzner, F. C. (1977). *Performance content for job training* (R & D Ser. 121-125, Vols. 1-5). Columbus, OH: Center for Vocational Education.

Anderberg, M. (1973). *Cluster analysis for applications.* New York: Academic Press.

Arnowitz, S., & DiFazio, W. (1994). *The jobless future.* Minneapolis, MN: University of Minnesota Press.

Arrindell, W. A., & van der Ende, J. (1985). An empirical test of the utility of the observations-to-variables ratio in factor and components analysis. *Applied Psychological Measurement, 9,* 165–178.

Arthur, J. B. (1994). Effects of human resource systems on manufacturing performance and turnover. *Academy of Management Journal, 37,* 670–687.

Arthur, W., Doverspike, D., & Barrett, G. V. (1996). Development of a job analysis-based procedure for weighting and combining content-related tests into a single battery score. *Personnel Psychology, 49,* 971–985.

Arvey, R. D., Maxwell, S. E., Gutenberg, R. L., & Camp, C. (1981). Detecting job differences: A Monte Carlo study. *Personnel Psychology, 34,* 709–730.

Ash, R. A., & Edgell, S. L. (1975). A note on the readability of the position analysis questionnaire. *Journal of Applied Psychology, 60,* 765–766.

Ash, R. A., Levine, E. L., & Sistrunk, F. (1983). The role of jobs and job-based methods in personnel and human resource management. In K. M. Rowland & G. R. Ferris (Eds.), *Research in personnel and human resources management* (Vol. 1, 45–84). Greenwich, CT: JAI Press.

Ashkenas, R., Ulrich, D., Jick, T., & Kerr, S. (1995). *The boundaryless organization*. San Francisco: Jossey-Bass.

Asimov, I. (1988). *The relativity of wrong*. New York: Windsor.

Baehr, M. E. (1967, March). *A factorial framework for job description*. Paper presented at the meeting of the Industrial Section, Illinois Psychological Association, Springfield, IL.

Baehr, M. E., & Orban, J. A. (1988). Municipal transit bus operator. In S. Gael (Ed.), *The job analysis handbook for business, industry, and government* (Vol. 2, pp. 1229–1241). New York: Wiley.

Baird, L., & Meshoulam, I. (1988). Managing two fits of strategic human resource management. *Academy of Management Review, 13*, 116–128.

Barrett, R. S. (1996). *Fair employment strategies in human resource management*. Westport, CT: Quorum.

Bartel, A. P. (1994). Productivity gains from the implementation of employee training programs. *Industrial Relations, 33*, 411–425.

Bartlett, M. S. (1950). Tests of significance in factor analysis. *The British Journal of Psychology, 3*, 77–85.

Bartlett, M. S. (1951). A further note on tests of significance in factor analysis. *The British Journal of Psychology, 4*, 1–2.

Bass, B. M., Cascio, W. F., & O'Connor, E. J. (1974). Magnitude estimations of expressions of frequency and amount. *Journal of Applied Psychology, 59*, 313–320.

Beatty, G. O. (1996, April). *Job analysis sample size: How small is large enough?* Poster presented at the 11th annual conference of the Society for Industrial and Organizational Psychology, San Diego, CA.

Beatty, R. W., Coleman, S. C., & Schneier, C. E. (1988). Human resources planning and staffing. In S. Gael (Ed.), *The job analysis handbook for business, industry, and government* (Vol. 1, pp. 138–156). New York: Wiley.

Becker, B., & Gerhart, B. (1996). The impact of human resources management on organizational performance: Progress and prospects. *Academy of Management Journal, 39*, 779–801.

Bendig, A. W. (1952). A statistical report on a revision of the Miami instructor rating sheet. *Journal of Educational Psychology, 43*, 423–429.

Bendig, A. W. (1953). The reliability of self-ratings as a function of the amount of verbal anchoring and the number of categories on the scale. *Journal of Applied Psychology, 37*, 38–41.

Bendig, A. W. (1954). Reliability and number of rating scale categories. *Journal of Applied Psychology, 38*, 38–40.

Bernardin, H. J. (1988). Police officer. In S. Gael (Ed.), *The job analysis handbook for business, industry, and government* (Vol. 2, pp. 1242–1254). New York: Wiley.

Bernardin, H. J., & Beatty, R. W. (1984). *Performance appraisal: Assessing human behavior at work*. Boston: Kent.

Blashfield, R. K. (1976). Mixture model tests of cluster analysis: Accuracy of four agglomerative hierarchical methods. *Psychological Bulletin, 83*, 377–388.

Blashfield, R. K., & Aldenderfer, M. S. (1988). The methods and problems of cluster analysis. In J. R. Nesselroade & R. B. Catell (Eds.), *Handbook of multivariate experimental psychology* (pp. 447–473). New York: Plenum.

Bloom, R., & Prien, E. P. (1983). A guide to job-related employment interviewing. *Personnel Administrator, 28,* 81–86.

Boorstin, D. J. (1983). *The discoverers.* New York: Random House.

Borgen, F. H., Weiss, D. J., Tinsley, H. E. A., Dawis, R. V., & Lofquist, L. H. (1968). *The measurement of occupational reinforcer patterns.* Minneapolis: Vocational Psychology Research, Department of Psychology, University of Minnesota.

Borman, W. C., & Brush, D. H. (1993). More progress toward a taxonomy of managerial performance requirements. *Human Performance, 6,* 1–21.

Borman, W. C., Dorsey, D., & Ackerman, L. (1992). Time-spent responses as time allocation strategies: Relations with sales performance in a stockbroker sample. *Personnel Psychology, 45,* 763–777.

Boudreau, J. W. (1991). Utility analysis in human resource management decisions. In M. D. Dunnette & L. M. Hough (Eds.), *Handbook of industrial and organizational psychology* (Vol. 2, pp. 621–745). Palo Alto, CA: Consulting Psychologist Press.

Boudreau, J. W., & Ramstad, P. M. (1997). Measuring intellectual capital: Learning from financial history. *Human Resource Management, 36,* 343–356.

Boyatzis, R. E. (1982). *The competent manager: A model for effective performance.* New York: Wiley-Interscience.

Bridges, W. (1994). *Jobshift.* Reading, MA: Addison-Wesley.

Brooking, A. (1996). *Intellectual capital.* London: International Thompson Business Press.

Brown, W. (1910). Some experimental results in the correlation of mental abilities. *British Journal of Psychology, 3,* 296–322.

Brush, D. H., & Schoenfeldt, L. F. (1980). Identifying managerial potential: An alternative approach to assessment centers. *Personnel, 57,* 68–76.

Burns, T., & Stalker, G. M. (1961). *The management of innovation.* London: Tavistock.

Butler, S. K., & Harvey, R. J. (1988). A comparison of holistic versus decomposed rating of position analysis questionnaire work dimensions. *Personnel Psychology, 41,* 761–777.

Carson, K. P., & Stewart, G. L. (1996). Job analysis and the sociotechnical approach to quality: A critical examination. *Journal of Quality Management, 1,* 49–64.

Cattell, R. B. (1965). Factor analysis: An introduction to essentials. (1) the purpose and underlying models, (2) the role of factor analysis in research. *Biometrics, 21,* 190–215, 405–435.

Christal, R. E. (1974). The United States Air Force occupational research project. *Selected Documents in Psychology, 4*(61), 1–66.

Civil Rights Act of 1991 (Pub.L. 102–166) (CRA).

Colihan, J., & Burger, G. K. (1995). Constructing job families: An analysis of quantitative techniques used for grouping jobs. *Personnel Psychology, 48,* 563–586.

Conley, P. R., & Sackett, P. R. (1987). Effects of using high- versus low-performing job incumbents as sources of job analysis information. *Journal of Applied Psychology, 72,* 434–437.

Cook, T. D., & Campbell, D. T. (1979). *Quasi-experimentation: Design and analysis issues for field settings.* Chicago: Rand McNally.

Cordery, J. L., & Sevastos, P. P. (1993). Responses to the original and revised job diagnostic survey: Is education a factor in responses to negatively worded items? *Journal of Applied Psychology, 78,* 141–143.

Cornelius, E. T. (1983). *Canonical correlation as a job classification technique.* Paper presented at the annual meeting of the American Institute of Decision Science, San Antonio, TX.

Cornelius, E. T., & Lyness, K. S. (1980). A comparison of holistic and decomposed judgment strategies in job analysis by job incumbents. *Journal of Applied Psychology, 65,* 155–163.

Cortese, A. (1996, February 26). Here comes the Intranet. *Business Week,* pp. 76–84.

Cosgrove, H. R. (Ed.). (1997). *Encyclopedia of careers and vocational guidance.* Chicago: J. G. Ferguson.

Cragun, J. R., & McCormick, E. J. (1967). *Job inventory information: Task and scale reliabilities and scale interrelationships* (PRL No. TR-67-15). Lackland Airforce Base, TX: Personnel Research Laboratory.

Cranny, C. J., & Doherty, M. E. (1988). Importance ratings in job analysis: Note on the misinterpretation of factor analysis. *Journal of Applied Psychology, 73,* 320–322.

Cronbach, L. J. (1951). Coefficient alpha and the internal structure of tests. *Psychometrika, 16,* 297–334.

Cronshaw, S. F. (1997). Job analysis: Changing nature of work. *Canadian Psychology, 39,* 5–13.

Cunningham, J. W., Boese, R. R., Neeb, R. W., & Pass, J. J. (1983). Systematically derived work dimensions: Factor analyses of the occupation analysis inventory. *Journal of Applied Psychology, 68,* 232–252.

D'Aveni, D. (1994). *Hypercompetition.* New York: Free Press.

Davids, M. (1997). Money, money everywhere. *Journal of Business Strategy, 18,* 49–51.

Davidson, W. N., Worrell, D. L., & Fox, J. B. (1996). Early retirement programs and firm performance. *Academy of Management Journal, 39,* 970–984.

Davis, L. E., & Wacker, G. J. (1988). Job design. In S. Gael (Ed.), *The job analysis handbook for business, industry, and government* (Vol. 1, pp. 157–172). New York: Wiley.

DeCotiis, T. A., & Morano, R. A. (1977). Applying job analysis to training. *Training and Development Journal, 31,* 20–24.

Delery, J. E., & Doty, D. H. (1996). Modes of theorizing in strategic human resource management: Tests of universalistic, contingency, and configural performance predictions. *Academy of Management Journal, 39,* 802–835.

Department of Labor. (1996). *Occupational outlook handbook.* Washington, DC: U.S. Government Printing Office.

Descartes, R. (1960). *Discourse on methods and meditations* (L. J. Lafleur, Trans.). Indianapolis, IN: The Liberal Arts Press.

Dixon, W. J. (1985). *BMDP statistical software: 1985 printing.* Berkeley, CA: University of California Press.

Drauden, G. M., & Peterson, N. G. (1974). *A domain sampling approach to job analysis.* St. Paul, MN: State of Minnesota Personnel Department. (Available through the Journal Supplement Abstract Service, Catalogue of Selected Documents in Psychology, MS1447.)

Drucker, P. F. (1977, September-October). The future that has already happened. *Harvard Business Review,* pp. 19–32.

Duncan, R. B. (1972). Characteristics of organizational environments and perceived environmental uncertainty. *Administrative Science Quarterly, 17*, 313–327.

Dunnette, M. D., & Motowildo, S. J. (1975). *Police selection and career assessment.* Washington, DC: U.S. Government Printing Office.

Dunnette, M. D., Hough, L. M., & Rosse, R. L. (1979). Task and job taxonomies as a basis for identifying labor supply sources and evaluating employment qualifications. In G. T. Milkovich & L. Dyer (Eds.), *Affirmative action planning.* New York: Human Resource Planning Society.

Equal Employment Opportunity Commission, Civil Service Commission, Department of Labor, & Department of Justice. (1978). *Uniform guidelines on employee selection procedures.* Federal Register, *43*(166), 38295–38309.

Feild, H. S., & Gatewood, R. D. (1989). Development of a selection interview: A job content strategy. In R. W. Eder & G. R. Ferris (Eds.), *The employment interview* (pp. 145–157). Newbury Park, CA: Sage.

Ferguson, L. W. (1963). *Psychology and the army: Classification of personnel.* New York: The Heritage of Industrial Psychology.

Fine, S. A., & Cronshaw, S. (1994). The role of job analysis in establishing the validity of biodata. In G. S. Stockes, M. D. Mumford, & W. A. Owens (Eds.), *Biodata handbook* (pp. 39–64). Palo Alto, CA: CCP Books.

Fine, S. A., & Wiley, W. W. (1971). *An introduction to functional job analysis: A scaling of selected tasks from the social welfare field.* Kalamazoo, MI: W. E. Upjohn Institute for Employment Research.

Finn, R. H. (1972). Effects of some variations in rating scale characteristics on the means and reliabilities of ratings. *Educational and Psychological Measurement, 32*, 255–265.

Flanagan, J. C. (1954). The critical incident technique. *Psychological Bulletin, 51*, 327–358.

Fleishman, E. A., & Quaintance, M. K. (1984). *Taxonomies of human performance.* Orlando, FL: Academic Press.

Fleishman, E. A., & Reilly, M. E. (1992). *Handbook of human abilities.* Palo Alto, CA: Consulting Psychologists Press.

Fleishman, E. A., Wetrogan, L. I., Uhlman, C. E., & Marshall-Mies, J. C. (1995). In N. G. Peterson, M. D. Mumford, W. C. Borman, P. R. Jeanneret, & E. A. Fleishman (Eds.), *Development of prototype occupational information network content model* (Vol. 1, pp. 10.1–10.39). Utah: Utah Department of Employment Security (Contract Number 94-542).

Flesch, R. (1948). A new readability yardstick. *Journal of Applied Psychology, 32*, 221–233.

Fletcher, J., Friedman, L., McCarthy, P., McIntyre, C., O'Leary, B., & Rheinstein, J. (1993, April). *Sample sizes required to attain stable job analysis inventory profiles.* Poster presented at the eighth annual conference of the Society for Industrial and Organizational Psychology, Miami, FL.

Ford, K. J., MacCallum, R. C., & Tait, M. (1986). The application of exploratory factor analysis in applied psychology: A critical review and analysis. *Personnel Psychology, 39*, 291–314.

Ford, K. J., & Wroten, S. P. (1984). Introducing new methods for conducting training evaluation and for linking training evaluation to program redesign. *Personnel Psychology, 37*, 651–665.

Friedman, L. (1990). Degree of redundancy between time, importance, and frequency task ratings. *Journal of Applied Psychology, 75*, 748–752.

Gael, S. (1988). Job descriptions. In S. Gael (Ed.) *The job analysis handbook for business, industry, and government* (Vol. 1, pp. 71–89). New York: Wiley.

Gael, S. (1988). *The job analysis handbook for business, industry, and government* (Vol. 2). New York: Wiley.

Gael, S. (1990). *Job analysis: A guide to assessing work activities.* San Francisco, CA: Jossey-Bass.

Garwood, M. K., Anderson, L. E., & Greengart, B. J. (1991). Determining job groups: Applications of hierarchical agglomerative cluster analysis in different job analysis situations. *Personnel Psychology, 44*, 743–762.

Gatewood, R. D., & Feild, H. S. (1994). *Human resource selection.* Fort Worth, TX: The Dryden Press.

Gerhart, F., & Milkovich, G. T. (1993). Employee compensation: Research and practice. In M. D. Dunnette & L. M. Hough (Eds.), *Handbook of industrial and organizational psychology* (Vol. 3, pp. 481–569). Palo Alto, CA: Consulting Psychologists Press.

Ghemawat, P. (1991). *Commitment: The dynamics of strategy.* New York: Free Press.

Gilbreth, F. B., & Gilbreth, L. E. (1919). *Motion study for the handicapped.* New York: E. P. Dutton.

Goldstein, I. L. (1993). *Training in organizations* (3rd ed.). Monterey, CA: Brooks/Cole.

Goldstein, I. L., & Buxton, V. M. (1982). Training and human performance. In M. D. Dunnette & E. A. Fleishman (Eds.), *Human performance and productivity* (pp. 135–177). Hillsdale, NJ: Lawrence Erlbaum Associates.

Gorsuch, R. L. (1974). *Factor analysis.* Philadelphia, PA: W. B. Saunders.

Gorsuch, R. L. (1997). Exploratory factor analysis: Its role in item analysis. *Journal of Personality Assessment, 68*, 532–560.

Green, S. B., & Stutzman, T. (1986). An evaluation of methods to select respondents to structured job analysis questionnaires. *Personnel Psychology, 39*, 543–564.

Green, S. B., & Veres, J. (1990). Evaluation of an index to detect inaccurate respondents to a task analysis inventory. *Journal of Business and Psychology, 5*, 47–61.

Greengard, S. (1994). The next generation. *Personnel Journal, 73*, 40–46.

Greengard, S. (1995). Catch the wave as HR goes online. *Personnel Journal, 74*, 54–68.

Guadagnoli, E., & Velicer, W. F. (1989). Relation of sample size to the stability of component patterns. *Psychological Bulletin, 103*, 265–275.

Guertin, A. A., Guertin, W. H., & Ware, W. B. (1981). Distortion as a function of the number of factors rotated under varying levels of common variance and error. *Educational and Psychological Measurement, 41*, 1–9.

Guion, R. M. (1998). *Assessment, measurement and prediction for personnel decisions.* Mahwah, NJ: Lawrence Erlbaum Associates.

Hakstian, A. R., Rogers, W. T., & Cattell, R. B. (1982). The behavior of number-of-factors rules with simulated data. *Multivariate Behavioral Research, 17*, 193–219.

Hamel, G. (1995, October). *Tomorrowday 1995.* Paper presented at the Masters Forum, Minneapolis, MN.

Hamel, G., & Prahalad, C. K. (1994). *Competing for the future.* Boston: Harvard Business School Press.

Harvey, R. J. (1986). Quantitative approaches to job classification: A review and critique. *Personnel Psychology, 39*, 267–289.

Harvey, R. J. (1991). Job analysis. In M. D. Dunnette & L. M. Hough (Eds.), *Handbook of industrial and organizational psychology* (Vol. 2, pp. 71–163). Palo Alto, CA: Consulting Psychologists Press.

Hemphill, J. K. (1960). *Dimensions of executive positions* (Research Monography No. 98). Columbus: Ohio State University, Bureau of Business Research.

Henderson, R. I. (1988). Job evaluation, classification and pay. In S. Gael (Ed.), *The job analysis handbook for business, industry, and government* (Vol. 1, pp. 90–118). New York: Wiley.

Hoovers Business Press Staff. (1997). *Hoovers handbook of American business.* Austin, TX: Hoovers.

Horn, J. L. (1965). An empirical investigation of various methods for estimating common factor scores. *Educational and Psychological Measurement, 25,* 313–322.

Howard, A. (Ed.). (1995). *The changing nature of work.* San Francisco: Jossey-Bass.

Hughes, G. L., & Prien, E. P. (1989). Evaluation of task and job skill linkage judgments used to develop test specifications. *Personnel Psychology, 42,* 283–292.

Hughes, G. L., Prien, E. P., & Hicks, J. (1987). Compensation and benefit plans in nonprofit organizations. In E. W. Anthes & J. Cronin (Eds.), *Personnel matters in the nonprofit organization* (pp. 279–312). West Memphis, AR: Independent Community Consultants.

Hunter, J. E. (1986). Cognitive ability, cognitive aptitudes, job knowledge, and job performance. *Journal of Vocational Behavior, 29,* 340–362.

Huselid, M. A. (1993, August). *Estimates of the impact of human resource management practices on turnover and productivity.* Paper presented at the annual meeting of the Academy of Management, Atlanta.

Huselid, M. A. (1995). The impact of human resource management practices on turnover, productivity, and corporate financial performance. *Academy of Management Journal, 38,* 635–672.

Huselid, M. A., & Becker, B. (1995, August). *High performance work systems and organizational performance.* Paper presented at the annual meeting of the Academy of Management, Vancouver, Canada.

Huselid, M. A., & Becker, B. E. (1996). Methodological issues in cross-sectional and panel estimates of the HR-firm performance link. *Industrial Relations, 35,* 400–422.

Jackson, D. N., & Morf, M. E. (1973). An empirical evaluation of factor reliability. *Multivariate Behavioral Research, 8,* 439–459.

Johnson, J. W., Schneider, R. J., & Oswald, F. L. (1997). Toward a taxonomy of managerial performance profiles. *Human Performance, 10,* 227–250.

Jones, L. V., & Thurstone, L. L. (1955). The psychophysics of semantics: An experimental investigation. *Journal of Applied Psychology, 39,* 31–36.

Kaiser, H. F. (1974). Little Jiffy, Mark VII. *Educational and Psychological Measurement, 34,* 111–117.

Kane, J. A. (1983). *A job analysis for the police officer job in the city of Washington, DC.* Unpublished manuscript.

Kane, M. T., Kingsbury, C., Colton, D., & Estes, C. (1989). Combining data on criticality and frequency in developing test plans for licensure and certification examinations. *Journal of Educational Measurement, 26,* 17–27.

Katz, D., & Kahn, R. L. (1978). *The social psychology of organizations* (2nd ed.). New York: Wiley.

Kenny, D. A. (1979). *Correlation and causality.* New York: Wiley.

Kim, J. O., & Mueller, C. W. (1978). *Factor analysis: Statistical methods and practical issues* (Sage University Paper Series on Quantitative Applications in the Social Sciences). Beverly Hills, CA: Sage.

Kim, J. O., & Mueller, C. W. (1978). *Introduction to factor analysis: What it is and how to do it* (Sage University Paper Series on Quantitative Applications in the Social Sciences). Beverly Hills, CA: Sage.

Kleiman, L. S., & Biderman, M. (1989). Job analysis for managerial selection: A guidelines-based approach. *Journal of Business and Psychology, 3,* 353–359.

Kleiman, L. S., & Faley, R. H. (1985). The implications of professional and legal guidelines for court decisions involving criterion-related validity: A review and analysis. *Personnel Psychology, 38,* 803–831.

Knoke, D., & Kalleberg, A. L. (1994). Job training in U.S. organizations. *American Sociological Review, 59,* 537–546.

Kraut, A. I. (1996). Planning and conducting the survey: Keeping strategic purpose in mind. In A. I. Kraut (Ed.), *Organizational surveys: Tools for assessment and change* (pp. 149–176) San Francisco: Jossey-Bass.

Landy, F. J. (1988). Selection procedure development and usage. In S. Gael (Ed.), *The job analysis handbook for business, industry, and government* (Vol. 1, pp. 271–287). New York: Wiley.

Landy, F. J., & Vasey, J. (1991). Job analysis: The composition of SME samples. *Personnel Psychology, 44,* 27–50.

Langeland, K. L., Johnson, C. M., & Mawhinney, T. C. (1998). Improving staff performance in a community health setting: Job analysis, training, goal setting, feedback, and years of data. *Journal of Organizational Behavior Management, 18,* 21–43.

Latham, G. P., & Fry, L. W. (1988). Measuring and appraising employee performance. In S. Gael (Ed.), *The job analysis handbook for business, industry, and government* (Vol. 1, pp. 216–233). New York: Wiley.

Lawrence, P. R., & Lorsch, J. W. (1967). *Organizations and environments.* Boston: Division of Research, Harvard Business School.

Lawrence, P. R., & Lorsch, J. W. (1986). *Differentiation and integration in complex organizations.* Cambridge, MA: Harvard Graduate School of Business Administration.

Lawshe, C. H. (1989). *Describing work behavior: How to prepare job activity or task statements.* West Lafayette, IN: Author.

Lengnick-Hall, C. A., & Lengnick-Hall, M. L. (1988). Strategic human resource management: A review of the literature and a proposed typology. *Academy of Management Review, 13,* 454–470.

Levine, E. L. (1983). *Everything you wanted to know about job analysis.* Tampa, FL: Mariner Publishing.

Levonian, E., & Comrey, A. L. (1966). Factorial stability as a function of the number of orthogonally-rotated factors. *Behavioral Science, 11,* 400–404.

Locklear, T. S. (1992). The exploration and evaluation of an index to detect inaccurate respondents to structured job analysis questionnaires. *Dissertation Abstracts International, 53*(5-B), 2572.

Lodge, M., Cross, D., Tursky, B., & Tanenhaus, J. (1975). The psychophysical scaling and validation of a political support scale. *American Journal of Political Science, 19,* 611–649.

Lodge, M., & Tursky, B. (1981). The social psychophysical scaling of political opinion. In B. Wegener (Ed.), *Social attitudes and psychophysical measurement*. Hillsdale, NJ: Lawrence Erlbaum Associates.

London, M. (1988). Career planning and development. In S. Gael (Ed.), *The job analysis handbook for business, industry, and government* (Vol. 1, pp. 234–242). New York: Wiley.

Lopez, F. M., Kesselman, G. A., & Lopez, F. E. (1981). An empirical test of a trait-oriented job analysis technique. *Personnel Psychology, 34,* 479–502.

Lozada-Larsen, S. R. (1992). *The Americans With Disabilities Act: Using job analysis to meet new challenges*. Presentation at the IPMA Assessment Council Conference, Baltimore, MD.

MacDuffie, J. P. (1995). Human resource bundles and manufacturing performance: Organizational logic and flexible production systems in the world auto industry. *Industrial and Labor Relations Review, 48,* 197–221.

Macey, W. H. (1996). Dealing with the data: Collection, processing, and analysis. In A. I. Kraut (Ed.), *Organizational surveys: Tools for assessment and change* (pp. 204–232) San Francisco, CA: Jossey-Bass.

McCormick, E. J. (1979). *Job analysis: Methods and applications*. New York: AMACOM.

McCormick, E. J., Jeanneret, P. R., & Mecham, R. M. (1972). A study of job characteristics and job dimensions as based on the Position Analysis Questionnaire (PAQ). *Journal of Applied Psychology, 56,* 347–368.

McIntire, S., Bucklan, M. A., & Scott, D. (1995). *Job analysis kit*. Lutz, FL: Psychological Assessment Resources.

McLagan, P. A. (1990). Flexible job models: A productivity strategy for the Information Age. In J. P. Campbell & R. J. Campbell & Associates (Eds.), *Productivity in organizations* (pp. 369–387). San Francisco, CA: Jossey-Bass.

McLaughlin, D. J., McLaughlin, B. L., & Lischick, C. W. (1991). Company values: A key to managing in turbulent times. In R. J. Niehus, & K. F. Price, (Eds.), *Bottom line results from strategic human resource planning* (pp. 261–274). New York: Plenum.

McLaughlin, G. H. (1969). SMOG grading: A new readability formula. *Journal of Reading, 12,* 639–646.

Micklethwait, J., & Wooldridge, A. (1996). *The witch doctors*. New York: Times Books.

Milligan, G. W. (1981). A Monte Carlo study of thirty internal criterion measures for cluster analysis. *Psychometrika, 46,* 187–199.

Mintzberg, H. (1979). *The structuring of organizations*. Englewood Cliffs, NJ: Prentice-Hall.

Mintzberg, H. (1994). *The rise and fall of strategic planning*. Hemel Hempstead: Prentice-Hall.

Mitchell, T. W. (1991). Comprehensive job analysis: Multipurpose or any purpose? *The Industrial Psychologist, 29,* 69–74.

Mobley, W. H., & Ramsey, R. S. (1973). Hierarchical clustering on the basis of inter-job similarity as a tool in validity generalization. *Personnel Psychology, 26,* 213–225.

Morgan, R. B., & Smith, J. E. (1996). *Staffing the new workplace: Selecting and promoting for quality improvement*. Milwaukee, WI: ASQC Quality Press.

Morgeson, F. P., & Campion, M. A. (1997). Social and cognitive sources of potential inaccuracy in job analysis. *Journal of Applied Psychology, 82,* 627–655.

Morsh, J. E., & Archer, W. B. (1967). *Procedural guide for conducting occupational surveys in the United States.* Lackland AFB, TX: Personnel Research Laboratory, Aerospace Medical Division, PRL-TR-67-11.

Moskowitz, M., Levering, R., & Katz, M. (1990). *Everybody's business.* New York: Doubleday.

Mullins, W. C., & Kimbrough, W. W. (1988). Group composition as a determinant of job analysis outcomes. *Journal of Applied Psychology, 73,* 657–664.

Mumford, M. D., & Peterson, N. G. (1995). Introduction. In N. G. Peterson, M. D. Mumford, W. C. Borman, P. R. Jeanneret, & E. A. Fleishman (Eds.), *Development of prototype occupational information network content model* (Vol. 1, pp. 1.1–1.16). Utah: Utah Department of Employment Security (Contract No. 94-542).

Narayanan, V. K., & Fahey, L. (1994). In L. Fahey & R. M. Randall (Eds.), *The portable MBA in strategy* (pp. 195–223). New York: Wiley.

Nunnally, J. C. (1978). *Psychometric theory* (2nd ed.). New York: McGraw-Hill.

Osborne, A. F. (1953). *Applied imagination.* New York: Charles Scribner's Sons.

Overall, J. E., & Klett, C. J. (1972). *Applied multivariate analysis.* New York: McGraw-Hill.

Page, R. C., & Caskey, D. T. (1988). Computer programmer. In S. Gael (Ed.), *The job analysis handbook for business, industry, and government* (Vol. 2, pp. 1192–1205). New York: Wiley.

Page, R. C., & van De Vroot, D. M. (1989). Job analysis and HR planning. In W. F. Cascio (Ed.), *Human resource planning employment and placement.* Washington, DC: Bureau of National Affairs, Inc.

Pass, J. J., & Robertson, D. W. (1980). *Methods to evaluate scales and sample size for stable task inventory information* (Report No. NPRDC TR 80-28). San Diego, CA: Naval Personnel Research and Development Center.

Pearce, J. A., & David F. (1987). Corporate mission statements: The bottom line. *Academy of Management Executive, 1,* 109–116.

Pearlman, K. (1980). Job families: A review and discussion of their implications for personnel selection. *Psychological Bulletin, 87,* 1–28.

Pine, D. P. (1995). Assessing the validity of job ratings: An empirical study of false reporting in task inventories. *Public Personnel Management, 24,* 451–460.

Plato (1973). *The republic and other works* (B. Jowitt, Trans.). New York: Anchor.

Porter, M. E. (1980). *Competitive strategy.* New York: Free Press.

Porter, M. E. (1985). *Competitive advantage.* New York: Free Press.

Prien, E. P. (1988). *Job analysis manual.* Unpublished manuscript.

Prien, E. P. (1991). *Action verb starter list.* Memphis, TN: Author.

Prien, E. P. (1997). Clerical inventory. Memphis, TN: Author.

Prien, E. P. (1997). Sales inventory. Memphis, TN: Author.

Prien, E. P., Goldstein, I. L., & Macey, W. H. (1987). Multi-domain job analysis: Procedures and applications. *Training and Development Journal, 41,* 68–72.

Prien, E. P., & Ronan, W. W. (1971). Job analysis: A review of research findings. *Personnal Psychology, 24,* 371–396.

Prien, E. P., & Schippmann, J. S. (1987). Hiring—Screening and selecting staff for the nonprofit organization. In E. W. Anthes & J. Cronin (Eds.), *Personnel matters in the nonprofit organization.* West Memphis, AR: Independent Community Consultants.

Primoff, E. S. (1975). *How to prepare and conduct job-element examinations* (U.S. Civil Service Commission, Technical Study 75-1). Washington, DC: U.S. Government Printing Office.

Primoff, E. S., & Fine, S. A. (1988). A history of job analysis. In S. Gael (Ed.), *The job analysis handbook for business, industry, and government* (Vol. 1, 14–29). New York: Wiley.

Ramstad, P. M., Janz, T., & Neumann, D. (1998). *Surviving the shift to a human asset economy.* Unpublished manuscript.

Rath, G., & Stoyanoff, K. (1983). The Delphi technique. In F. L. Ulschak (Ed.), *Human resource development: The theory and practice of needs assessment* (pp. 111–131). Reston, VA: Reston Publishing Company.

Raymark, P. H., Schmit, M. J., & Guion, R. M. (1997). Identifying potentially useful personality constructs for employee selection. *Journal of Applied Psychology, 50,* 723–736.

Reagan, R. T., Mosteller, F., & Youtz, C. (1989). Quantitative meanings of verbal probability expressions. *Journal of Applied Psychology, 74,* 433–442.

Reddon, J. R. (1990). The rejection of the hypothesis of complete independence prior to conducting a factor analysis. *Multivariate Experimental Clinical Research, 9,* 123–129.

Rifkin, G. (1997). How to "truck" the brand: Lessons from the Grateful Dead. *Strategy & Business, 6,* 51–57.

Rifkin, J. (1995). *The end of work: The decline of the global labor force and the dawn of the post-market era.* New York: Putnam.

Robbins, S. (1980). On eigenvalues greater than unity and the true structure of tests. *Educational and Psychological Measurement, 40,* 875–877.

Rosenberg, S., & Sedlack, Z. (1972). Structural representations of perceived trait relationships. In A. K. Romney, R. N. Shepard, & S. B. Nerlave (Eds.), *Multidimensional scaling* (Vol. 2, pp. 133–162). New York: Seminar.

Rouleau, E., & Krain, B. (1975, September–October). Using job analysis to design selection procedures. *Public Personnel Management,* pp. 300–304.

Rugman, A. M., Kirton, J., & Soloway, J. A. (1997). NAFTA, environmental regulations and Canadian competitiveness. *Journal of World Trade, 31,* 129–144.

Rummel, R. J. (1970). *Applied factor analysis.* Evanston, IL: Northwestern University Press.

Sackett, P. R., Cornelius, E. T., & Carron, T. J. (1981). A comparison of global judgment vs. task oriented approaches to job classification. *Personnel Psychology, 34,* 791–804.

Sanchez, J. I. (1994). From documentation to innovation: Reshaping job analysis to meet emerging business needs. *Human Resource Management Review, 4*(1), 51–74.

Sanchez, J. I., & Fraser, S. L. (1992). On the choice of scales for task analysis. *Journal of Applied Psychology, 77,* 545–553.

Sanchez, J. I., & Levine, E. L. (1989). Determining important tasks within jobs: A policy-capturing approach. *Journal of Applied Psychology, 74,* 336–342.

SAS Institute, Inc. (1985). *SAS SR user's guide: Statistics, version 5 edition.* Cary, NC: Author.

Sayles, L. (1964). *Managerial behavior.* New York: McGraw-Hill.

Schippmann, J. S. (1996). *Key decision points in job modeling.* Unpublished manuscript.

Schippmann, J. S., Hughes, G. L., & Prien, E. P. (1987). The use of structured multi-domain job analysis for the construction of assessment center methods and procedures. *Journal of Business and Psychology, 1,* 353–366.

Schippmann, J. S., Hughes, G. L., & Prien, E. P. (1988). Raise assessment standards. *Personnel Journal, 67,* 68–79.

Schippmann, J. S., & Prien, E. P. (1986). Psychometric evaluation of an integrated assessment procedure. *Psychological Reports, 59,* 111–122.

Schippmann, J. S., Prien, E. P., & Hughes, G. L. (1991). The content of management work: Formation of task and job skill composite classifications. *Journal of Business and Psychology, 5,* 325–354.

Schippmann, J. S., Vinchur, A. J., Smalley, M. D., & Prien, E. P. (1988). Using structured multidomain job analysis to develop training and evaluation specifications for clinical psychologists. *Professional Psychology: Research and Practice, 19,* 141–147.

Schippmann, J. S., & Vrazo, G. J. (1995). Individual assessment for key jobs. *Performance & Instruction, 35,* 10–15.

Schmitt, N., & Cohen, S. A. (1989). Internal analyses of task ratings by job incumbents. *Journal of Applied Psychology, 74,* 96–104.

Schmitt, N., & Landy, F. J. (1993). The concept of validity. In N. Schmitt & W. C. Borman (Eds.), *Personnel selection in organizations* (pp. 275–309). San Francisco: Jossey-Bass.

Schmitt, N., & Ostroff, C. (1986). Operationalizing the "behavioral consistency approach": Selection test development based on content-oriented strategy. *Personnel Psychology, 39,* 91–108.

Schneider, B. (1976). *Staffing organizations.* Santa Monica, CA: Goodyear.

Schneider, B., & Konz, A. M. (1989). Strategic job analysis. *Human Resource Management, 28,* 51–63.

Senge, P. M. (1990). *The fifth discipline: The art and practice of the learning organization.* New York: Doubleday.

Silverman, S. B., Wexley K. N., & Johnson, J. C. (1984). The effects of age and job experience on employee responses to a structured job analysis questionnaire. *Public Personnel Management, 13,* 355–359.

Society for Industrial and Organizational Psychology. (1987). *Principles for the validation and use of personnel selection procedures* (3rd ed.). College Park, MD: Author.

Sparks, C. P. (1988). Legal basis for job analysis. In S. Gael (Ed.), *The job analysis handbook for business, industry, and government* (Vol. 1, pp. 37–47). New York: Wiley.

Spearman, C. (1910). Correlation calculated from faulty data. *British Journal of Psychology, 3,* 271–295.

Spector, P. E. (1976). Choosing response categories for summated rating scales. *Journal of Applied Psychology, 61,* 374–375.

Spencer, L. M., McClelland, D. C., & Spencer, S. (1994). *Competency assessment methods: History and state of the art.* Boston: Hay McBer Research Press.

Spreitzer, G. M., McCall, M. M., & Mahoney, J. D. (1997). Early identification of international executive potential. *Journal of Applied Psychology, 82,* 6–29.

SPSS, Inc. (1986). *SPSS user's guide, edition 2.* New York: McGraw-Hill.

Steiner, G. (1969). *Top management planning.* London: Macmillan.

Stevens, J. P. (1996). *Applied multivariate statistics for the social sciences.* Hillsdale, NJ: Lawrence Erlbaum Associates.

Stewart, T. A. (1997). *Intellectual capital: The new wealth of organizations.* New York: Doubleday/Currency.

Super, D. E. (1947). The validity of standard and custom-built inventories in a pilot selection program. *Education and Psychological Measurement, 7,* 735–744.

Swanson, R. A. (1994). *Analysis for improving performance.* San Francisco, CA: Berrett-Koehler.

Tabachnick, B. G., & Fidell, L. (1989). *Using multivariate statistics.* New York: Harper & Row.

Taylor, F. W. (1911). *The principles of scientific management.* New York: Harper.

Terpstra, D. E., & Rozell, E. J. (1993). The relationship of staffing practices to organizational level measures of performance. *Personnel Psychology, 46,* 27–48.

Thompson, J. D., & McEwen, W. J. (1958). Organizational goals and environment: Goal setting as an interaction process. *American Sociological Review, 23,* 23–31.

Title VII of the Civil Rights Act of 1964 (Pub.L. 880352), as amended, 42 U.S.C. 2000e et. seq.

Tryon, R. (1939). *Cluster analysis.* New York: McGraw-Hill.

Tucker, L. R., Koopman, R. F., & Linn, R. L. (1969). Evaluation of factor analytic research procedures by means of simulated correlation matrices. *Psychometrika, 34,* 421–459.

Tufte, E. R. (1997) *Visual explanations.* Cheshire, CT: Graphic Press.

Tukey, J. W. (1977). *Exploratory data analysis.* Reading, MA: Addison-Wesley.

Uhrbrock, R. S. (1922). The history of job analysis. *Administration, 3,* 164–168.

U.S. Department of Labor. (1971). *Equal pay for equal work under the Fair Labor Standards Act.* Washington, DC: Author.

United States Civil Service Commission. (1976). *Job analysis for improved job-related employee development.* Washington, DC: Author.

Velicer, W. F. (1976). Determining the number of components from the matrix of partial correlations. *Psychometrika, 41,* 321–327.

Velicer, W. F. (1977). An empirical comparison of the similarity of principal component, image, and factor patterns. *Multivariate Behavioral Research, 12,* 3–22.

Velicer, W. F., & Jackson, D. N. (1990). Component analysis versus common factor analysis: Some issues in selecting an appropriate procedure. *Multivariate Behavioral Research, 25,* 1–28.

Velicer, W. F., Peacock, A. C., & Jackson, D. N. (1982). A comparison of component and factor patterns: A Monte Carlo approach. *Multivariate Behavioral Research, 17,* 371–388.

Vinchur, A. J., Prien, E. P., & Schippmann, J. S. (1993). An alternative procedure for analyzing job analysis results for content-oriented test development. *Journal of Business and Psychology, 8,* 215–226.

Vinchur, A. J., Schippmann, J. S., Switzer, F. S., & Roth, P. L. (1998). A meta-analytic review of predictors of job performance for salespeople. *Journal of Applied Psychology, 83,* 586–597.

Voss, H. (1996, July–August). Virtual organizations: The future is now. *Strategy and Leadership,* p. 14.

Weiss, D. J. (1976). Multivariate procedures. In M. D. Dunnette (Ed.), *Handbook of industrial and organizational psychology* (pp. 327–362). Chicago: Rand McNally.

Welbourne, T. M., & Andrews, A. O. (1996). Predicting the performance of initial public offerings: Should human resource management be in the equation? *Academy of Management Journal, 39,* 891–919.

Werner, J. M., & Bolino, M. C. (1997). Explaining U.S. Courts of Appeals decisions involving performance appraisal: Accuracy, fairness, and validation. *Personnel Psychology, 50,* 1–24.

Wexley, K. N., & Silverman, S. B. (1978). An examination of differences between managerial effectiveness and response patterns on a structured job analysis questionnaire. *Journal of Applied Psychology, 63,* 646–649.

Wilson, M. A., Harvey, R. J., & Macy, B. A. (1990). Repeating items to estimate the test-re-test reliability of task inventory ratings. *Journal of Applied Psychology, 75,* 158–163.

Wooten, W. (1993). Using knowledge, skill, and ability (KSA) data to identify career pathing opportunities: An application of job analysis to internal manpower planning. *Public Personnel Management, 22,* 551–562.

Wright, P. M., & McMahan, G. C. (1992). Theoretical perspectives for strategic human resource management. *Journal of Management, 18,* 295–320.

Youndt, M. A., Snell, S. A., Dean, J. W., Jr., & Lepak, D. P. (1996). Human resource management, manufacturing strategy, and firm performance. *Academy of Management Journal, 39,* 836–866.

Zemke, R. (1982). Job competencies: Can they help you design better training? *Training, 19,* 28–31.

Zerga, J. E. (1943). Job analysis, a resume and bibliography. *Journal of Applied Psychology, 27,* 249–267.

Author Index

Numbers in parenthesis are reference numbers and indicate that an author's work is referred to although the author's name is not cited. Number in italics show the page on which the complete reference is listed.

A

Ackerman, L., 123, (22, 27), *151*
Ackerman, P. L., 123(19), *151*
Age Discrimination in Employment Act of 1967, 6(27), *13*
Aldenderfer, M. S., 199(25), *229*, 268(34, 36), 270(37), *273*
American Psychological Association, 7(34), *13*
Americans with Disabilities Act of 1990, 6(29), *13*
Ammerman, H. L., 73(34), *115*, 139(34), *152*
Ammerman, N. L., 168(18), *187*
Anderberg, M., 268(31), *273*
Anderson, L. E., 268(35), *273*
Andrews, A. O., 4(20), *13*
Archer, W. B., 168(16), *187*
Arnowitz, S., x(9), *xvi*, 117(4), *150*
Arrindell, W. A., 261(5), *272*
Arthur, J. B., 4(13), *12*
Arthur, W., 73(25), *115*
Arvey, R. D., 198(20), *229*
Ash, R. A., 5(24), *13*, 123(16), *151*
Ashkenas, R., 117(1), *150*
Asimov, I., 3(1), *12*

B

Baehr, M. E., 9, 10, 11, 120(13), *151*
Baird, L., 4(9), *12*
Barrett, G. V., 73(25), *115*
Barrett, R. S., 21(5), *32*, 104(7), *114*
Bartel, A. P., 4(6), *12*
Bartlett, M. S., 264(19, 20), *272, 273*
Bass, B. M., 168(24), *188*

Beatty, G. O., 179(36), *188*
Beatty, R. W., 72(11), 74(44), *114, 116*
Becker, B. E., 4(12, 18, 19), *12,13*
Bendig, A. W., 168(19, 20, 21), *187, 188*
Bernardin, H. J., 73(38), *116*, 120(10), *151*
Biderman, M., 72(20), *115*
Blashfield, R. K., 199(25), *229*, 268(32, 34, 36), 270(37), *273*
Bloom, R., 72(16), *115*
Boese, R. R., 9, 10, 11
Bolino, M. C., 7(39), *14*
Boorstin, D. J., 190(1), *228*
Borgen, F. H., 9, 10, 11
Borman, W. C., 120(7), 123(22, 27), *150, 151*, 238(2), *259*
Boudreau, J. W., 3(2), *12*, 233(1), *237*
Boyatzis, R. E., 20(3), *32*
Bridges, W., x(8), *xvi*, 117(3), *150*
Brooking, A., 233(3), *237*
Brown, W., 196(14), *229*
Brush, D. H., 120(7), *150*, 159(6), *187*, 238(2), *259*
Bucklan, M. A., 139(37), *152*
Burger, G. K., 73(28), *115*, 266(29), *273*
Burns, T., 37(4), *67*
Butler, S. K., 8(52), *14*
Buxton, V. M., 162(14), *187*

C

Camp, C., 198(20), *229*
Campbell, D. T., 71(1), *114*
Campion, M. A., 123(31), *152*
Carron, T. J., 198(22), *229*
Carson, K. P., 74(44), *116*

Subject Index

A

Abilities, people pyramid, 22
Across-group profile, 206
Action planning, 166
Amalgamation coefficients, 269, 270, *see also* Cluster analysis
Amazon.com, 51
ANOVA, *see* Repeated-measure analysis of variance
Application relevance matrix, 78, 79
Applications for desired outcome, 69–74
    detail of information required, 102–105, 106, 107–108, 109–110
    job modeling methods, 80, 82–83, 84–98
    types of information required, 98–102
    validity and relevance, 71, 75–76, 77
    where to start, 76, 78–80, 81
Appraisal, performance, 73, 83, 101
Assessment Method Matrix, 158, 180

B

Background information, 175, 177, *see also* Questionnaire
Baker's Dozen, 88, 91–92
Banking industry
    background information on questionnaires, 175, 177
    cluster analysis, 268–270
    outcomes, 75
    Q-factor analysis, 263, 264, 266
    vision and competitive strategy, 43, 54, 56
Behavior, manifest and vision/competitive strategy, 50
Boundaries, changing, 117

B (second column top)

Business, *see also* Organization
    mission and vision/competitive strategy, 48–49
    strategy map, 39–40
    strategy web, 58, 59

C

Can-do competency, 21, *see also* Competency; Job modeling, strategic
Canonical correlation, 197, *see also* Information, analysis/display
Capabilities, person-related, 16–17, *see also* Job modeling, strategic
Capacity-driven organization, 51, 62
Career management
    human resource management, 74
    information type and detail for intervention, 101–102
    job modeling method for human resource applications, 83
Case study, 88, 90, *see also* Job modeling
Categorization, factor analysis, 265
Charting, human capital, 234
Cheshire Model, 27–31, *see also* Job modeling, strategic
Citibank, 51
Classification/placement
    human resources
        applications, 82–83
    information type and detail for intervention, 100
    potential questions, 168, 169
Client/server networks, 235–236
Cluster analysis, 199–200, 268–271, *see also* Data reduction; Information, analysis/display

294